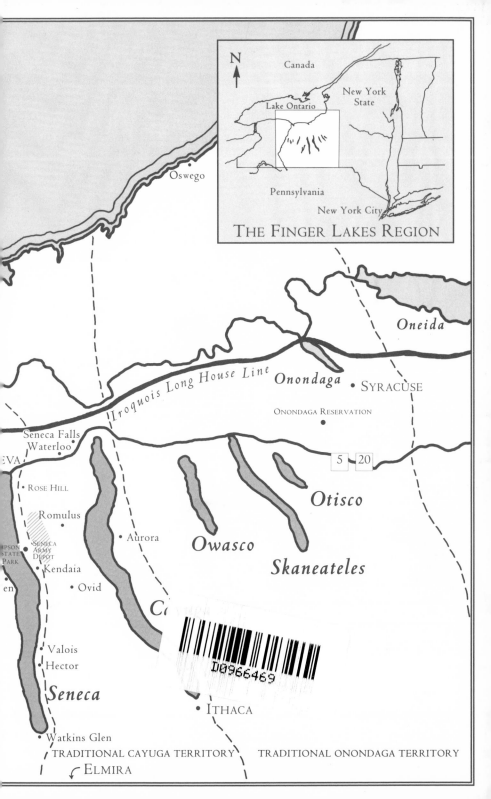

N

Canada

New York
State

Lake Ontario

Oswego

Pennsylvania

New York City

THE FINGER LAKES REGION

Oneida

Iroquois Long House Line

Onondaga • SYRACUSE

ONONDAGA RESERVATION •

Seneca Falls
Waterloo

EVA

5 · 20

ROSE HILL

Otisco

Romulus

•Aurora

Owasco

IPSON
STATE
PARK

SENECA
ARMY
DEPOT

Skaneateles

•Kendaia

•Ovid

C

en

Valois
•Hector

Seneca

•ITHACA

•Watkins Glen

TRADITIONAL CAYUGA TERRITORY   TRADITIONAL ONONDAGA TERRITORY

ELMIRA

From Where We Stand

FROM WHERE
WE STAND

Recovering a Sense of Place

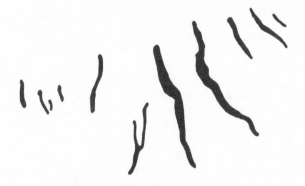

DEBORAH TALL

ALFRED A. KNOPF

NEW YORK

1993

Grateful acknowledgment is made to the following for permission to reprint
previously published material:

Harcourt Brace & Company and Faber and Faber Ltd.: Excerpt from "Little Gidding"
from *Four Quartets* by T. S. Elliot, copyright © 1943 by T. S. Eliot, renewed 1971
by Esme Valerie Eliot. Rights outside the U.S. administered by Faber and Faber
Ltd., London. Reprinted by permission of Harcourt Brace & Company and
Faber and Faber Ltd.

Alfred A. Knopf, Inc.: Excerpt from "The Poem That Took the Place of a
Mountain" by Wallace Stevens from *The Collected Poems of Wallace Stevens*, copyright
© 1952 by Wallace Stevens. Reprinted by permission.

T. C. McLuhan: Seven excerpts from pages 156, 100, 131–3, 100, 131, 37, and 54 from
Touch the Earth: A Self-Portrait of Indian Experience by T. C. McLuhan (New York:
Outerbridge & Dienstfrey, 1971). Reprinted by permission of the author.

W. W. Norton & Company, Inc.: Excerpt from "From an Old House in America"
from *The Fact of a Doorframe, Poems Selected and New, 1950–1984* by Adrienne Rich.
Copyright © 1984 by Adrienne Rich. Copyright © 1975, 1978, by W. W.
Norton & Company, Inc. Copyright © 1981 by Adrienne Rich. Reprinted by
permission of the author and W. W. Norton & Company, Inc.

Syracuse University Press: Excerpts from *American Indian Environments* by Christopher
Vecsey and Robert Venables (Syracuse, New York: Syracuse University Press, 1980).
Reprinted by permission.

Turtle Quarterly: Excerpts from "Humans and the Earth" by Lisa M. Aug (volume 3,
number 2, Spring/Summer 1989). Copyright © 1989 by Lisa M. Aug. Reprinted
by permission.

Library of Congress Cataloging-in-Publication Data
Tall, Deborah.
From where we stand: recovering a sense of place/Deborah Tall.–1st ed.
p.   cm.
ISBN 0–394–57738–8
1. Tall, Deborah.–Homes and haunts–New York (State)–Finger Lakes Region.
2. Poets, American–20th century–Biography.   3. Finger Lakes Region (N.Y.)–
Biography.   4. Finger Lakes Region (N.Y.)–History.
I. Title.
PS3570.A397Z465   1993
811'54–dc20   [B]   92–54784   CIP

For David, Zoe, and Clea,
partners in this place

and in memory of my father, Max Tall

It is by knowing where you stand that you grow able to judge where you are.

—*Eudora Welty*

Contents

Acknowledgments

I have relied on the generosity of many people in the making of this book. My colleagues at Hobart and William Smith Colleges in Geneva, New York, have warmly shared their knowledge and helped in many ways. I thank especially Bill Ahrnsbrak, Marvin Bram, Elena Ciletti, Jim Crenner, José de Vinck, Toni Flores, Rebecca Fox, Stephen Kuusisto, Frank O'Laughlin, Mara O'Laughlin, John Loftus, Eric Patterson, Lee Quinby, Don Woodrow, and the library and secretarial staffs. The Colleges supported me with research grants, and several students helped—Miriam Karmel, Uzma Khan, and Jennifer Miller.

Enormous aid came from the Geneva Historical Society, especially its archivist, Eleanor Clise, and former director, Michael Wadja, and from Cayuga chief Frank Bonamie, Sherwin Cooper, Jeri Engle, Madeleine Grumet, Andrew Harvey, Peter Jemison, Tamar March, Christopher Millis, Fran Nicolucci-Aspromonte, Stephen Scully, Christopher Vecsey, Rosanna Warren, and Rebecca Weiner. For their patience and encouragement, I thank my agent, Stuart Krichevsky, and editor, Corona Machemer.

I am extremely grateful as well to the Ingram Merrill Foundation and to Yaddo for providing much-needed writing time.

And I have relied, as always, on my husband, David Weiss, for his critical astuteness and countless generosities. My children helped by being themselves.

FROM WHERE WE STAND

I

HERE

———

A here from which the world discloses itself.
—*Eric Dardel*

UPSTATE NEW YORK—"anything north of the Bronx," as Ed Koch once put it—terra incognita. Miles of it feathered out from the car window of my first visit, wheaten, gray, mauve of March, lit only by persistent sumac and the gold plaint of wintering willows. I was interviewing for a teaching job in Geneva, New York. I'd never been up here before. The kind student driving me chattered apologetically about how it wasn't much of a place, not much going on.

On the map I'd studied the night before, there were lakes, the so-called Finger Lakes, eleven long claw marks left where glaciers gouged blue water out of the hard land. Or the scratch of an eleven-fingered god. Elsewhere in New York State, lakes meander like question marks, but here they are unequivocal exclamations. The book I consulted said they are edged by gorges and waterfalls, that two of them are so deep they're below sea level, that they are "a topographically unique occurrence . . . without parallel elsewhere in all the wide world." Promising stuff. Seneca Lake, the one I was coming to, is longest and deepest: nearly forty miles north-south, three miles across, more than six hundred feet deep, one of the deepest lakes in the country. It has frozen over completely only four times in re-corded history.

At my first glimpse of it, I felt tremendous relief. It stretched into the southern horizon, a startling sheet of blue held by hills. Long a walker of shorelines, I had feared the loss of coast this move upstate from the city would mean—that edge from which new continents can be journeyed to, a precipice, the avant-garde. Over two hundred miles into upstate New York, it might as well be the Midwest, landlocked, adrift in that large blob of country I'd no means to orient myself to. "Centrally isolated," the region boasts of itself. It was a vague mass to me, uncharted by any sense of its cities or history. I knew only that it was big, thinly populated, and cold, and that my mother once got stranded in it for three days by a snowstorm.

When the job was offered and we decided to come, the lake was what I kept telling my husband, David, about, not the slightly seedy town that hung on to the side of the campus like an embarrassing stepparent. That lively inland sea would be my consolation for the loss of ocean. It gave me hope. I imagined it would help me feel "somewhere."

Imagination gathered fact. Officially, it turned out, we wouldn't be landlocked after all. Through canals, rivers, Lake Ontario, and the St. Lawrence Seaway, with a sound boat and time to spare, one could reach the Atlantic easily. Rumor even persists of a subterranean passage to the sea from the Finger Lakes. There are mysterious tides in Seneca Lake, a sudden rise in the water of as much as a foot, which some locals like to ascribe to its hidden oceanic connection. Saltwater fish have a number of times been caught. Louis Agassiz, on one of his famous research trips through western New York, found small herring in the lake, seawater natives that quickly died in the fresh water; he too hypothesized a passage to the sea. And it's not hard to imagine in the hardly imaginable depths of the lake, 174 feet below sea level. Even at the recorded bottom there is no rock, but built-up sediment, so the lake is thought to go down another 400 feet at least. The Seneca Indians called it bottomless.

All of this was reassuring to my mind's geography, even after a local geoscientist explained away the lake's mysterious tides as an internal long-wave phenomenon—which scientists can't fully explain either. "While men believe in the infinite," says Thoreau, "some ponds will be thought to be bottomless." For the moment, that suited me fine.

Like so many Americans raised in suburbia, I have never really belonged to an American landscape. The narrow strips of spared trees buffering my several childhood housing tracts from nearby highways don't qualify as much of a landscape. Nor does landscaping, clumped shrubbery from the nursery transplanted under maternal directive on Saturday mornings—a row of squat evergreens screening the house's cement foundation. Bulldozed, paved, it was a terrain as homogeneous and orderly as the developer's desktop model. As Gertrude Stein says, "When you get there, there is no there, there." The land's dull tidiness was hard to escape, except in the brief adventures of childhood when I could crawl beneath a bush or clothe myself in a willow tree. Before long, tall enough to look out the kitchen window, I saw the tree tamed by perspective, the bush that could be hurdled, my yard effectively mimicked up and down the block: one house, two trees, one house, two trees, all the way to the vanishing point.

A stripped landscape is a grief for a dreamy child. I searched our yard for magic, gravitated to the mimosa tree which mysteriously closed its leaves when I touched them. It seemed a kind of friend. At dusk it closed itself, and I would close up too, go inside.

The moments I was touched by the larger natural world were few and far between: days at the beach, plunging far out into the ocean past human voices to lie back alone with the sky; or vacations in the country, rapt in the back seat of the car, taking in the sweep of scenery as if it held an answer to my undefined disquiet ("A penny for your thoughts"—"Nothing, just looking at the trees . . ."). "Just looking" was a lie. Every molded mountain and tree-spoked hillside was alive, boldly

beckoning me away from the tedium of my known world. I was
slowly turning into a writer—nature was my ready muse, an
invitation to fly.

As soon as I was of age I went into exile. I followed an Irish
writer to rural Ireland, desperate to live a life close to the land
and far from middle-class niceties. I longed to escape indistinct-
ness, to feel the world as unavoidably real, even if ferocious. I
was no mountain-scaling backpacker; what I dreamed of was a
stone house on open land, modest means, time to write. Though
by temperament domestic, I nonetheless longed to put myself at
risk, to let nature have its sway, to rid myself of excessive props.
It was the early seventies. I'd spent my college years soul-
searching and demonstrating and trying to write poetry. Defiant,
romantic, I landed on an Irish island, an outcrop of rock and
bog in the untamed Atlantic, a place still loitering in the nineteenth century with its heart exposed to weather. The island's
climate matched my Sturm und Drang: gales, downpours, the
constant land-bashing sea, ecstasies of clouds lifting over an
enduring rocky village that had no choice but to observe the
landscape's rhythms and facts in its every routine. There were
no comfortable buffers—the houses leaked, there was no electricity or plumbing, little heat. When storms raged, we were
often cut off from the mainland for days or weeks at a time,
dependent on what food and fuel we'd stored. When the sky
cleared, we stood outside, stunned, under a blessing of stars. It
was a place that had to be constantly attended to—one couldn't
muddle along ignoring it. I felt as if I'd awakened after years of
sleepwalking.

I tilled it; I fished it; I addictively walked its coast, dirt
roads, and fields, day and night. It was dazzlingly beautiful,
brutally poor. I learned its stories, repeated them to whoever
would listen. I could hardly bear to be away from it, even for
a week. What had I found there? Though I spent hours of each
day writing, I didn't have the language yet to say.

It is still hard to wholly tell. How do we accurately evoke land we love? What should we even call the world we walk and drive through—scenery, landscape? A snippet from *The New Yorker*, recorded about thirty years ago, gets me thinking. Here are two secretaries in conversation after their vacations:

> "But you get so tired with nothing but scenery all the time."
> "Yes, but you get even more tired and bored without any scenery."
> "Well, I guess. But I like it better when there's mostly landscape and not so much scenery."
> "Well, I guess. But then most of the scenery was gone when we were there. There were just mountains and things."

"Scenery," from the Greek word for "stage." The set, the illusory flap. In choosing where to live or vacation, we may merely be setting the stage for the play of ourselves, treating nature as prop. "The idea that the world contains scenery," comments Paul Shepard, "converted the human habitat into a kind of coinage. . . . Scenery comes with science and museum art."

Take the idea too far and here comes Video Vue Tours, a busload of sightseers on the New York Thruway—are they watching videotapes as they travel? Or does the name derive from the squared windows of the bus, each a suggestive frame for the film of the passing view? From a speeding car, with the blaring sound track of radio or tape deck, nature becomes little more than cinema, or a startling photo in the rearview mirror, receding. It is thrilling backdrop, but backdrop only, for the real action—the hurry through. It is scenery.

Maybe "landscape" is a better word. The view, the surround, from the German *Landschaft:* land sculpted into fields, clustered around houses; then the Dutch *landschap:* land shape, the painter's organizing, accentuating eye, teaching us what's there to see—a vista, a composition, from a carefully chosen viewpoint. Landscape: "Strictly speaking," says geographer D. W. Meinig, "we are never in it."

No, that's not what I'd felt in Ireland at all.

Reconsider. Leslie Marmon Silko, the Native American writer, maintains that the word "landscape" as we use it is misleading, assuming as it does that the viewer necessarily stands *"outside* or *separate from* the territory he or she surveys." In truth, we live inside that which for *another* is view. On the island, I always had the pleasing dual sensation of being self-contained, indisputably situated, while at the same time knowing we were part of a view, a shape drifting in and out of focus, admired from the mainland. On the island, the shifting colors of main-land mountains were decorative—scenery. Landscape was where we were—hauling seaweed into a field, cutting turf, skipping across a causeway of stones.

We use the word "landscape" as if we could disconnect ourselves from it, stand far enough back to see it clear, instead of looking at the ground beneath our feet. Nowadays we prefer to speak of the "environment," but it too, in its original mean-ing, is what surrounds us, rather than what we are inextricably involved in.

Where's a word for a wholeheartedly lived-in landscape? Maybe simply *place*—which we're willing to say has a "spirit," a character evinced in the lives of its people—*place,* which is humanly defined by buildings and customs but is also firmly attached to and in part defined by the piece of earth on which it sits. In Ireland, I felt I got inside a landscape for the first time, became a living part of a living place. Joined to it by work, friends, curiosity, and staying power, by living out its rituals and long silences, I learned how to look, how to dwell, how to think about land.

But after five years there, soaked, sated, curiosity and restlessness pushing me in other directions, I began to spend weeks in Dublin, weeks in Paris. In the end, I returned to the United States in order to go back to school. I felt compelled, finally, to try to make a place for myself in the country I'd fled, to find a place to live as richly as I had in Ireland. No doubt it was going to be a very different life. I joked that I'd retired into idyllic isolation before I'd ever had a job. Now I needed to backtrack, to take up the path most of my friends already had—toward a career and some version of American adulthood.

I began by subjecting myself to the island's polar opposite—Manhattan. There I plunged into the nonstop man-made, bedazzled by people who dwelled solely in their minds, fascinated to meet other young writers scraping by on dull jobs while waiting for—what? For what I'd just given up, probably. But I was loving the city's energy and my return to museums, music, and film. I knew I could never entirely give all that up again.

For many, nowhere is more defined, more obviously a place, than a city. Yet given my experience of the island, I quickly became disoriented, overwrought. I was living five stories adrift above the pavement, landless, hovering. I craved silences, the sound and touch of unimpeded weather, animals, an open sky of unbuilt-on distances. This wasn't going to be easy. Newly married to a New Yorker, a poet who imaginatively thrived on the subway's whining rattle and the geometry of abandoned buildings, I tried to adapt; we switched cities three times in five years, finished graduate school, began teaching, wondered what next. Secretly, I studied maps. Before long I also studied the ads for teaching jobs in the country.

So now after passing through five years of the urban, we've agreed to come to semirural America, hoping to discover in Geneva some surviving version of a traditional farming community alongside a small town, a workable compromise in a fairly unspoiled American place. No housing tracts here, hardly a mall.

A modest, slow-moving town, still on the fringes of corporate America, set in a lush landscape. Naively, or perhaps nostalgi- cally, I long for this to be a place where the natural world still informs human life, a place whose community lives attuned to a beautiful landscape. David tilts his head with doubt—he's as interested in decaying downtown Geneva as in the lake. He doesn't share my insistent need to try to connect to this land- scape, or for this move to be "significant." I'm the one who's nudged us in this direction; I desperately hope it will work, that this will be a place we'll want to stay in for longer than a year or two. It's 1982, I'm thirty-one. We're about to take up our first full-time teaching jobs, reluctantly become full-fledged adults. We're thinking about having children, and we're trying to stop thinking about ourselves as on the way somewhere, but as actually having gotten somewhere. And so arriving here feels to me like a milestone—the possible solution to where in this country I might embark on the next phase of my life.

———

Our stacks of cartons from a city liquor store block the view of the lake. We quickly abandon the settlement of our new world and walk outside. "Here I am!" I want to shout to water, stone, and sky. But *where* am I? I'm still not altogether sure, nor am I sure how I can find out. Not from the change-of-address packet delivered by the post office, or the barely memorized network of roadways between home and office and shopping plaza. Not from the realtor's hallowed hierarchies of neighborhoods, or a colleague's who's-where car tour. A first tentative exploration, standing still and taking a deep breath.

Start small. Here: a house perched on the western edge of Seneca Lake, ten miles south of Geneva, New York, and the college we've come to teach in. We've chosen the edge of this edge, avoiding even the slight clutter of town in favor of a lakeside cottage. Pitched high up, with huge windows, the house

seems dreamily afloat, a glass boat on a mild sea. Sunrise impos-
sibly pinks the kitchen, and in the evening, in westerly windows,
the hue of last chances is as magnificent as morning was. We
pace about our plot. Two dozen steps to the precipice above the
lake, a drop of thirty feet down a cliff face to the cold lapping
water, a stairway to get to it. Below and above, a generous
helping of water and sky, both today the undoubting blue of a
newborn's eyes. A line of upright evergreens shows where the
yard stops and the wild tangle of woods begins—here, inside,
is the space we're meant to take as our own.

Out there, the space the lake takes, that unbridged, unalterable blank—an interruption, a respite. A space we're forced to
drive around. A lake wide enough so I almost feel islanded, the
other shore just half decipherable, tiers of patched fields in their
several greens and the vague blue of ridges rounded by centuries
of cultivation, a high path between Seneca and the next lake
over, Cayuga. What's felt of islands can be felt of a house by a
lake. Woods enclose us on three sides, the lake's our only
window on the rest of the world, the scale of it small enough
to grasp in the mind, imaginatively hold.

Nearby, a short walk out, there's a countryside part farmed,
part wooded, part dotted with a motley array of houses. It is
broad and open, without many surprises. Unlike other regions
of New York, there are no nearby intimate hills and winding
valleys, land sneaking up on you. Instead, the long rippling of
single-minded ridges, the slow dip to the lakes between them.
Vineyards rise from the shorelines and take the morning sun—
at their height, they have a Tuscan richness. This is wine country. But this is also poverty country. For all the fecundity of the
vineyards and nearby corn and cabbage fields, the human habitat
is in disrepair. Houses may boast a graceful colonial front, but
around the side is the sagging porch holding a broken washing
machine and a snarling chained dog, windows fluttering with
last winter's polyethylene covers, three or four wrecked cars

stalled in the backyard. Aluminum siding and rusting trailers are neighbor to the indigenous—a few beautiful old houses built with cobblestones from Lake Ontario. Most houses lack the need for pretensions. One has a car engine tied up to a tree in the front yard, presumably for repair; it sways in the wind, eerily resembling a deer carcass from afar, except it doesn't rot and stays there for more than a year. On weekends, all manner of junk is exhibited on front lawns, for sale cheap. Some lawns remain permanently littered with everything from colored glass vases to the kitchen sink, a perpetual yard sale.

Though our new address is Penn Yan (equitably named for that town's early mix of immigrants from Pennsylvania and New England), we're nearly as far from Penn Yan as from Geneva. There is no gathered village out here, just dirt roads running off the highway into the trees where a dozen houses stake a row against the lake. The railroad runs just yards behind them, built so close to shore, originally, to make it a tourist draw for passengers traveling up from Watkins Glen. Now it carries two or three freight trains a day, startling the cupboards and floorboards into motion and substantially reducing the value of lakefront property.

There's lots for sale up here, and property stays on the market for years. With just a two-year initial contract at the college, people warned us not to buy a house, even though we could have gotten one for almost nothing—the problem would be unloading it later. A damaged economy spackles the natural beauty of this land with rusting "For Sale" signs and sagging, unused barns. On the road we drive to Geneva there are but a handful of businesses: a hazardously smoky convenience shop appended to what's called Darwin's Motel—five doorways in a peeling white box—which gradually metamorphoses into Darwin's Flea Market; a tiny restaurant, Chi Chi's Kashong Inn, that we fail to try before it closes; a gas station that warns "Last Gas Stop"—till what?; Fredie's [sic] Shack, whose sign always says

"Open," though it rarely is; and, ludicrously, two tropical fish shops in view of the cold lake, shoulder to shoulder.

But back here: a strip bound by railroad tracks and lake, a narrow slice of verdant territory. Burrowed and denned, home to deer and woodchucks. Construction site to woodpeckers. Ours to inhabit for a while. Embraceable. Knowable.

"Paradise" comes from the Old Persian word for "enclosure," and gardens derive from the same notion. In the unimaginably large world, people need graspable space. We sit around the campfire, ring-around-the-rosy, make of ourselves a boundary, create places. More concretely, we surround ourselves with walls and bushes, make our homes a private paradise, even though we know the fragility of the enterprise—the twilight glimpse of Hooker Chemical cars rumbling just yards from the kitchen window. It is not insignificant that the traditional god of the garden has over the years evolved into the scarecrow.

Making a place. I want to do it consciously, with the best of intentions. Geographer Yi-Fu Tuan, a notable explorer of the notion of place, says: "If we think of space as that which allows movement, then place is pause; each pause in movement makes it possible for location to be transformed into place." I don't walk too far afield yet. I hold still to listen and look: gurgle of brook and cowbirds in the cottonwoods, a southern border; geese at dusk whining their way diagonally across the yard to bed down on the lake; a tree frog chirping at the edge of distance. But under sun, moon, or steel-plate gray of weather, my eye returns always to the lake, the center that for the moment defines this place for me. I pause.

Late dusk. Driving home from teaching, fatigued. Suddenly in the headlights, a woman, white-haired, on the other side of the road, not hitchhiking exactly—improbable—but waving (hailing?) and at the last moment's sixty-miles-per-hour glimpse, blood streaming from her left eye. Can this be true? My foot, disbelieving, stays frozen on the accelerator.

By the time I pull over and U-turn back, minutes have passed, and when I get to where I think she was, there's no trace of her. No wrecked car, no pool of blood. A hallucination. Or she's been saved—though I passed no one going the other direction, saw no headlights from behind. I search for some way to confirm her reality, some stain on the asphalt, something to mark where she was. But I can find nothing.

Next evening I check the local paper for news—nothing. So that I do not know if I failed her, or dreamed her up out of the dusk, a nightmare vision, a test. For which I failed to pause . . .

After years of pursuing myself through the world, I am ready to pause, to arrive once more, as in Ireland, at a *here*, and stay long enough so that "here" is all that need be said. I want to recognize my neighbors, not wake up in the morning and squint trying to remember where I am, not hesitate wondering how to answer when asked where I'm from. I have no original "from" of any lastingness, nor have I made myself one. Even my parents have been moving every couple of years for the past decade. What does "hometown" mean anymore? I want to stop the rolling camera. I want a close-up, a still life, and me in the picture.

Here: years of planted bulbs cresting our first April, the yard an unknown repository of care until now, patch by patch, the hands of its past tenders show up as crocus, jonquil, tulip, iris. Flowers chosen to bloom and fade, bloom and fade, each week as spring unfolds. A kind of map, perhaps, to lead us into the life of the place. All we know so far is something of the house itself—built in the twenties, lived in by just one family until they rented it to us, so that for our neighbors it will never be ours, but "the Smith house"—our truest address. Of the land itself, what can we discover beyond the graceful eye Mrs. Smith had for placing flowers? What's happened here? Who stalked deer, who first cleared the land, what stories attach to that pierced rock jutting into the water, that tree growing perpendicular to the cliff, the smelt-running creeks, the whalebacked mound of rock offshore . . . ?

No one's about to step out of the woods and tell us what in another place would be subject of song and legend—*oh whale who wandered from the sea, stalled in lake water, turned to stone . . .*—the landscape brought to life as story. I need to learn the plot and poetry of this place, the outlines of time passing on it, in order that it not be merely scenery. But my neighbors are reticent, sedentary. They mumble and nod the rare times we pass on the road. No one, as in my rural fantasy, has come by with a welcoming plate of homemade cookies, with chat and advice, not to speak of legends. By nightfall, their houses give off the platinum glow of television. We're left to our own devices.

No doubt, for the Seneca Indians who once lived here, the land was full of stories. But they are banished, silent. It will be hard to find their traces. A landscape reflects the history, for the most part, of those who have prevailed. The Seneca's fate is defined by their absence.

In acclimating myself to Ireland years ago, I relied on the centuries of stories the land told—every path and crag resonant with the history of what had happened on it, retold to children and newcomers each time it was passed: the rocks of shipwreck, the coves of drownings, the fields of killings, the beaches of seduction. All over Ireland, it's been said, people will point to large flat rocks and identify them as "beds" of Grainne and Diarmait, those famous lovers of mythology who slept their way across the country while pursued by Grainne's rightful fiancé. So powerful is the association that a young woman, asked by a male tourist to show him the site of such a bed, will decline with a blush, taking it for a proposition.

For the Pueblo, too, says Leslie Silko, stories are firmly attached to the land, always told as people pass the place where they happened. The date of the incident is much less important than its setting. Stories commemorate events, but they also inadvertently provide crucial geographical information, and thus function as maps.

The land's history guides. And it can do so quite literally. Among the Western Apache, for instance, it serves as a concrete moral force. Anthropologist Keith Basso describes as example how a chain of incidents turns the landscape into teacher.

A young woman, just returned to the reservation from boarding school, wears curlers in her hair during a sacred ceremony to which women traditionally wear their hair loose. Nothing is said at the time, though there are disapproving glances. But at a party two weeks later, her grandmother, seemingly out of the blue, casually tells a story—about a man who once lived atop a nearby hill, a man who had allied himself with whites against a fellow Apache. The young woman abruptly leaves the gathering, stricken, and her grandmother explains, "I shot her with an arrow."

Basso doesn't understand what's happened, but two years later, he finds himself giving the young woman a lift in his car, passing the hill connected with the grandmother's story. He asks her about that night, the meaning of the story, and her response. She simply points to the hill and says, "I know that place. It stalks me every day."

Still perplexed, Basso finally asks an elder, who explains that the grandmother, and her story's implicit warning against betraying Apache culture, are now permanently evoked for the young woman by the presence of the nearby hill. Her flouting of tradition had been likened by the grandmother to a kind of treason. By remembering the story whenever she sees the hill where it took place, she is continually guided by her grandmother, reminded of how she should behave. "You won't forget that story," he says. "You're going to see the place where it happened, maybe every day. . . . If you don't see it, you're going to hear its name and see it in your mind. It doesn't matter if you get old—that place will keep on stalking you like the one who shot you with the story. Maybe that person will die. Even so, that place will keep on stalking you. It's like that person is still alive."

The landscape, then, embodies the voice of ancestors, is myth and history, is practical, moral advice. Human foibles recur—it happened before, right there. Take note.

Marshall McLuhan once described the advisory function of myths and epics as the ancient equivalent of Ann Landers. Here that role is extended to include the land itself; the landscape acts as a cultural binding force understood as almost literally alive. Thus one can say, as the Apache do, "The land looks after us." For people like the Apache to be displaced from their territory would mean losing the "indispensable mnemonic pegs on which to hang the moral teachings of their history."

That, for me, is a compelling ideal—the landscape as true repository, the cultural and spiritual revelations of its human history as vivid as the rocks and trees you can touch, the past made visible, a family tree, and the future into which you can confidently walk.

The need for an identity rooted in a known place is evident in almost all cultures. Among some people, says Amos Rapoport, "anyone who leaves his native region is treated as dead and receives funeral rites; exile is equivalent to a death sentence." A South African Ronga ritual expresses well the deep identification most people in the world make with their native land: a man, marrying a woman from another region, will first bring her some earth from his home. "The woman must eat a little of it every day in her porridge, in order to accustom herself to her new abode. This earth provides the transition between the two domiciles." To leave the home place, to abandon one's ancestors, is repugnant to most peoples, though in many cultures women are frequently called upon, by marriage, to do just that.

I've wandered far trying to claim a place as home. I still feel adrift up here in Geneva. No nibbler of soil, I study the map, try to place myself through roads and the names of upstate towns: Troy, Rome, Syracuse, Ithaca, Romulus, Ovid, a Ulysses, and a Hector—all right here in New York State. No wonder I'm so confused. The classical zeal of New York's early settlers feels comic now. For them, the lightness of the Indians' touch, the near invisibility of the long pre-Columbian occupation, meant the continent was a blank page on which they could compose from scratch. They energetically humanized the so-called wilderness with what they knew and admired—cultural mementos of the Old World that couldn't have been more remote and irrelevant. They left us place-names that reveal nothing of the place itself, only evidence of their own homesickness and intellectual pretensions. In this, New York's settlers initiated a national tradition—classical names spread wildly from New York State to the rest of the country. There were eventually thirty-one American Troys, and plenty of old-world spin-offs like Geneva: our lakeside, but not-at-all-alpine, town.

The settlers' impulse is understandable. Names tame the chaotic, reorient. They are the quickest way to take possession of a new land, to make oneself at home. Importing a name from one's previous home provides a crucial sense of familiarity. Even the Masai of Kenya, forced to relocate, took the names of the hills and rivers of their territory with them and transplanted them into a new topography. And I confess to sometimes imagining my view of the eastern shore of Seneca Lake as the Connemara coast I stared at for five years from my Irish island. But in declining upstate New York, transplanted European names echo more and more ironically. After living here only a few months, hearing on the radio that a meeting of Nobel prize–winning scientists is taking place in Geneva, I gasp with pleasure, then wonder where they're staying—at the town's one hostelry, a dilapidated motel on Routes 5 & 20?

Townspeople call that place in Switzerland the *other* Geneva.

Nearby towns like Victor and Waterloo are shadowed by older names, of course. Gaosagao: In the Basswood Country. Skoiyase: Long Falls. More pleasant associations by far than the battered shade of Napoleon. *My brothers, the Indians must always be remembered in this land. Out of our languages we have given names to many beautiful things which will always speak of us. Minnehaha will laugh of us, Seneca will shine in our image, Mississippi will murmur our woes.* The name Seneca, in fact, was a Dutch misunderstanding. The Seneca's true name is Nundawaono, People of the Hill. Apocryphally, a Dutch doctor in search of the People of the Stone, *sinnekar* in his language, was sent progressively west in his quest and finally, exhausted, attached the name to the natives he found here. The name was transmuted to Seneca and stuck. Even where genuine native names have persisted, as in Canandaigua, they remain awkward loans, mispronounced, misspelled, undecodable. Few names of local origin were given by the people who settled here (Penn Yan is a notable exception), so there's little connection to the territory through its names—the sure way to communicate special features and one of the most intimate ways in which a people can belong to a place (the national anthem of India is simply a litany of place-names). Here: our local Ithaca so easily achieved by highway between the Charybdis of the lake and the Scylla of the Seneca Army Depot.

Americans still ignore the land they're on when they name places. Housing developments lean Britishly toward courts, manors, mews, and meres. The use of native names has steadily declined—shades of the Indians evidently don't attract buyers to new development frontiers. Rather, "parks" and "gardens" seem to steady the nerves of those venturing from city to suburb. "The practice of giving an attractive name to a prospective colony," says Arthur Minton, "goes back at least to Eric the Red, who, having found a new land . . . called it Greenland 'Because men would the more readily go there if the country had a good name.' " The advertiser's mentality still prevails and has resulted in names that are utterly irrelevant to their locations. When embarrassed Levittown, New Jersey, had had enough of its image as a bland replica of Levittowns in New York and Pennsylvania (the one I spent part of my girlhood in), the community itself decided to concoct something tonier—Willingboro.

There's a general propensity in suburban America for compound names like Wood Crest or Cedar Hill, suggesting that prestige is lent by topographical elevation and woodedness. Most often, though, the trees aren't anywhere to be seen, and the name is a consolation, what David Lowenthal dubs "linguistic landscaping." A good many of these names are comically paradoxical—the country is full of oxymoronic Ridge Dales and Glen Hills, and such high points as Sunken Meadow Heights. Well-known New York City suburb Forest Hills was built on a low-lying tract of reclaimed, treeless land.

We're not alone, of course, in our desire to prettify the bland with nice names. The nineteenth-century suburbs of London were jeered at for similar pretensions—by Byron, for instance, in *Don Juan:*

Through Groves, so call'd as being void of trees
    (Like *lucus* from *no* light); through prospects named
Mount Pleasant, as containing nought to please,
    Nor much to climb. . . .

I spent a good part of my childhood in the New Jersey suburb of Cherry Hill, which was flat as a pancake and home to no cherry trees.

With such deliberate obfuscations, how *can* one decipher the land's biography, the signature of those who have lived on it? If our place-names insist we reside on hills and crests, do we stop seeing the flat horizon of our lives? Do we notice there are no elms or cedars in our Elmhursts and Cedar Parks? With the land misnamed and chaotically cluttered, where can we find glimpses of how it was once lived on?

We hardly know what to look for, our vision is so atrophied. We might begin with a lesson from the Australian aborigines. Amos Rapoport: "Many Europeans have spoken of the uniformity and featurelessness of the Australian landscape. The aborigines, however, see the landscape in a totally different way. Every feature of the landscape is known and has meaning—they then perceive differences which the European cannot see. These differences may be in terms of detail or in terms of a magical and invisible landscape, the symbolic landscape being even more varied than the perceived physical space."

The distinguishable, symbolic landscape is the mythic territory of their ancestral gods. In aboriginal belief, the deities entered a void landscape and made the hills and trees and rivers. Wherever they walked they left their mark on the land; where they plunged their sacred poles, wells formed. The pathways they left tell the stories of their adventures. The repeated, ritualistic walking of these sacred pathways by generations of aborigines, and the singing of their associated stories, has made this symbolic landscape more "real" than the visible one. The paths are called songlines, dreaming tracks, or the footprints of the ancestors. Everyone is assigned a totem songline at birth. The preservation of the stanzas of one's song and the land they cross is a lifetime responsibility and a spiritual link to the "dreamtime," when the ancestors wandered the continent "singing the world into existence," as Bruce Chatwin lyrically describes it, obviously as attracted to the notion as I am—it's a moving metaphor for a writer. "Each totemic ancestor, while traveling through the country, was thought to have scattered a trail of words and musical notes along the line of his footprints," Chatwin explains. The song survives as a map to the sacred territory. Hundreds of such songlines crisscross the Australian continent, their topography and stories known only to initiates. "In theory, at least, the whole of Australia could be read as a musical score."

That's an imaginative vision most would be quick to dismiss when speaking of mere land. A culture teaches its people how to look, what to appreciate and what to ignore. Mountains, for instance, were for centuries shunned by Europeans as being hideous. Until Petrarch climbed one and experienced with the vista an expanded sense of self, and until Rousseau argued that mountain peaks were spiritually uplifting, travelers across the Alps would keep their carriage blinds down. Of this country, Henry James wrote in 1879, not untypically, that "History, as yet, has left in the United States but so thin and impalpable a deposit that we very soon touch the hard substratum of nature." For "history" read "colonial history." The supposedly raw and unstoried wilderness of North America dismayed most European settlers. But how hard is nature itself to fall back on? It's only in recent times that we've begun to regard the natural world as profane, inexpressive. Throughout human history, people have consistently made symbols out of natural terrain. "The ancient landscape was full of *numina* or local powers," notes Yi-Fu Tuan. "One could hardly move about in the countryside without meeting a shrine, a sacred enclosure, an image, a sacred stone, a sacred tree." While Americans developed a general sense of nature as godly, we never learned to read the sacred dimensions of what Native Americans had inscribed on and seen in the land.

All inhabited landscapes carry markers if we can learn their vocabulary—sculpted mounds, piles of stones, divided fields, a circle of ash, a single tree left in an open pasture to grow old. . . .

We need reading lessons.

From the air, I've always felt I understood the fundamental

conflict between the Irish and British by looking at how their land is arranged. The tidy evenness of England's squared fields evokes politeness—the steady grace of iambic pentameter, containment, control—whereas the unruly, wavering, pitchfork-fought-over boundaries between Irish fields, their shapes jagged with defiance, embody the ungovernable wild spunk of the Irish, the quick-shifting registers of their music. I've learned to watch for character in the lived landscape, to look to the ground for information. When I see two rows of rhododendrons flanking a strip of grass the width of a path, I know a house once stood at their head and look for signs of its foundation—a few rolled stones. When I'm climbing a hill and find the slight depression of a trail left by sheep, I follow it, trust that over time they've found the safest way up. I read the landscape to help me through, to know what's come before me there, to find my footing in time. The land can speak us back to ourselves, a kind of autobiography. To see it as mere scenery is like looking at the closed cover of a book.

My project is to find what's legible here.

———

Driving the perimeter of the lake, I pass through Watkins Glen, fading bastion at the head of Seneca Lake, and begin the steep climb through blasted stone to the eastern shore and the road back north. Soon I'm up among precipitous hillsides scored with grapevines, acres of vineyards pouring down the sunny hills. In the lake itself rests a painting of the other shore, its fields and trees afloat, still. I wind through groves, waterfalls, rushing creeks. It's dazzling. Then a roadside sign, a state historical marker, disturbs my attention: "Condawhaw—Iroquois Village Consisting of Corn Fields, Longhouse and Cabins, Destroyed September 4, 1779, by General Sullivan's Troops." If this is something I should recognize from American History

101, I fail to. Farther up the road, another sign declares this road, which the map calls simply Route 414, the "Military Trail." I hurry back to the library, my curiosity stung.

General John Sullivan: chosen by George Washington to lead a major expedition into New York State. The aim of what's come to be known as the Sullivan campaign: the destruction of the Iroquois Indians.

The Iroquois had hoped to remain neutral in the Revolutionary War but were pressured into alliances that divided their six-nation League. Two tribes joined with the colonists, while the Seneca and others sided with the British, who were well entrenched in the region and had earlier been their allies against the French. The Seneca reluctantly allowed the British to build a palisaded fort to use as a supply depot at the major village of Ganundasaga—the site of which would become Geneva. Ganundasaga was the staging point for several assaults in which the Iroquois participated, notably the massacres in the towns of Wyoming, Pennsylvania, and Cherry Valley, New York, which the Sullivan campaign was meant to avenge.

In late August 1779, more than 3,000 artillery-laden soldiers of the Patriot army converged near present-day Elmira and met their enemy—750 Iroquois and Loyalists. Sullivan's offensive was three-pronged, carefully prepared, well armed and financed. British and Iroquois preparations had been hasty, unrealistic. When the Indians were fired on and saw how overwhelmed in numbers they were, they quickly fled in panic, only intermittently harassing Sullivan's army as it triumphantly marched up the east side of Seneca Lake, on the trail I've just been driving, into the heart of Iroquois territory.

Horseheads, Catherine's Town, Condawhaw, Kendaia . . . only historical markers show where the old villages stood. Sullivan's men moved relentlessly north, discovering day after day the abandoned villages of the Seneca and Cayuga nations. They burned everything they found that could sustain life.

And what a life it was they found. Sullivan's men left journals rhapsodizing over the land they plundered. They described corn in the fields so tall that "a man riding through it on horseback would be hidden from sight," corn with eighteen-foot-high stalks and ears twenty inches long. Cornfields extended for miles around the villages. There were huge apple, peach, and plum orchards—fruits adopted from earlier European visitors—trees thick with ripe fruit. Nothing they'd seen in the coastal colonies compared with the fecundity they found here. "A veritable Eden," they called it.

All was destroyed. Along with the villages, entire fields of ripe, standing corn were burned; granaries of stored corn, beans, squash, melons, and cucumbers were likewise burned; and the orchards were cut down. As historian Barbara Graymont wryly notes, "the business of this campaign would prove a strange task indeed for men at arms—a warfare against vegetables."

Who'd have thought they'd find such bounty? Early visitors to the region had, in fact, described the extent of Indian agriculture and how the Indians far surpassed the English in caring for their fields, "not suffering a weed to advance his audacious head above their infant corn." And though corn was the Iroquois' staple, huge amounts of squash and beans were also grown, along with pumpkins, sunflowers (for their oil), thick-rinded gourds that could be used as containers, Jerusalem artichokes, melons, and cucumbers. Sweet corn was reportedly unknown to colonists until Sullivan's army found it here in Seneca fields.

For the Iroquois, corn, beans, and squash held a special place in the diet and mythology. Grown together they constituted what was known as the Three Sisters, a sacred triad said to have grown from the grave of the first woman on earth. Lewis Henry Morgan, who published the classic study of the Iroquois in 1851, reports that the spirits of these vegetables were imagined as three beautiful women who were "very fond of each other." They were known collectively as Deohako, Our Life or Our

Supporters, and were never mentioned separately, having no individual names. The crops were cultivated together in small hills, a technique still, for practical reasons, recommended in gardening handbooks and practiced locally—the bean vines can climb into the sun on the cornstalks instead of stakes, and the squash sprawls happily over the ground between corn and beans, its tangled vines discouraging incursions by raccoon and deer. Companion planting also acts as a natural pesticide.

The Indians Sullivan had been sent to conquer were a lot more sophisticated, it turns out, than we've been taught to think. The Iroquois had for centuries inhabited all of upstate New York, parts of Pennsylvania, and eastern Ohio. Their own name for themselves was (and remains) the Haudenosaunee, the People of the Longhouse, in recognition of their much admired sixty- to one-hundred-foot-long bark houses that were home to several families. The longhouse, as well as being a practical home to an extended family, was also the symbol of the Iroquois League, a confederacy of five distinct tribal nations—the Mohawk, Oneida, Onondaga, Cayuga, and Seneca (later, with the addition of the Tuscarora, six). The tribes of the League envisioned their territories as bridged by pact into a figurative longhouse, the sky its ceiling, the earth its floor, each tribe a "fire"—a family hearth—within the extended household. The Seneca, who lived in the territory I've moved into, were the largest tribe of the group, their numbers perhaps greater than the other four tribes combined. And they were logistically crucial, situated at the western end of the symbolic longhouse, west from Seneca Lake all the way to Ohio. They were thus known as "the keepers of the western door."

The metaphor of the single house was understood almost literally, as when in 1652 the Mohawk, keepers of the eastern door, jealous about direct trade between Canada and the Onondaga across Lake Ontario, warned the French:

Is not the door the proper entrance to the house, and not the chimney or the roof of the cabin, unless the visitor be a thief and wishes to surprise the people? We constitute but one house, we five Iroquois nations, we build but one fire and we have through all time dwelt under the same roof. Well, then, will you not enter the cabin by the door, which is on the ground floor of the house? It is with us, the Mohawks, that you should begin. You would enter by the roof and by the chimney if you begin with the Onondagas. Have you no fear lest the smoke may blind you, our fire not being extinguished? Do you not fear to fall from the top to the bottom having nothing solid whereon to plant your feet?

This literal sense of the structure persists, even in the fragmentations of contemporary Iroquois reservation geography. When a group of Navajo recently came to Onondaga to speak to the League about their own territorial crisis, they entered Iroquois territory as tradition demanded—through the western door of a Seneca reservation, to be properly greeted and escorted to the house's central hearth, kept by the Onondaga, now in the midst of industrial Syracuse.

The Iroquois League was a political organization so astutely developed that Governor Clinton of New York famously termed the Iroquois "the Romans of the West" (though Clinton was also a prime instigator of the Sullivan campaign, and his brother was second in command). With detailed procedures for replacing leaders and guaranteeing equity, the Iroquois maintained a remarkably peaceful balance among themselves for many centuries. The framers of the U.S. Constitution are now thought to have been inspired by their laws and principles. Benjamin Franklin early on championed the Iroquois model when he presented the Plan of Union to the Albany Congress in 1754: "It would be a strange thing if six nations of ignorant savages should be capable of forming such a union . . . and yet a like union should be impractical for ten or a dozen English colonies." Some have called the League the world's first United Nations.

The Iroquois preserve the League's origins in the myth of Deganawida, usually called simply the Peacemaker, a visionary born of a virgin, who along with Hiawatha brought the nations into their unusual alliance. Most versions have it that Hiawatha's daughters had all been killed and he was inconsolable. ("He threw himself about as if tortured . . . no one came near him, so awful was his sorrow.") It's said, too, that years of intertribal strife and revenge warfare had left the Iroquois inured to death. So Hiawatha wandered away alone in his grief until he met Deganawida, who consoled him and converted him to a vision of peace built around a ritual of condolence.

Now when a person is in deep grief the tears blind his eyes and he cannot see. By these words we wipe the tears away from your eyes that you may again see.

When a person is mourning the loss of a loved one his ears are stopped and he cannot hear. By these words we remove that obstruction so that you may again hear.

The ritual of condolence became a mechanism for communal peace as Deganawida and Hiawatha traveled among the Iroquois promoting it as a means of comforting the bereaved and thus ending the habit of revenge killings ("mourning war"). Because the ceremony heals intertribal griefs, explains Christopher Vecsey, "condolence" became the equivalent of "alliance" in Iroquois thinking. The condolence ceremony also helps ensure the allied League's stability by simultaneously mourning a chief's death while investing his successor.

Since our brother has died the light has dropped from the sky. We now lift up the light and replace it in the sky.

The foundation date of this deliberate, humane league is disputed, but certainly antedates European contact. Most scholars estimate its origins between the fourteenth and sixteenth centuries.

Cars now rumble along the trail marched by Sullivan. I drive it again, enlightened but burdened by what I've learned. The scorched land has revived itself, though it took a generation or more for some of it to become fertile again. Now it is littered with abandoned farms and gas stations, leaning barns. Though near Valois: "Gadiodjiyada—a Peach Orchard Where Sullivan Camped September 3, 1779," and there it still stands, broad-trunked knobby peach trees perfectly aligned, a glimpse of lake at the end of each corridor, branches twittering in the breeze, an orchard of ghosts.

It took days for the army to march this route that's now a half-hour drive. By the time they reached Ganundasaga, the population of four to six hundred had fled, though only just— valuables were abandoned, food was left cooking over fires. The village's sixty or seventy bark huts, log buildings, and huge stores of food were burned by Sullivan's men on September 8, 1779, and the residents of Ganundasaga joined two to three thousand other displaced Iroquois.

The entire Indian population of the Finger Lakes had been forced to migrate in a matter of days. Most sought refuge at English military installations up by Lake Erie, but the British were unable, or unwilling, to accommodate their stricken native allies, and the winter that followed was the most severe in memory. Hundreds are said to have died of starvation, scurvy, dysentery, and exposure. All told, by the end of the war, the Iroquois population had been halved (in the seventeenth century it had already been halved by smallpox epidemics, the virus carried in by missionaries). Indian habitation of central New York had been virtually eliminated; where there had been thirty thriving villages, there were now two. "I flatter myself," Sullivan reported to Congress, "that the orders with which I was entrusted are fully executed."

The orders, direct from George Washington, had been that the land of the six nations not be "merely *overrun* but *destroyed*."

"Have we, the first holders of this prosperous region, no longer a share in your history?" intoned Cayuga chief Peter Wilson fewer than seventy years later:

> Glad were your fathers to sit upon the threshold of the Long House, rich did they then hold themselves in getting the mere sweeping from its door. Had our forefathers spurned you from it when the French were thundering at the opposite end to get a passage through and drive you into the sea? Whatever has been the fate of other Indians, the Iroquois might still have been a nation; and I instead of pleading for the privilege of living within your borders—I—I might have had a country!

When Britain made peace with the United States in 1783, no provision was made for the Iroquois. And when, the next year, the Treaty of Fort Stanwix was signed, it included major Iroquois land cessions, ensuring the virtual termination of the League's political existence. Seneca chief Red Jacket is well remembered for his eloquence about the consequences—though he was one of those who negotiated the treaty:

> We stand a small island in the bosom of the great waters—we are encircled—we are encompassed. The evil spirit rides upon the blast, and the waters are disturbed. They rise, they press upon us, and the waves once settled over us, we disappear forever. Who then lives to mourn us?—None. What marks our extinction?—Nothing. We are mingled with the common elements.

It is in the common land that I search for the spirit of the Iroquois now.

Conquered, virtually denuded, the land was wide open for settlers, and a number of Sullivan's soldiers, who had seen it in its glory, were among the first to move in. Some of the decapitated orchards sprouted new trees, six or seven from a single root, and within fifteen years settlers were making a bundle off the fruit. When one John McIntosh found a wonderfully sweet apple growing here, supposedly wild, he named it after himself—an appropriation as lasting as other colonial rebaptisms of Iroquois land.

Hector, Ulysses, Scipio, Marcellus, Brutus—the names of townships east of Seneca Lake commemorate bloodshed. For here are the so-called military tracts, the six-hundred-acre gridiron parcels into which the land was carved to reward the soldiers who'd fought in the Revolution. As it happened, most of the rewarded soldiers sold their plots to speculators without having ever seen them. But the gridded fields survive, and the twenty-eight tracts remain as a shadowy underpinning. They are the basis of contemporary township borders, cut at right angles across the rolling land, indifferent to streams and hills, dividing local governments into illogical units—a prototype for the great carving up of America with "remorseless rectangularity," as geographer Wilbur Zelinsky describes it, "and with the greatest possible disregard for the sphericity of the earth and the variable qualities of its surface."

The U.S. Land Ordinance Act of 1785, which followed local examples like upstate New York in dividing vast tracts of the American landscape into standard-sized farms, has been thought of as part and parcel of American democracy. J. B. Jackson, that great thinker about landscape, sees the grid as an expression of equality of opportunity countrywide, the symbol of a Jeffersonian agrarian utopia. But one can also read an imperialist underside to it. Historically, the other great makers of grids were the Romans, the Chinese, and the Spanish in the Americas—in each case colonizers, highly centralized powers with a pressing need to organize large areas of land. And as Tocqueville, worrying about the future of American democracy, said: "Every central government worships uniformity." The grid plan made it possible to lay out land in advance of its settlement—a peculiarly abstract exercise—and for speculators to buy and sell it sight unseen. The system was a cheap and easy way to identify parcels; its mathematical regularity reduced border disputes; and record keepers knew where everyone was, what they owned. It guaranteed "coherence" in the settlement pattern—a very much controlled plan for settling the frontier despite our myth of individualism. And not everyone ended up with an equal square, of course, despite the ideal. Speculators moved in quickly, divided, profited. Grids also created a maddeningly dull aesthetic for the land, which we've not yet been able to shake.

The roads I drive here are for the most part the perfectly aligned boundaries between rectangular fields; the corners I turn are right angles. Cars zip across perpendiculars, toys on a board. I quickly become so used to this configuration that I'm surprised to hear a friend from Massachusetts complain about the tedious linearity of my daily commute. The pattern here, as in much of the country, is a given, and a striking reminder of how this land was settled following the Revolution.

Both east and west of Seneca Lake, huge waves of settlers, inspired by early reports, arrived to tame the land with alarmingly quick success. Hillsides were cleared by burning so vigorously that some compared the landscape in those years to a crematorium or to Hades—"None would suspect that these workers in fire and smoke had anything in common with tillers of the soil. . . ." It was boasted that three men with a yoke of oxen could, in four or five weeks, clear, fence, and sow ten acres and build a comfortable house as well. The newly cleared land yielded bumper crops. But when crops weren't rotated, the soil failed, so more land was cleared. The logging industry took care of what the farmers didn't, and the countryside was soon almost entirely stripped of trees. Those first-growth trees were giants by our current standards, many comparable to California redwoods. Only a few were left, as markers, or to shade a farmhouse. An observer in 1810 wrote: "As I stand on the hilltop, the farms are mosaiced up to the river bank and even through the deepest wrinkles in the anatomy of land. As for the trees, as far as my eye can reach, I can count them on my two hands."

The local Indians had also slashed and burned forests to clear farmland; but about every ten years, as the soil and firewood supply became exhausted, they picked up their villages and moved ten miles or so in order to let the land recover. They did have population on their side. Iroquois numbers, though not known exactly, were probably never greater than 25,000, a population the region could easily sustain. Their abandoned land restored itself fairly quickly, and so accommodated both them and the deer they needed to hunt.

The new European population west of Seneca Lake boomed from 1,000 in 1797 to perhaps 300,000 by 1810. And the ambitions of the new settlers were great. So successful were their farms that for a time the area's fecundity and strategic location on waterways made it the breadbasket of the developing nation. Food was exported to the entire East Coast and even to Europe. Fresh fruit and wheat were available in greater quantities than even the well-developed transportation network could handle, so thirteen distilleries were busy processing the surplus in Geneva by the early nineteenth century. "No army in the history of the world," extols agricultural historian Ulysses Hedrick, "has made conquests of so great importance to civilization as did the men who turned the forests of New York into farms during the half century that followed the American Revolution."

But the greed of the farming ensured the region's quick demise. As early as 1791, George Washington wrote, "The aim of the farmers in this country (if they can be called farmers), is, not to make the most they can from the land, which is or has been cheap, but the most of the labour, which is dear; the consequence of which has been, much ground has been scratched over and none cultivated or improved as it ought to have been." Letters to the editors of local newspapers urged crop rotation, ample sowings of clover for cover, and reforestation too, but their prophetic advice was ignored. Attitudes were probably something like those still being expressed by a group of West Texas cattlemen a century later: *"Resolved,* that none of us know, or care to know, anything about grasses, native or otherwise, outside the fact that for the present there are lots of them, the best on record, and we are after getting the most out of them while they last." By the middle of the nineteenth century, New York's wheat fields were being devastated by the midge (an attack prepared for by earlier failures of management), and major cultivation of grain had moved to the Midwest. The people had moved too. They had surprisingly little loyalty to the region they had pioneered. An English traveler was startled to observe that "There is as yet in New England and New York scarcely any such thing as local attachments—the love of a place because it is a man's own—because he has hewed it out of the wilderness, and made it what it is or because his father did so, and he and his family have been born and brought up, and spent their happy youthful days upon it. Speaking generally, every farm from Eastport in Maine to Buffalo on Lake Erie, is for sale."

The region's brief heyday did impressive damage, though. By 1880 there were no deer left, though it's thought that deer had been native to the area since 4000 B.C. Loss of habitat and overkilling had also eliminated wild turkeys, beavers, wolves, eagles, elk, bobcats, and the now-extinct passenger pigeon, flocks of which had once blackened the sky for hours at a time each spring and fall. Early visitors mistook the roar of their migrations for tornadoes. Squirrels existed in like numbers— "Any tolerable marksman could go out to Fort Hill of a morning and bring in as many as he could conveniently carry, before breakfast." Destruction of animals was encouraged to prevent any return of the "hunter class" (Indians). Bounties awarded for killing wolves cost struggling young towns tens of thousands of dollars.

So great was the effect of these settlers that, despite the sprawling development of towns in recent decades, the quality of natural life here has in fact improved significantly since the nineteenth century. A quarter of all the settlers' farms were abandoned by 1925, their tools often dropped in the fields, left lying there for us to trip and wonder over. Farms, which previously accounted for seventy percent of the land, now constitute fifteen or twenty percent. Gradually, the land has come closer to its prerevolutionary state. Deer have returned, found sumac, dogwood, and apples in the revived orchards. Wild turkeys (with the help of the state trap-and-transfer program) have come back to find abundant cover, nuts, and berries. Seventy percent of the land is again forested, enough to support a high population of wildlife.

I look for evidence: on the way into town, lawns just barely rescued from the woods, fertilized and trimmed, enormous expanses dwarfing the typical three-bedroom ranch, grass studded with replicas of those animals home owners would drive off if they dared wander in—the ubiquitous chubby plastic deer, the newfangled fabric geese set on posts so that they swivel and billow with the breeze, seemingly nodding, but never soiling the grass, and chic, upscale polyester-stuffed sheep, life-size. Plywood wells complete the scene, along with mushrooming female derrieres, those silhouettes of a woman's capacious hips covered by a polka-dot dress, poised as if to pull a weed from a flower bed, bloomers peeking beneath the hem, always for a moment wincingly realistic. Because I now do too much driving through the world instead of walking, I see plastic and plywood far more often than the real thing. On the road, I only rarely glimpse a live shuffling woodchuck or dreaming pheasant. More often, tracks, a fleeting white tail, or in twilight, the detached orange slits of eyes that waver in front of my headlights, unreal as the front-lawn phantoms.

In the morning, road kills border the grass—raccoon, possum, rabbit, crumpled doe.

Despite the carnage of cars and hunting, we're assured by officials that forest dwellers are prospering, that there are in fact too many deer here for their own good—that's another story. But what of the fish in the lakes?

"A handsome sheet of wholesome water," one early traveler described Seneca Lake, and indeed it's difficult not to believe the beautiful healthy. Given the lake's grace and size and lively shifts of mood, it's natural to think it full of treasure. (How I've come to cherish its daily dramatics, its blessings of spray, its calming of the eye like a poultice.) True that it's ringed by highways and railroad tracks, that it suffers chemical runoff from farms, is tainted with pesticides and PCBs. Still, the lakeshore has been little enough spoiled that it harbors nearly extinct flora—one of the last surviving colonies of Leedy's Roseroot is here, a cliff-dwelling, flowering plant that came with the glaciers ten thousand years ago, flourished across the northern part of the continent, and then all but vanished as the glaciers retreated.

The lake has been an important source of fish for longer than we know. The earliest sign of habitation beside it is a fishing camp apparently used by Indians around 2500 B.C. The wealth of Seneca Lake's fish is such that a New York State fisheries guide declares it "world renowned" for three-pound perch and twenty-pound northern pike. Geneva, though, prides itself most on the lake's abundant trout, and even posts a sign at the entrance of the town, declaring itself "The Lake Trout Capital of the World." Doesn't a place have to be inspected before committing such claims to billboard paint? Geneva has as substantiation, at least, an annual trout derby on Memorial Day weekend that draws more than two thousand fishermen (the lake suddenly garbled with boats and wake). But it turns out that even the much-touted trout are dependent on New York State's restocking program: "natural reproduction of all important coldwater species is either nonexistent or inadequate." Twenty-pounders were often caught in the old days; the all-time record is thirty-two pounds. Divers say the big ones are still down there—hiding out in the depths.

I was excited to hear about the trout, kept looking for them at local stores, but with no success. There were plenty of boats out there fishing, bunches of them clustered each evening directly beyond the end of our dock. So we briefly took up fishing ourselves, three weekends in a row, each Saturday morning going into town for tackle and bait, rowing out to where we thought we'd seen the locals lingering, each Saturday afternoon having lost all our equipment to unfamiliar weeds, deciding to try again next week.

I finally asked my neighbors where I could buy fish and discovered that as with most sporting fish in New York State, because of high pollution levels in the lakes, they're not permitted to be sold. Even if you're lucky enough to catch them yourself, New York recommends you eat no more than one meal per week from any water in the state, and none at all if you're a woman of childbearing age or a child under fifteen.

So much for being fed by the lake in any literal way. If we weren't fortunate enough to be living beside it, there would be few enough places we'd even be able to get access to swim in it. What it gives most freely is the chance to muse. Over time, it has yielded its myths: monsters sighted, hoaxed into existence, or actually caught—heart-stopping giant sturgeons, for instance. And oddities suggesting communication with the sea are still periodically nabbed and bragged of, as in this yellowed newspaper clipping I found:

> The theory advanced by prominent scientists and geographers that Seneca Lake, that wonderful body of water, whose phenomena are inexplicable, is connected by some underground or subterranean passage with larger and presumably saline bodies of water, has been again and peculiarly substantiated.
>
> However much the doubting Thomases may cavil and sneer at the supposition that there exists such a passage, the incontrovertible and substantial facts still remain.
>
> No less a person than E.C. Havens, trustee of the village of Watkins and a prominent druggist, vouches for the following facts.
>
> During a fishing excursion down Seneca Lake, Mr. Havens witnessed the capture of a strange and peculiar species of the piscatorial tribe.
>
> This fish was of the general form of a trout or perch, but there the likeness ended. The fish possessed a mouth with a hooked lower jaw . . . the jaws were supplied with teeth which were pointed backward, indicating that the fish was used to feeding on the larger form of the finny species. . . . Research by local scholars reveals the fact that the only fish which approaches the description of this one is the species Mustelus hinnulus. This fish is known by several names such as smoothhound, skate tooth shark and raytooth dog, the two latter titles being appropriately given on account of its curious and beautifully formed teeth. The habitat of this species of the shark tribe is the waters off . . .

Here the clipping beguilingly ends, torn. But we get the point. And the point seems to have been made every decade or so, leaving those of us with little knowledge of the "piscatorial tribe" to merely nod, wide-eyed.

The lake's direst legend is that it refuses to give up its dead. The drowned are held fast, or turn up in other Finger Lakes long after. Some say the water's so cold and deep that bodies don't bloat, don't rise to the surface. The lake may be littered with dead.

Rochester journalist Arch Merrill added comically to the lake's lore in recent years, reporting that because it only rarely freezes, some have claimed that "Seneca water, placed in an automobile radiator, makes a sure-fire anti-freeze." Well, I wouldn't trust my car to that one. As for the lake being bottom-less, my colleague at the college, Bill Ahrnsbrak, putters around in his research boat and says there's always a bottom on the meter. I ask him instead about the mysterious, quick tides.

Ahrnsbrak holds a whiskey bottle horizontally in front of me; it's half-filled with water, a layer of Mazola oil floating on top. He sloshes it back and forth, illustrating long waves. The top seventy-five or one hundred feet of the lake, he says, are warmer, lower in density, and float atop the deeper, colder water. Where these two layers meet, an internal long wave is created. The wave moves so quickly it can travel the length of the lake (nearly forty miles) in half an hour. As the wave passes, the temperature in the water drops twenty-five degrees. See? He tilts the bottle. All I see is sloshing water and oil, enough to make me feel seasick.

What makes the wave start? Why does it happen here but not in the other lakes? Well, no one's entirely sure, he admits, but it happens in a handful of lakes that are deep and long and narrow like Seneca and where there's a large temperature differ-ence between the surface and the depths. It also happens in Loch Ness.

Stories like this make the lake a dramatic, compelling presence. Windy days it threatens the docks, turns into a vengeful sea. Summer evenings it can be so still, to dive into it is to send out shuddering rings as far as the eye can follow. Winter mornings, when its relative warmth hits the cold air, it hoods itself in an eerie cloak of mist. Sunsets, it's painted with heartbreak. It is, above all, a focus, organizer of the view.

I've come to count on the lake. But geologists casually remind us that lakes are short-lived affairs. The memorized contours of the shore that become dear to us are, in the grand scheme of things, fleeting. Seneca Lake, alive with small changes all the time, has changed radically over the eons. Don Woodrow, another colleague here, finds seashells and lake sediment in soils miles from the current shoreline. It's thought that the Finger Lakes were at times so high and deep that several of them merged. Woodrow predicts that Seneca Lake will eventually become a mere swamp. The idea pains me.

Swampy brown sediments stripe the lake's deep blues when the creeks are running hard, water rushing through tiny falls, churning uneasily beneath the dock where I often sit. I let myself be mesmerized by the moving water, transfixed by the color shifts of the other shore. But at dusk, from the blur of ridges, something red pricks my eye. On, off, on, off. It takes me weeks to track it down, drive to its source, place it—the pulsing lights of the radio tower at the Seneca Army Depot, the sole visible sign of what's going on across the lake that four miles of nonchalant water cannot pretend to distance me from.

Though I'd like to think, as poet Cesare Pavese wrote, that "at night the earth has no owners," here the night is owned by the army. We've heard the transport planes coming in and taking off at two or three in the morning, their improbably long, low lumbering down the seven-thousand-foot runway, laden with threat. Pershing missiles, neutron bombs, the lot. From here right to Europe. The radio tower signals us, the world: on off on off, yes no yes no, a pole of monstrous fireflies, jittery on and off like the buttons on the consoles of those machines used in psychology experiments that pit you against an unknown competitor, on and off ruthlessly proving aggression, you, me, you, me, everything taken, nothing left. What have we won? Reportedly the largest depot of nuclear weapons in the eastern half of the country, built on the farmland of Kendaia, once the site of a thriving Seneca village.

Kendaia, destroyed by Sullivan—a sign posted at the weedy edge of a narrow rest area along the highway all that acknowledges it now—a village so well known for its orchards that it was called Apple Town. It was an important tribal center too—Sullivan's men noted unusual, gorgeously painted tombs for chiefs buried there.

Eleven thousand acres around the former Kendaia are now guarded by more than 250 military police authorized to shoot to kill to keep anyone from approaching the five hundred underground bunkers of bombs there. I think I can see where the bombs are . . . in the Landsat satellite photo sold locally as a poster—the big oval ring of the depot distinctly set off from the quilt of gridded fields, the area's biggest single swath of land, gouged out like one of the lakes, though not a bit blue. Inside the first ring there's a second boundary, and there, in telltale lines, are pale brown dots, five clumpings of them, contained and orderly, clearly visible from this extraterrestrial angle, but never from the ground by the likes of us. Helicopters whir round the perimeter of the base to protect it. The sky is crisscrossed by contrails, the distant glint of speeding jets. Dogs roam the barbed-wire fences, and guards peer from towers. Pulling over onto the shoulder of the road is deemed suspicious—friends have reported the quick swoop of a copter, questioning.

The military has been here since 1941 when the depot and Sampson base across the road were built at panic speed. The uranium for the Manhattan Project was stored here, and thousands of men boot-camped at Sampson. The army had favored the site's rural, inland setting and the "all-American" makeup of its neighboring population. Some all-American families long settled on the land chosen for the depot, though, said they were treated "rottenly." A number of them got as little as three days' notice to give up their homes and farms. They raced to harvest what they could from their fields, abandoning the rest to bulldozers in a spirit eerily reminiscent of Sullivan's march through, 162 years before.

Many felt undercompensated for their land, but money wasn't their only grievance—"That black walnut there came up from some nuts dumped on the ground when my girl was young. It's such things as that get you attached to a place." Sampson base devoured twenty additional farms, twelve more houses, seventy-five lakefront cottages, and two general stores. Some of the houses seized dated from the first white settlement in the late eighteenth century. And the land included the unusual Indian cemetery that had so impressed Sullivan's soldiers. The first settlers had vowed to the last of the local Indians that they'd protect the cemetery. And they had. Until during the building of the base, when excavations for a water line intersected the mounds.

After the war, the bombs stayed in the so-called igloos, and the navy stayed to work on the lake—it's deep enough to simulate submarine experience. Of that work, we can only see what's happening on the surface: a huge barge, not far from us, which never moves from its anchor. At night it rolls under a single orange light, my landmark as I drive down from Geneva, time to turn onto the road home. It's a kind of companion on the emptiness of the water, a stalwart. We can see a few small boats tied up to it, men motoring in and out to shore. Things are going on. One night in the moonless dark we hear it—an eerie, nerve-jangling music, soprano, moaning, coming in slow

spurts, fragmenting into the trees, pausing long enough to persuade us we're going mad, then there it is again, for terrifying
real. They say it's experimental work with sonar equipment. But
I imagine that if bombs could sing, this might be their music.

All we can see at the depot itself is a herd of odd-looking
all-white deer grazing the perimeter fence—aberrations, images
of our fear. They are not, experts insist, albinos. But they are
pure white, and their antlers are heavy and irregular compared
with those of other deer. It's tempting to wonder if they're
victims of radiation. But scientists say they're a natural mutation
that has flourished because the herd is unnaturally restricted
within the high fences of the depot. The first white fawn was
sighted in 1956. Now there are hundreds, and none is permitted
to be shot. So they are increasingly visible, loveliness behind
barbed wire, set into panic by helicopters and transport planes,
caged with bombs. They are our heart pang. Or our sci-fi vision
of the nuked world, wan, entrapped.

They are also the local symbol of the depot. See them on
T-shirts, or in white Styrofoam as a leaping silhouette, gold
antlered, dressing up the window of a convenience store down
the road, sporting a decal—"We Love the SEAD" (SEneca
Army Depot). Though only about six hundred low-skilled jobs
are open to locals, the depot is one of the largest employers in
impoverished Seneca County, so it is embraced by the community, vociferously defended. For peace groups, it is a focus of
demonstrations. A women's peace encampment, modeled on
Greenham Commons, was established near the depot gate in
1983, and marches through the eighties drew thousands, including peace activists like Dr. Spock, who climbed the depot fence
as an act of civil disobedience. But most local people are unquestioning supporters of the military. In 1982, when the storage of
nuclear weapons at the base was indisputably established, only
a few citizens raised the issue of an emergency evacuation plan
for the area. None has ever been made; it is probably pointless.

Nor did anyone say a thing in 1989 when the Environmental Protection Agency recommended that the depot be added to the Superfund list of the nation's worst hazardous-waste sites. An investigation focused on a ninety-acre open area where explosives "and related wastes" were burned and detonated for thirty years. Monitored wells revealed unacceptable levels of several carcinogens. As for radiation, no one's talking. Earlier, the depot apparently managed to get rid of the remains of the Manhattan Project—what has been called "the world's most historic waste"—by dumping it at Lewiston, just north of Niagara Falls. Niagara County, home of Love Canal, has long been a favorite upstate dumping ground because of its heavy clay soil. Until the seventies, the more than twenty-two thousand tons of radioactive waste used to build the country's first nuclear bomb took no advantage of that soil, though—it was lying about on open ground or sitting in an old water tower. Not until the tower was shown to be emitting radon, and the exposed waste to be washing into nearby Lake Ontario, did the government finally agree to a containment plan. Now assembled in a ten-acre mound, the waste will remain radioactive for 150,000 years.

Forgive me if I panic when a crowd of pickups in front of an abandoned farmhouse, a stone's throw up the road from the depot, is joined by a van labeled "Emergency Spill Response." We're not going to see any explanation of *this* in the paper.

Tonight the Big Dipper hangs over the Seneca Army Depot, a scoopful of dark. Behind me the bright red of Mars; demurely to the right, Venus. Suddenly the light of a small city is switched on in the emptiness, and I can see a transport plane slowly lowering itself like a huge, awkward moth onto the long runway. As soon as it touches down, the lights go out. Something's been delivered. We're in the dark again. I should try to sleep. But I'm up for hours, unable to rest, groping for description, solace. I rummage the bookshelf, settle at last on Rilke, that poet for whom invisible presences spoke louder than planes, and find words to focus my unease: "Killing is a form of our wandering sorrow."

What danger has there been, I have to ask, in my own form of wandering? What land would I defend? Will I ever be "a local"? Do I even want to be, with the term's implication of provinciality? Thought of another way, though, the local defines a circle of obligation, a territory of responsibility. The local versus the passing through—how you know which you are:

A car pulls out right in front of you on a two-lane road. You have to slam on your brakes to avoid hitting it. It creeps along at twenty miles per hour, turns off a few hundred yards down the road. You lean on the horn, let them have it.

Next day, you only have to go a short way down the road to pick up a neighbor. You pull out of the driveway as you do every morning and meander down, indignant at the out-of-state Buick that races up onto your bumper, honking. You let them have it.

The boundary between these two indignations is thin. Ten miles down the road, we can easily lose our sense of territory, become the one hurrying elsewhere.

Never having been settled long enough on a piece of land to see a tree grow from a dropped nut, to lie down before the bulldozers, I'd have to ironically echo the Cree who, asked his address by a Canadian court, replied, "I have come from what I have survived on." For me it has been friends, poems, certain paintings and melodies, horizon lines . . . Home is a bed to lie down on, a desk to write at, a few talismanic objects hovering nearby. When I think back, images of my life line themselves up like photographs on the mantle, the landscapes of three decades a backdrop to self-portraiture, the land gone miniature, segmented into its inspirational moments.

"In part, at least," writes Richard Wilbur, "all men [and women] approach the landscape self-centeredly or self-expressively, looking for what agrees with their temperaments, what seems to embody their emotions, what suits them as decor or theatre of action. Some have the luck to be born, and to remain, in country which is continuous with their personalities; others ramble about until they can say at last . . . 'This is the place.' "

If we find it, do we know to stay? Is it right for a lifetime? I can't be sure. I thought I'd found my place once, in Ireland; now I'm wondering if I can find it here, touched as I am by this area's poignancy and abiding beauty. Maybe we need different places for different phases of our lives. Maybe cherished places remain alive inside us even if we have to move on—our attachment to the earth not thinned, but widened. Still, I worry over the pile of fragments in my past, the running of one place into another. Wherever I am is cluttered with the memory of dozens of other landscapes. Where was it I saw her, the woman bleeding by the side of the road . . . ? Okay, I admit it, I didn't turn back at all, I convinced myself she was a phantom, my overworked imagination bringing the landscape to life, an Indian mother shot in the eye by Sullivan, a nineteenth-century adulteress abandoned . . .

No, come off it, she was a housewife who slipped on the ice.

I drive back the next day. And the day after. I drive around this landscape relentlessly, looking. Next time I'm determined to know her. I'm going to recognize the place and know what to do. I'm going to know where in the world I stand.

II

A Pretty Place

———

It would be fine here if it were fine here.
—*Arthur Dove, in Geneva, New York,*
1935

Geneva is a pretty place, a very pretty place, and the Genevans know it right well; and so does every traveller though as blind as a mole in five minutes after his arrival; for they tell him so.... [Another] amiable trait is the sovereign contempt they entertain for all the surrounding villages. . . .

That's from the *Penn Yan Democrat* in 1835. I've begun to look more closely at this odd little town we've landed in. True, I don't think of myself as a resident of Geneva, exactly, having settled my heart out on the lake and in the surrounding hills and valleys, but this is where I work and shop; this is where, officially I suppose, I'm from now.

In its heyday, Geneva apparently had genuine elegance and a grand sense of itself. One can see the outlines of those days still on the south side of town, where the college is, on well-coiffed South Main Street. There, atop a ridge overlooking the lake, are storied row houses and mansions, graciously broad, and a lovely semicircular park, the early, strolled, showy heart of the town, gathered, secure. It has something of a New England village cohesion to it, not a classic green, but a congenial gathering place unlike the slapdash market center that lies at the heart of so many American towns. Geneva, actually, is made up of both those kinds of towns. The topography of the ridge and the swampy lakeshore below early on divided it into two essentially separate entities—the realm of commerce in the flats and "civility" above. Up on the ridge, architectural pleasures abound, from Federalist symmetries to the ginger-bread of High Victorian Gothic. The columns of the Greek Revival intersect the horizontals of lake and ridge in a white-washed calm. Upstate New York, along with classical names, has the greatest concentration of classical architecture in the country, and Geneva boasts plenty of Greek Revival houses. They are beautifully set, too. In the backyards of South Main Street, winding paths descend steep gardened slopes to the lake, where pleasure boats wait. It all speaks of leisure, old-style aristocracy, an unlikely pocket of European elegance in this largely undeveloped landscape.

But walk downhill—a quarter mile north—to the downtown area, and there's a very different picture. Fun Food Grill, Club LTD (Love to Dance), Bambu's Place, Daniel's Den—there are more bars per capita in Geneva than anyplace I've known, but few shops of any substance. What were once well-proportioned, sturdy brick buildings, offices, and factories are now a crumbling, painted-over jumble of storefronts and apartments, sickly gray and beige, stuck together with neon and plastic. Where the old buildings have deteriorated beyond repair, they've been replaced with shipped-in blank glass faces, so the streets have become a sorry mishmash. Nothing holds the eye, distinguishes one stretch from another. The scene is uncomposed, decomposing. People who've lived here as long as twenty years still have trouble remembering whether a shop is on Seneca Street or Castle Street, each is so unremarkable—and this in a shopping district of only three streets.

"For Rent" signs pepper the formerly prosperous Exchange Street, so named in honor of the volume of business once conducted behind its doors. Business, though, as in so many American towns, has been siphoned off by the highway and routed out to shopping plazas. A mile and a half of strip begins just west of the college with the Town and Country Plaza—a former frontier edge—and continues along so-called 5 & 20,

U.S. Route 20 here coinciding with New York Route 5, both offspring of the Genesee Road, which by and large traces the Iroquois longhouse trail. Once the symbolic and literal aligning route of the League, the trail across which Iroquois runners ferried information the three hundred miles from Buffalo to Albany in just three days, the road now connects in a matter of hours the major cities and towns of upstate New York, flanked by car dealerships and junk-food outlets.

Oddities are mostly what remain in business downtown: a restaurant supply store (in a town that has perhaps the fewest restaurants of any its size—our misery); a factory outlet party store, where plastic birthday favors sell ten for a dollar; the Linden Exchange, where contorted mannequins pose in kelly-green and orange castoffs. Those who gather on Exchange Street these days do so in the doors of bars, thrift shops, and porno magazine stores. Often drunk by midday, they leer at those who still think to shop and walk downtown. At night, under sulfurous streetlights, the drug dealers move in and fights spill out of the bars.

It's curious—we came to the periphery optimistic about a town that had been spared anonymous development. But instead the place feels overlooked, abandoned. Lack of development means thumbs down, decay. Though a dubious economy has saved Geneva from most of the chain stores, local entrepreneurs haven't stepped in in their place. It's an isolated town of only fifteen thousand people with little to sustain itself. Despite the efforts of the college, much of the common culture as we've known it elsewhere in America is missing—there's little theater, live music, or food that hasn't come off a production line. The town supports just one movie house and one small department store. Geneva has many of the griefs of a city—drugs, violence, the despair of the unemployed—but none of the advantages. Penn Yan, closer to its agricultural tradition and so more appealing in some respects, has even less to offer by way of entertainment. While it's been novel and fun to spend Saturday nights with farmers at Penn Yan's auction barn, listening to a local woman musically huckster everything from antique rockers and sleds to grab bags of buttons and lace, after a few months, we look around for Saturday-night alternatives, find ourselves driving the hour to Rochester or Ithaca for ethnic cuisine, a concert or foreign film.

At first glance, the slight tawdriness of Geneva, its lack of pretension and avoidance of all things chic, had been reassuring. It had made me believe that another kind of culture must be thriving here, one I might feel at home in. But I now realize that behind the plainness there's very little at all—mostly the remains of a swankier past and a sense of damage, a depression and frustration that hang over the place like sheeting. "Everyone in Geneva dead or dying or just walking around," the painter Arthur Dove described it in the thirties. Two guys with death-rattle coughs sitting in the bus station over coffee and cigarettes say the same thing: this town is dead, gotta get out, go somewhere else—to the bus station coffee counter of another town.

I'd hoped to find real distinction here. Instead, as in so many places in the world, one increasingly feels the denial of the "here." The lovely, bay-windowed but falling-apart Seneca Hotel, still standing when we arrived in 1982, was soon after razed and replaced with a featureless nine-story apartment block for senior citizens. They wander out blankly onto Exchange Street, no grocery store within walking distance—a completely misguided setting, and the building itself a major contribution to the downtown's growing blandness. Geneva seems to think that buying into contemporary bland is the way to rate. It lobbies for junk-food chains; its own restaurant menus never reflect the season or what's grown here. A nearby eatery, perched above the lake, advertises New England lobster—of course nothing from the lake (presented as view in the restaurant's picture windows) can be offered.

When a new mall is built in Syracuse right at the central hearth of the Iroquois League, I'm startled to discover that it's a virtual replica of the mall near my parents' home in Florida—same pink marble floors, same shops. Even the seafood house, which had struck me as fairly Floridian, is up here serving the same fish and biscuits.

We've been so conditioned by now to think of shops and restaurants as universal, impersonal, that it comes as a shock to drive up to the Dunkin' Donuts here for my coffee one morning and find it darkened, a hand-lettered sign on the door: "Closed Due to Death in Family." That a family stands behind the franchise counter is altogether unexpected. The twenty-four-hour services of our life seem unconnected to individual people. "Variety is disappearing from the human race; the same ways of acting, thinking, and feeling are to be met with all over the world." That was Tocqueville in 1830. It's myopic to think our present predicament is news. Yet what is dismaying is the relentlessness of the commercial blenderizing of the world, the increasing rarity of any flavor of the local. The impulse behind it has frightening possibilities—Den Fujita, head of McDonald's in Japan, in 1976 predicted of the Japanese: "If we eat hamburgers for a thousand years we will become blond. And when we become blond, we can conquer the world."

As places lose distinction, even the boundaries between them blur. Towns like Geneva don't *end* in any definite way; they dribble themselves out into farmland. Larger towns run into neighboring sprawl, so that a sign denoting a boundary seems arbitrary, pointless. Places are hemorrhaging.

Some upstate towns still seem wholesome and livable in the way I'd hoped Geneva would be. They retain the grace of their nineteenth-century architecture and fit in new buildings harmoniously. They have a comfortable neighborly feeling, storefronts where one can casually meet and loiter under the shade of old trees. Penn Yan, Canandaigua, other towns in the area, welcome you in from the country with an impressive run of Victorian houses and gentle downtown hubbub. But Geneva's lost that feel. Economically, it never recovered from the agricultural collapse of the mid-nineteenth century. As well, the bypassing of the town by the builders of the Erie Canal shifted commerce slightly north. Up until then, Geneva's fortuitous siting on the never-frozen Seneca Lake, where steamers plied year-round, had made it an important trade center. But by midcentury, with the growing dominance of the railroads, the lake was bereft of traffic. And when the New York Thruway chose the same bypassing route as the canal, Geneva's marginality was sealed. The economy crumbled, and so did many of the old buildings and the town's spirit. In recent times it's perhaps the nearby army base which has most shaped the town's ambience—the number of bars, the sense of the temporary. Temporary too are the thousands of farm workers who migrate in from Florida each summer for the apple harvest. By first frost they're gone.

Though in some respects there is still a strong sense of the local in the Finger Lakes region, and many extended families live within a few miles of one another, even setting up trailers for grown children at the edge of their plots, the love of one's home place up here tends to have a defensive, narrow tone; it easily becomes boosterism. There isn't enough in the life, it seems, to be proud of. The local paper gropes. "Days of Yore," the daily salute to local history, publishes such rich facts as "Ten years ago today L.J. of Waterloo was the winner of a 'Lard Makes It Better' pie baking contest at the Swine Field Day and Picnic in Pulteneyville." Every Saturday, the week's best "news tip" is awarded ten dollars and recognition on the front page—like the time someone was quick enough to alert the paper that a pair of Geneva citizens, on vacation in Atlantic City, had had a cocktail on the Trump Princess. In places like this, traditions strained by TV culture, things of significance occur too often somewhere else.

Railroad cars assemble each morning on the siding by the lake—Erie Lackawanna, Susquehanna, Sioux City, Milwaukee, Amarillo—a mural of names elongating itself, churning up noise and gravel. Their painted place-names seem as real as the ground the cars shift over, the dream of distance. What freight is secreted inside we'll never know. They're just passing through.

Also passing at a mere thirty miles per hour, a truck pulling a huge tank flanked by four state-police cars, lights flashing—something dangerous, heading toward the depot. Materials for nuclear weapons are said to be shipped through the area routinely, by truck, train, and air.

In town, shell-shocked veterans from halfway houses stand on street corners waiting for a bus to take them off to their excuse for a day. They smoke and wobble, big stubbled babies, their pants stained and sagging. At night they gather on the front porches of their state-owned houses, TV carried outside with an extension cord, watching the traffic and the thrillers.

Soldiers zoom by in pickups with bumper stickers advertising how great family life in the army is (a new home per year?) and proclaiming how much they love babies—born and unborn. College students in catalog clothes zoom by in new Saabs calling for a clean environment and announcing "I ♥ Soweto."

Geneva's a place where you can find a bit of anything, but all of it remains forlornly in bits. It's the kind of town where when a boy is critically hurt in a car accident, a church telephone chain quickly spreads the news with requests for prayers. There are still farming families on the margins in coherent, small communities, here for generations, glimpsed at the hardware store. In town, trapped in low-paying jobs, women spend their money at tanning parlors. Their morals are old-fashioned, politics conservative, but they long for the gloss of the up-to-date, the stamp of the middle class. Others, the inner- and edge-of-town poor, seem to long for little. They're plagued with alcoholism and obesity and indifference. Day in, day out, lines of unemployed men fish from a crumbling cement pier that once held a row of swank boathouses, old hats pulled down over their eyes, the view blocked.

Geneva is a goulash with too many flavors, too little meat. Its immigrant groups—Puerto Rican, Syrian, Italian—stand apart, unwilling to mix. The whole town holds off the college suspiciously. There's no common vision of the place that could rally the effort necessary to revive it. Every few years Geneva tries to stir itself up, add a little this or that, a downtown revitalization plan, a row of antique street lamps. But it only gets sadder, thwarted by its contradictions. Well-intentioned renewal either fails to materialize or interferes with what's genuinely attractive from the original stew.

We academics are probably the greatest misfits of all. The vagaries of the job market being what they are, we often end up far from home, teaching in unexpected corners of the country, where, by inaction or inevitability, we stay for life.

When a luminary from the big city arrives on campus in Geneva, many of my colleagues are quick to disavow this place. Their quips, their whole demeanor, say, "I may live here, but don't assume I like it, that I'm anything like *them.*" Any emissary of the cosmopolitan unnerves internal exiles, makes them feel provincial.

Many who've stayed here—even twenty years—are still in part pledged to escape. They know little about Geneva beyond their own small circle; they need to maintain at least a mild disdain for it.

Americans have a striking ability to ignore the place they're in. It's plainly visible in our homes, which regard the givens of local topography and climate as mere impediments to be overcome. Our houses rarely emerge from or hold to the land the way, for instance, Pueblo towns do. We blithely put picture windows in subarctic and tropical climates alike, toil to grow lawns in the desert. Reproducing the ideal home everywhere may make moving across state lines less jarring, but it effectively shields us from the influence of geography, makes it easy to define our places by their interiors, to turn our back on where we physically are. English writer Stephen Potter has expressed amazement at Americans' general ignorance of what watershed they're in, which way rivers flow—"which left me, as an Englishman who is uneasy unless he knows which ocean will receive his urination, somewhat scandalized." Knowledge of watersheds seems esoteric given our fundamental indifference.

Curiosity about and loyalty to an accidental place of residence *is* difficult, especially for people like us, who are, often, culturally and politically at odds with the communities that house us. We spend the day talking progressively, then hear our neighbors being narrow-minded and inflexible. We are threatening oddities to many of them, while in our eyes they often represent bigotry, puritanism, and selfishness. In the circumstances, it is tempting to isolate ourselves within the campus walls. Physicist Edward Witten probably spoke for many of us when asked to compare his life in suburban Princeton with the urban environment at Harvard from which he'd just come: "In Princeton, I sit at my kitchen table at night doing physics instead of going down to Nassau Street. At Harvard, I sat at my kitchen table at night doing physics instead of going to Harvard Square."

———

From certain angles, Geneva is full of promise. Approaching from the east, there's a skyscape of spires and stony blue-grays and the long cliff hovering over the lake spotted with clapboard, stone, and adobe houses. There is a lakeside park with a border of fat old willows, and there is the undeniably riveting blue of the lake itself with its big arena of sky. A town nestled up beside an open page of light. It should be beautiful.

It's not until you get up close that you see the empty rubbled lots, the unpainted backsides of warehouses and stores shoving themselves out toward the lakeshore, stagnant puddles along the railroad tracks, dusty shop windows. It's the grief of disuse, of attention turned elsewhere, the blight of so many American towns and cities. It's the incoherence of the unintentional, the accidents of two hundred years of habitation, so much rushing through, so many western horizons to aim for, so little staying power. The whole town turns its back on the lake and surrounding landscape, aimed claustrophobically inward, viewless. There's a slackness, a lack of belief. Even the church spires don't proclaim "Here!" They seem to say "Maybe." (Wrote Dove: "They are spending $2,000 putting up lights and Christmas trees which would support two families. They couldn't cheer this goddamn town up with $50,000 worth of lights.")

Through the 1920s, Geneva was still fairly prosperous and a well-known resort. An express train came up directly from New York City, and the town actually had more than a hundred hotels, some with casinos. It was a place where the rich and artistic mingled. F. Scott Fitzgerald came once to vacation at a casino, but he must not have been too impressed—when he wrote *Tender Is the Night*, he had Dick Diver end up, in utter defeat, practicing medicine in Geneva and environs. By the time Arthur Dove came back for five years in the thirties, things had evidently faded considerably. Dove had grown up in Geneva and did his first revolutionary abstract paintings here after an eighteen-month visit to Europe, camping in the woods on the edge of town to recover from homesickness and to bind his love for the local landscape to his newfound ideas about painting. Those Geneva paintings made him the first American to develop a nonrepresentational style before the Armory Show, "the most radical American painter of the first decade of this century." Some of his best paintings date from his return to Geneva as a mature painter, a return made to settle his parents' estate. The estate's unexpected debts, and the economic paralysis of the depression, turned the visit into a five-year ordeal of poverty, bone-numbing cold, and continual interruptions of family business. But Dove managed to paint brilliantly in spite of it, stimulated by his return to the loved land and lake. Georgia O'Keeffe came to visit, proclaiming Dove "the only American painter who is of the earth," and Alfred Stieglitz was a steady correspondent; their devotion kept him going. Most Genevans hated his work, considered it an ugly distortion of the local landscape. But O'Keeffe saw the density and exploding energy of his paintings as altogether representational of the region—"He was up there painting, doing abstractions that looked just like that country, which could not have been done anywhere else." Nevertheless, those years in Geneva were for Dove an intolerable exile from his chosen home in Long Island. He loved the landscape but found its inhabitants unbearable—"It is swell from 3 a.m. until 6—then the people begin to appear." He repeatedly damned the narrowness of Geneva society in his letters, clearly threatened by its puritanical strictures and its censure of his life (he had left his Geneva-born wife and was living with another woman)—"Think I'd better not *try* to like Geneva" (a sentiment still audible on campus today).

Geneva's glitzier days can be resurrected only from books or in the late-night talk of longtime bartenders. It is now one of New York State's most economically depressed towns. There remains but a handful of factories. The whole flattened-out northern end of town is crisscrossed by railroad tracks and disintegrating houses. A large tract of land designated as an industrial park lies nearly empty.

What went so wrong here? The town seems to have been unlucky almost from the start.

———

After Sullivan's successful campaign against the Iroquois, there began a period of intense land speculation. The site of Ganundasaga/Geneva was regarded as the gateway to Genesee Country, the great fertile territory running west from Seneca Lake to the Genesee River. The first attempt to appropriate the land was by the New York Genesee Land Company, which in 1787 tried to persuade the Iroquois to sign a 999-year lease, a lease declared illegal by the New York state legislature. There followed the legal but financially precarious and indifferent speculators Oliver Phelps and Nathaniel Gorham, who bought two and a half million acres from the Iroquois for a pittance and opened the first commercial land office in America in 1789. When Phelps and Gorham failed to profit quickly enough, however, they sold Genesee Country to Robert Morris, who quickly turned around and sold it to a group of English investors under the name of Pulteney Associates. The Pulteney Land Office, a cut-stone mansion, still stands just behind Main Street.

Geneva was at that time only minimally settled: "a small, unhealthy village containing fifteen houses, all log excepting three," according to visitor Elkanah Watson. Its sickliness was frequently noted, its inhabitants described as "a gang of lawless adventurers, who were prostrated by the fever and ague. The place was then notoriously unhealthy, from the proximity of an extensive marsh." Watson looked forward to the day "when the borders of the lake will be stripped of nature's livery, and in its place rich enclosures, pleasant villas, numerous flocks, herds, etc. . . ." Perhaps Watson was distressed by how different Geneva was from its European pastoral counterpart; or perhaps it was the local accommodations, his group having been "troubled most of the night by gamblers and fleas, two curses to society." Frequent illness was indeed a reality here. A dysentery epidemic in 1795 nearly wiped Ge-

neva out. Early travelers refer repeatedly to the terrifying
"Genesee fever." Malaria and other illnesses became synony-
mous with the name Genesee Country.

But the Pulteney Associates' agent, Charles Williamson,
overcame this inauspicious start. By 1804, Geneva was a town
of seventy houses, described as "handsomely situated" with "a
large and elegant hotel, kept in the best manner, two school-
houses, . . . several well supplied stores, three considerable
distilleries, a brewery, and a market for butcher meat, of which
1,500 pounds is killed weekly." Growth continued spectacularly,
so that by 1818, when Elkanah Watson returned, he described
Geneva as "not only an elegant but a salubrious village, and
distinguished for the refinement and elevated character of its
society." It still at that point far exceeded future cities like
Rochester and Syracuse as a trading center.

Relentlessly enthusiastic, Williamson designed the town,
got it built, and then promoted its qualities far and wide. The
land of Genesee Country, he boasted, furnished "the best situa-
tions imaginable for farms." Interestingly, memory of the land's
immediate past had already vanished; Williamson expressed
perplexity at the abundant evidence of former Seneca cultivation—"The openings, or large tracts of land, found frequently
in this country free of timber, and showing great signs of having
been once in a state of cultivation, are singularly curious." Early
settlers assumed that these tracts were bare because they were
barren, wrote Williamson, but on attempting to cultivate them,
"were agreeably disappointed on finding they had got a good
crop, and in numberless instances they have continued to reap
plentiful crops every year for seven years past. . . . It is difficult
to account for these openings, or for the open flats on the
Genesee River, where ten thousand acres may be found in one
body, not even encumbered with a bush, but covered with grass
of such height, that the largest bullocks at thirty feet from the
path, will be completely hid from the view." It was promotional

letters like this, unknowingly boasting of the Seneca's steward-ship of the land, that persuaded many to emigrate to Geneva.

Once Williamson's ambitious plans for Main Street had taken shape, once a well-appointed inn was dispensing hospi-tality, and roads were opened south to Baltimore, the town boomed. Williamson was criticized by other upstate develop-ers for requiring little or no down payment from settlers—it was feared he'd attract absentee speculators and undesirables. It's true that there seems to have been great flux here for a time, land frequently changing hands. It was part of the gen-eral restlessness of the era, but partly due as well to Geneva's location. Strategically perched on the ice-free lake and the great east-west Genesee Turnpike, Geneva was a convenient first stop on the way to the developing western territories. Many arrived only to move on.

In addition to regularly arriving boats, thousands of sleighs crammed the turnpike each winter. Emigrants generally pre-ferred winter travel when the mud and marshes were frozen over. In other seasons, the roads—stumps often left in their midst, or "corduroyed" with logs hastily thrown down into marshes—were atrocious to travel. Tourist Charles Dickens reported on the horror, recommending that all visitors to the New World travel by boat whenever possible, specifically warn-ing them against the notorious corduroy road—"The very slightest of the jolts with which the ponderous carriage fell from log to log, was enough, it seemed, to have dislocated all the bones in the human body. . . ."

Despite the hardships, migration west was so intense along the Genesee Turnpike that journeyers heading east against the tide had a hard time getting by, and it was often difficult for travelers to find a night's shelter along the way. Many stopped here in Geneva, though, and many chose to stay in the rapidly expanding town. Immigrants from the South—Williamson's prime target—mixed with New Englanders and contributed considerably to the town's growing wealth and pretensions. Geneva's so-called southern connection is unique in upstate New York. As early as 1802, the large Rose and Nicholas families came with their entire plantations, slaves and all, to become gentry of the new North. Descendants of their slaves remain as part of the local African-American population, much of it impoverished and shoved up into the northeastern corner of the town, onto a wasted strip between Geneva and Waterloo called Border City. The story behind that name reveals something of Geneva's plight—it's the story of Preemption Road.

At the Penn Yan end, fifteen miles south, they write it as two words and pronounce it "Pre *H*emption." In Geneva, at the intersection of 5 & 20, it's marked by a sign erected by the State Education Department: "Preemption Line, Boundary Drawn Between Massachusetts and New York December 16, 1786, Cause of Long Controversy in Western New York." Massachusetts? Halfway across New York State? The first few times I glimpse the sign I am utterly baffled. I head back to the library.

> When the colonial charters were granted by the English kings in the seventeenth century, they were often written in such a way that the northern and southern boundaries of the territory were indicated, but no western boundary was delineated. Since there was no conception of the width of the North American continent, the charters often stipulated that the granted territory ran "from sea to sea."

Massachusetts was particularly adamant about its sea-to-sea rights and went into a protracted battle with New York over title to the western part of the state. After years of negotiation, a compromise was arrived at whereby Massachusetts ceded sovereignty of the land to New York, but New York ceded to Massachusetts "the right of preemption of the soil from the native Indians" for the western portion of the state.

That is, Massachusetts could buy or steal it from the Indians, resell it, and reap a fortune, but the land would then become New York's. Early settlers in the area apparently found the ambiguity of the border as amusing as we do: "I arose early this morning and took a walk to Massachusetts and back before breakfast," reads a local diary entry of the time, leaving descendants to doubt the writer's sanity. Another: "Today I cut wood in Massachusetts."

The eastern boundary of Massachusetts' portion was to run from eighty-two miles west of Pennsylvania's northeastern corner, all the way north to Lake Ontario. A Colonel Maxwell began the necessary survey in 1788 to confirm the exact location of the line. It was assumed from the start by Massachusetts and the waiting hagglers that Geneva would certainly be part of the western territory. It was by far the largest settled town in the region and considered essential as a headquarters for land speculators. But Colonel Maxwell's survey team emerged from their trek in 1789 one mile *west* of Geneva, excluding the town from the Massachusetts territory and thereby economically and politically stranding it.

The survey was immediately and furiously attacked, especially by Phelps and Gorham, the team who'd already bought rights to the territory from Massachusetts. "Not a line; rather a succession of thrusts," one writer described it. "Fraud, error or hard liquor?" another asked. Fraud is a possibility; one of the team was loyal to the New York Genesee Land Company, which still hoped to make a comeback by undoing Phelps and Gorham. And there were ample kegs of whiskey along for the ride. In any case, the line was a disaster for Geneva. It meant that Canandaigua, seventeen miles to the west, became regional headquarters for land dealers and businessmen, and eventually county seat. Geneva's growth was from that moment limited, which was all the more frustrating when, a couple of years later, after Morris took over, the line was resurveyed and the error discovered—Geneva was in fact part of the great developing territory and should have been its major town. Moreover, the correct line, running a mile *east* of Geneva, created an eighty-five-thousand-acre triangle, called the Gore, that should have gone to Massachusetts, but didn't, and whose titles remained in complicated dispute for a century. The correct line, mirrored in the current Preemption *Street*, runs through Border City, a meaningless boundary in the midst of housing projects and railroad sidings.

The name and circumstance of Preemption Road are so unusual that when a letter arrived from Denmark in 1967 addressed to a man on "Preemption Road, U.S.A.," it was successfully delivered because a New York City postal employee recognized the name and sent it to Geneva. Most local residents, though, don't even know the name's origin. A man who'd spent his whole life on the road is reported to have said, "I have always maintained that the correct name should be Prevention Road, but I've never been able to find out what it was there to prevent."

It prevented no injustices to the Iroquois; it prevents nothing now. "Father!" protested Seneca chief Cornplanter to George Washington in a 1791 speech in Philadelphia, "the voice of the Seneca nation speaks to you. . . . You told us . . . that the line drawn from Pennsylvania to Lake Ontario, would mark it [our land] forever on the East; and the line running from Beaver Creek to Pennsylvania, would mark it on the West, and we see that it is not so. For first one, and then another, comes and takes it away. . . ."

————

High on a ridge over town, Preemption Road takes the brunt of the wind, gives the fullest of views. From up here, squint the plastic away and look back: Seneca Lake, Cayuga Lake, the ridge between—three giant steps east. Beyond, a long recession of illegible hills, white, blue, gray, black, or briefly orange under a contused sky. Vista blurs our tracks, lets us start over. From up here, I can't make out the arches of McDonald's, the trash dumped in the margins of fields; there's no strife, no poverty, hardly a building to interrupt the sweep of color, the canvas on which weather shows itself. Up here, heady on distance and the story of Preemption Road, I can ignore the traffic, the shopping center that marks this boundary now, ignore even the grand cobblestone house stranded on this hilltop, its stately Greek columns rising anomalously from the loud horizontals of mall and parking lot. Sometimes I come up here early in the morning, park the car on the one undeveloped corner of weeds, and look down over the lake and hills, catch the last dawn slick on the water, the ridges and drumlins taking their place in the light for the long march north.

I felt from the start that the lake would be my center here, my point of orientation in an unknown landscape. I imagined myself afloat in the middle of it, the shore encircling me, my own body a kind of *axis mundi.* But except for the infrequent boat ride and far-out swim, I perch on the rim of that circle, peering in, or, as here, high up, take in the large sweep of it. And this has left me feeling oddly unbalanced, not yet settled, even after two years. How easy it was on my Irish island to feel myself at a hub, the island a charmed circle afloat in the ocean, at the center of an arc of watery horizon and ringing mountain ranges. First thing in the morning, walking out the door, I knew exactly where I was, the island a separate fact in the middle of a huge all. It's not as easy to locate myself again, to feel such certitude. There is too much crowding the edges, breaking into the middle.

I'm a mother now, and that has changed things considerably. For months last winter it meant I raced home after classes seeing nothing but my daughter's infant face hovering in the windshield, beloved, absent. The landscape was static on the radio, she a chime of feeling so piercing I didn't know how I could contain it. Evenings I would walk Zoe into the yard, hold her out to the lake and sky—this her place of origin. I feel more profoundly part of the land now, having made her here. But those first months, my world contracted to her blue eyes. I drew the curtains, turned up the heat, and found my place in her gaze.

By spring, my mind bolted. I began to look for a way back into the landscape, together with her. I learned where strollers could function, where I'd have to haul her on my back. She, David, and I were going to have to belong to this place as a trio now, on new terms. We'd have to embrace town life—its day-care centers and playgrounds—along with our lakeside woods. My choices could no longer come solely from my moody heart.

To transfer my loyalty from sea to inland lake already demanded a reining in—giving up my youthful grasping at the infinity of ocean and accepting limitation, a boundary on aspiration. Now, juggling work and motherhood and writing, the task of finding a way to bind myself to this land seems all the more daunting, but all the more necessary. The arena has necessarily shrunk, but thereby intensified. I rely on the lake as imaginative hearth. The horizon of middle age knows how much we can really take in at a time: a good four-mile stretch.

Still, at the crest of Preemption Road, pausing for a moment between the morning with Zoe and my first class, distance contracts, hands me the land on a platter. I can dream again, return for a moment to the unsurveyed world, no possibility preempted. I can feel keenly the Iroquois' love of this territory, the poignancy of their loss. I reassure myself that there are still plenty of things to discover here, to muse on, become attached to and grounded by. And I feel, as Peter Handke wisely describes it, "that moment of unspecified love without which there can be no justified writing."

As always, it is a fragile moment. A semi guns past me. The unlovable specific intrudes.

In this case, turning around to the west, it's specifically the Pyramid Mall. In fact, the Pyramid Mall, with fewer than a dozen shops, is as flat and unaspiring as a leftover soufflé and is more commonly referred to by its largest store: Kmart, here called *the* Kmart, so powerfully does it monopolize our material lives. "K for Kmart," children chant as they learn their alphabet. "H for horsey," the yellow plastic one spasmodically galloping by the front door.

Across the road stands a Ponderosa Steak House on the site of what was once another great house up here, the Charles Bean Mansion, with its famous Lafayette Tree—a balsam poplar supposedly rested under by Lafayette as he approached the city of Geneva in 1825 during his welcome-back-to-the-New-World tour. Or, alternatively, the tree where the townsfolk shaded themselves, having walked a mile west to greet him. (They even composed an ode for the occasion, sung by "a bevy of young ladies"—"Columbia's sons shall ne'er forget / the brave illustrious LaFayette.") However it happened that day, the tree grew legendary. It grew over a hundred feet tall, its trunk more than twenty feet around. And it survived until 1965. It even made the National Hall of Fame for trees. In all likelihood, before its Lafayette association, it was a council tree for the Seneca. In pioneer days, a church met weekly in the chapel of its shade. And even if Lafayette himself didn't rest under that tree, he had to have *passed* it to get into Geneva, so the Lafayette Tree remains a favorite item of local sentiment, its photo proudly tacked up on the town-office wall.

Charles Bean probably perpetuated the tree's brush with fame to enhance the value of his land and the questionable Endymion Military Academy he tried to found there. Advertisements for the school show brawny young men resting around a swimming pool (an eighteen-inch wader especially created for the brochure photo). Photos of Bean show him as pale and moon-eyed. He wrote numerous local histories with little basis in fact and erected a monument to Sarah Bernhardt. For his school, he built classrooms, a stage, dormitories, a gym, even put class mottoes up over doorways. But though he interviewed teachers, listed a board of governors, and had diplomas printed up, the school never really opened. Despite that minor detail, classes were "graduated" each year from 1884 to 1917. Numbers of Genevans were listed as alumni. One admitted that while "trimming hedges and lawns at Endymion, he was instructed on occasion by Mr. Bean who read from a text book." "Bean's Folly," the locals call it, one of the oddities that constitute Geneva. They distinguish themselves from outsiders by calling this intersection, with its larded air, Bean's Hill.

As hub, Bean's Hill actually represents a shift of focus. The great Seneca village of Ganundasaga lay half a mile to the north. It would be easy, though, to live here a lifetime and never see sign of it nor hear tell of it. I'd read there was a burial mound still visible at the site and was curious to see it. But on my first few quests I could find nothing. Follow Old Castle Street, I was told by a local—"Castle" is what the early settlers had respectfully called the Seneca stronghold and the road that led to it. But following Castle Street out to the corner of Preemption Road just brings you to the Castle Street Mini Mart. It wasn't until my third baffled attempt that I finally saw the telltale state historical marker in the convenience store parking lot, the sign tilted tenuously ground-ward, obviously having been hit by a car. So it's another of those sites you risk your life for as the dirty blue and gold of information abruptly comes into focus and you slam on your brakes. A fallen sign marking the spot of the fallen empire.

Hidden behind the mini mart and the cattycorner Kalama-zoo Furnace Company lies the low mound, a swell of earth bearing a modest plaque set by a club earlier this century. Gusts of passing traffic riffle its grasses. Across the street, where the tribe sowed corn, lie fields of the New York State Agricultural Experiment Station with red warning signs:

EXPERIMENTAL ORCHARD—INEDIBLE FRUIT

I labor to imagine Ganundasaga, its earlier orchards and cornfields stretching up to Bean's Hill and past the Pyramid Mall, its regal longhouses and palisades crowning this plot. But nothing except the mound remains to mark the village—a squeezed-in remnant, a pile of dirt. Nothing in this cramped site can remotely suggest Ganundasaga's size or power.

The land the mound is on, I later discover, is not even under public protection—it's owned by the Kalamazoo Furnace Company, outsiders. Fortunately they take their stewardship seriously. They keep the lawn mowed in summer, and when school-children come by to visit, maybe once a year, they kill weeds for the occasion.

It is told: There was once a giant taller than the tallest trees who split a hickory for his bow and used pine trees for arrows. On a visit to the Hudson River, he saw a huge bird on the water, flapping its wings as if it wanted to get out. So he waded in and lifted the bird ashore. But then he saw that there were many terrified men riding atop the bird who gestured to him to return them to the water. When he did, they gave him a sword and a musket in thanks and the bird swam away. The giant returned to Ganundasaga and showed his tribe the sword and gun. When he fired the gun, though, he provoked terror and reproach. Calling him an enemy of the nation, the tribe ordered him to take the terrible thing away. Dejected, the giant left the council with his weapons and lay down in a field. The next morning he was found there, dead. A mound was raised over his body. It is said that if the mound is ever opened, his huge skeleton and the dreaded weapons will be found beneath it.

The mound's been in private hands since not long after the destruction of Ganundasaga by Sullivan. Verbal promises were made to the Seneca in 1795, at the time of its sale as part of a farm, that the burial site would not be tampered with. And a small band visited yearly until about 1850 to pay their respects and ensure that the promise was kept. It more or less was until 1920, when some ditchdigging in the area unearthed a large number of skeletons—none of giants. At once, a group of Seneca arrived from the reservation to rebury the dead and angrily demand that the old promise be kept.

Local historian George Conover had earlier tried to ensure that violations of the grave wouldn't occur, even though he himself had been part of a group in 1879 that dug into the mound and removed a few relics and bones to "confirm the legend" that it was indeed a burial site. Contrite, however, Conover made a public appeal in 1888 to the New York State Agricultural Experiment Station to buy the site—the farms of the station virtually surround the mound, and the addition of the contiguous land seemed an obvious way to ensure the mound's protection. Only three or four acres needed to be purchased. Seneca chief and U.S. general Ely S. Parker (who was Lewis Henry Morgan's informant about Iroquois culture) seconded Conover's appeal in an eloquent letter to then governor Hill:

> It matters very little to the people of this State, or to the undersigned, whether this be done or not, but to the historian and future generations, it is a matter of moment, to know what people lived here. . . . The amount required to initiate this matter is but a trifle, and to maintain it hereafter is a mere bagatelle for the great Empire State. . . . The Indians, as such, have left no memorial monuments. . . . The ancient Egyptians left to us their obelisks and pyramids, the Romans their buried cities, the Greeks their arts and literature, the English are leaving their relics in Westminster Abbey, the Americans have already planted a Washington Monument, and all that is

asked here of this Legislature is the purchase, preservation and consecration of this small piece of ground, where shall remain, undisturbed from vandal hands, the dust of the Seneca dead.

The appeal failed, and the historical record becomes sketchy at this point. It's something of a small miracle that the mound has in fact survived dozens of private owners, including in recent times the Indian Mound Restaurant. Its preservation remains dependent on the kindness of strangers.

The Indians have left no monuments? When Cayuga chief Dr. Peter Wilson heard that declared to an 1847 meeting of the New York Historical Society, he angrily replied: "That land of Ganono-o or 'Empire State' as you love to call it was once laced by our trails from Albany to Buffalo—trails that we had trod for centuries—trails worn so deep by the feet of the Iroquois that they became your own roads of travel as your possessions gradually eat into those of my people. Your roads still traverse those same lines of communication and bind one part of the Long House to another. The land of Ganono-o, the Empire State, then is our monument."

Another nearby site, Ganondagan, *has* recently become a more palpable monument. Geneva's ancestor, Ganundasaga— New Settlement Village—was founded only after the destruction of the larger Ganondagan about twenty miles to the west. Ganondagan was the Seneca's principal settlement and reputed capital in the late seventeenth century, "a city or village of bark, situate [*sic*] at the top of a mountain of earth," l'Abbé de Belmont described it in 1687, its fatal year. "It appeared to us, from a distance, to be crowned with round towers." Us, in this case, was the French, led by the Marquis de Denonville, governor of New France, who'd marched down from Montreal to wipe out the nettlesome Seneca with the largest European army ever assembled in North America up to that time, more than three thousand men. The city on the hill was probably home to thousands, containing up to 150 longhouses and a palisaded granary holding hundreds of thousands of bushels of corn. So great was the bounty at Ganondagan and three nearby villages that it took ten days for the French army to destroy their corn.

Now, after a lapse of three hundred years, Ganondagan has just been dedicated as a state historical site.

The August morning I drive out to it, the fields are striped with the gold of new corn and the dusky blue-green of cabbages. I'm playing Breton folk music on my tape deck, intricate, buoyant circle dances, sea-spray dances, and it's setting the mood. Birds seem to dip and dart to my sound track. Even the corn in the fields is nodding, concurring with the rhythm, wafting me out of suburban sprawl into a duet of land and song.

Yesterday, when I called to get directions, a man on the phone slowly spelled out the complicated web of back roads between me and the site and finished by saying, "At the top of the hill, by the flashing light, you'll see me on the right." For a confused moment, I imagined we'd unwittingly made an appointment, and he'd be there on the edge of Boughton Hill Road, waving me in. Then I recalled that it was just a handful of men and women, working for years, who had made the resurrection of Ganondagan a reality, and whomever I was talking to might well be tempted to use the first-person singular for the now-public park. Or perhaps this was evidence of the deepest sort of identification with a place—this old symbol of Seneca power, this reclaimed land: my tribe, me.

When I pull into the parking lot, the site's only visitor, there he is as he said he'd be—Peter Jemison, already striding out to meet me, a commanding beacon: manager and sole resident of Ganondagan, answerer of its every phone call, greeter of every guest, guard of its mission. He leads me into the small visitor's center with its modest exhibition of artifacts found at the site. For decades before its protection, the area was plundered of beads, axes, and arrow points, but some beautifully carved bone combs have been preserved. While I watch a videotape of the village's history, Jemison is outside pulling weeds from the flower beds, his clan amulet swaying against his broad chest— earning the right to call himself Ganondagan. Around him swirl the wonderful hills and meadows the state has bought to en- shrine this place, a memorial all the more poignant for the absence of much physical evidence of its inhabitants.

Though they'll allow no further excavation of graves, the Seneca firmly believe that Jikonhsaseh is buried here—the Peace Mother, or Mother of Nations, she who helped found the League of the Iroquois by convincing the recalcitrant and brutal Onondaga chief Tadodaho to join Hiawatha and Deganawida in their planned union. One interpretation of Ganondagan's name, in fact, is She Lived There. Jikonhsaseh had been well known for looking after and feeding warriors along the road, but Deganawida persuaded her not to support warfare in even that way. It was because she was the first to accept his message of peace, it's said, that clan mothers hold ultimate power in the League's political system. In her honor, this revived site is dedicated to peace.

The site feels as plain as peace, as comforting. Mowed paths through the fields, dotted with informational markers, lead to nothing but the land itself, land just now embroidered with blue, white, and yellow wildflowers and the busy music of cicadas. At the crest of a hill, a sign marks the spot from which the French invaders were first sighted. It was, like today, an oppressively hot afternoon, and the women were working in the fields. I imagine them here, singing and hoeing, and suddenly noise, terror . . . It's hard to envision violence on such minding- its-own-business land, hard to remember that men train for war beside the deep blue silence of Seneca Lake. A truck suddenly barrels up the road from Victor, from where the French came, deafening me. It happens like that; you can never prepare yourself. I turn back in to Ganondagan's paths, along which herbs and berries were gathered, get lost in their odors, in the enclosure of trees. Here are the plants and grasses they brewed to soak corn seed in—protection for the crop from insects. Here are the fields of food, lore, and practical science, the cattails used for diapers and torches, basswood bark curved into water pipes, sumac poultices, cherry-bark cough syrup. Padding along the single-file path, I descend decades with each quarter mile, down gullies, down into windblown talking grasses, down finally into windless silence—theirs. At noon, three short blasts of the firehouse horn in Victor and, faintly beyond, the drone of traffic heading into and out of Rochester—ours.

Nothing stands here. Postholes are all the archaeologists have found thus far, along with the small combs. The outline of one longhouse is marked by poles—the site's only verticals. It's fitting that this banished tribe be commemorated by a battle-stripped field, by emptiness. The dozens of other longhouses and the twelve-foot-high palisades that once stood here must be raised by imagination. I willingly set them where Jemison points and follow his fingertip to the top of Fort Hill, from which today, he guesses, after checking the sky, I'll be able to see Bare Hill down near the head of Canandaigua Lake. Bare Hill—the legendary birthplace of the Seneca Nation, another place that requires revival through imagination, and at the moment literal rescue.

Bare Hill has long been a sacred spot for the Seneca, site of council meetings and ceremonies; annual rites are reported to have taken place there through the 1870s. The village of Ganundagwa nearby, now the city of Canandaigua, was named for its proximity to the sacred birthplace—Place Set Apart or The Chosen Spot.

The popular version of the Seneca creation myth has it that the tribe broke out of the earth at Bare Hill—thus they are the Nundawaono, the People of the Hill. But the hilltop from which they emerged was surrounded by a serpent, entrapping them. When they tried to escape, all were devoured except for two children who were told, by oracle, how to kill the monster. Shot with a poison arrow, the serpent writhed and tumbled down the hill, destroying the slope's trees and vomiting up the heads of those it had eaten. The skulls of the dead are said to have petrified into the large round stones that lie on the bottom of Canandaigua Lake. The timber destroyed by the serpent never reappeared, so the hill remains "bare."

The details of the myth are debated; the traditional version is a closely guarded secret, seldom told, especially to anthropologists. But the hill remains a crucial part of Seneca identity. "Our Senecaness is tied into the area," says Peter Jemison.

Bare Hill has recently been chosen for a subdivision of luxury homes. Long disused, it's been littered with burned-out cars and soda bottles, torn up by ATVs. Despite that, many Canandaiguans value it as a place to walk and bird-watch, and out of a combination of ecological concern and respect for the Seneca, they are working to help block the housing project. There's some confidence the battle will be won. The dedication of Ganondagan is seen as a breakthrough, just a start in the process of protecting and commemorating sacred Seneca land. People like Peter Jemison have returned to work here from lives that were cut off from their land—Jemison from a career as a painter and gallery manager in New York City—and they bring skill and zeal to their efforts. It's especially touching to see Jemison in a leading role, but not entirely surprising. His quiet energy and determination match his Seneca lineage: he is a direct descendant of the legendary eighteenth-century captive Mary Jemison, the so-called White Woman of the Genesee. Mary Jemison not only willingly stayed with her captors but became an important, highly respected and trusted figure in Seneca life, even, for a time, holding wampum for the tribe. Going against the tide of inexorable appropriations by whites, she stands out as a salutary gesture, a healing link.

Mary Jemison was born at sea in 1742 or 1743 as her parents emigrated from Belfast to Pennsylvania. In 1755 she was kidnapped, along with her family and several friends, by an Indian raiding party. Only she and a neighbor boy were spared; the others were murdered, their bloody scalps displayed to the young Jemison the following morning. All that gave the girl fortitude was her mother's final admonition, when she saw her daughter moccasined and separated from them, not to forget how to speak English.

Brought to a village in Ohio in exchange for a murdered warrior, Jemison was adopted rather than killed, named Dehhewamis (Pretty Girl), and lovingly cared for by her two new Seneca sisters. Though she did remember English all her life, forcing herself to practice it nightly, she quickly became fluent in Seneca and acclimated herself to tribal life. Her recollections of her first years with the Seneca are of a life both affectionate and easygoing, though necessarily rigorous. The women worked together cheerfully in the fields and Jemison learned the skills that would later enable her to survive. After two or three years, she married a young man and bore a son, Thomas.

She speaks warmly of her husband and their relationship, despite the obvious biases of the transcriber of her autobiography—her account was dictated in the last decade of her life to a writer who tempered her recollections to fit popular taste. Kidnappings, in this literary genre, were played up for their horror; the embracing of "savage" life, and particularly miscegenation, was downplayed or denied. It was more than a little unsettling to American pioneers when white prisoners, like Jemison, chose to remain with their Indian captors.

She never tried to escape, never seriously considered leaving when later offered the choice. She remained fiercely loyal to her adopted family, even after an ordeal that she describes as more harrowing than her kidnapping. Her young husband was from the Genesee Valley, and it was decided she ought to return there with their baby in the company of his two brothers; he would follow and meet them in the spring. The group set out from Ohio on foot in early autumn, in thin clothing, the nine-month-old Thomas strapped to Jemison's back. But it became unseasonably cold and there was a constant downpour; nightly they slept on the bare ground in their sodden clothes. "Only those who have traveled on foot the distance of five or six hundred miles, through an almost pathless wilderness, can form any idea of the fatigue and sufferings that I endured on that journey," Jemison dictated. Worse suffering followed when, the spring after her arrival, her husband did not show up. Months later she learned he had become ill and died shortly after her departure. In grief, and in a strange village, she had to begin her life once again.

She had come to one of the most fertile and beautiful spots in New York State, the Genesee Valley (about fifty miles west of here), its name in Seneca meaning Shining Open Valley. She so quickly became attached to her new life there that when a bounty was offered by the English to "redeem" her and other prisoners, she hid lest she be returned by force to now-foreign white society. The village consequently embraced her. She was married to a renowned warrior, Hiokatoo, by whom she eventually bore six more children.

Jemison's autobiography offers a rare firsthand account of the suffering caused by the Sullivan campaign from the Indian perspective. Her village hid in the woods while the soldiers destroyed their homes and corn, and returned to find "there was not a mouthful of any kind of sustenance left—not even enough to keep a child one day from perishing with hunger." Jemison's response was characteristically courageous. As the rest of the tribe fled into the unwilling arms of the English, she "immediately resolved to take my children and look out for myself, without delay. With this intention, I took two of my little ones on my back, bade the other three follow, and traveled up the river to Gardeau Flats." There she found two escaped slaves living in a small cabin who accepted her help harvesting their corn in exchange for food and shelter.

> I have laughed a thousand times to myself, when I have thought of the good old negro who hired me, who, fearing that I should get taken or injured by the Indians, stood by me constantly when I was husking, with a loaded gun in his hand, in order to keep off the enemy; and thereby lost as much labor of his own as he received from me. . . .

At the Gardeau Flats, Jemison survived that uncommonly severe winter in which thousands died.

> The snow fell about five feet deep, and remained so for a long time; and the weather was extremely cold, so much so, indeed, that almost all the game upon which the Indians depended for subsistence perished, and reduced them almost to a state of starvation through that and three or four succeeding years. When the snow melted in the spring, deer were found dead upon the ground in vast numbers. . . .

That spring she built herself a cabin, carrying the boards five miles on her back with only the help of her children. She stayed there alone on the Gardeau Flats—the slaves having fled to Canada—and grew corn to survive.

When eventually some of her fellow villagers trickled back, they offered her the "freedom" to return to white society, though they insisted that her son Thomas, a promising warrior, stay with them. She was uninclined to go in any case. Pleased once again by her decision to stay with them, the tribe arranged in treaty negotiations that she be officially given the land on which she'd built—the Gardeau Tract, nearly eighteen thousand extraordinarily fertile acres along the Genesee River.

The Gardeau Tract is now part of Letchworth State Park, through which the Genesee River cascades over three waterfalls, cutting a canyon four hundred feet deep. It's a spectacular landscape, often called the Grand Canyon of the East. I had only known the Genesee River farther north, in Rochester, where it roars over a falls downtown, cutting a huge rock bowl around it, a gaping ravine between city blocks. Old mills and brick factories and the Genesee Brewery are edged up against the muddy, turbulent water—another world from the calm of Mary Jemison's place, two centuries and a river journey apart.

Though most visitors to Letchworth confine themselves to the waterfalls, one can hike down steep, muddy trails through head-high weeds to the bottom of the gorge and the lovely river where Mary Jemison farmed, fished, and raised her children. Down in the flats, the rush of rapids is only faintly audible behind the shush of wind in the weeds. The mud is soft, black, and fish tanged. Hawks circle slowly overhead, and the cries of crows echo off the rock walls. On summer evenings thunder cannons through the gorge, hammering it shut with a lid of sky.

Come to pay obeisance to Jemison, I have led David and Zoe down here. They are innocent of information, have no associations or sense of poignancy, only the place's inherent beauty—which is bountiful. Hot from the hike down, two-year-old Zoe tears off her clothes, wades into the river, squats, ritually pees. A butterfly lands on her shoulder, pauses, flies. She slowly squiggles her toes into the dark soft mud, is uncharacteristically silent. I put my hands in the river, finger stones. This is the place—where Jemison cleared the land, sowed corn, built her cabin. It's overgrown, unmarked. Fish pass, birds pass, and wind passes over the trees.

I momentarily shiver in the trapped isolation of the gorge, its high walls blocking out everything but a slice of sky. Maybe it takes a physical severance from the surrounding world—by water or walls of stone like these—to feel an unquestioning sense of place. I imagine living in this deep valley, imagine it in January filled with snow, wind turned to harrowing blast, the withered grasses, the land holding its breath for six months. Here at Gardeau, one might almost feel protected. Weather might look like something passing by, only incidentally depositing itself on your head. For Jemison this tract was a literal gift, a place set apart. For me, it is a reminder of how I felt on the island—placed—but also an invitation, a foretaste of what this whole region might slowly come to mean to me.

I watch Zoe trying to fish with a reed, the wind playing on her brown curls. What greater life could Jemison have given her children than this river and rock-edged bowl of sky? Offered freedom—from this? Of course she stayed, stayed till she was in her eighties; stayed, I guess, till she could no longer manage the trail out of the canyon.

We stay too, as long as we can, wandering, wading. I've been too long away from this sensation to want to move on. When we must, we struggle up the steep trail and at the top, panting, gaze back down wistfully into the wild flats. To disengage ourselves, we decide to drive a few miles up the road to visit the cabin Jemison built in the flats for one of her daughters, the building now transplanted to a more convenient site for tourists, and beside it, a memorial sculpture of Jemison herself, baby Thomas strapped to her back, looking as she did when she first arrived in Genesee Country. Strong, handsome. But in truth she is more easily envisioned back there in the curve of the river and the windblown reeds: a woman who found her place.

I would like to say she was left in peace finally, but she was not. Thomas was murdered by his competitive half brother John, her eldest son by Hiokatoo. The following year, John killed his youngest brother; he himself was murdered five years later. Only three of Jemison's seven children survived her.

While Jemison's life was extraordinary, so too was the book that recounted it. It was the "unrivaled best-seller of 1824," and for the rest of the decade "continued to sell as well as the novels of Scott and Cooper." Her story, according to Annette Kolodny, is "the first text in American literature to move a real-world white woman beyond the traditional captivity pattern to something approaching *willing* wilderness accommodations. . . ."

Jemison remains a brave example. Willing accommodation is a good description of what I've been trying to do here, cast by circumstance into this resonant land. My friend Marvin, a historian who's been teaching in Geneva for twenty years, calls this area "the most insulted place I know"—its environment abused and its history so compulsively ignored by most inhabitants that recent Iroquois land claims appear as if out of nowhere, colliding with communal amnesia. The abyss between us and the past of the land seems impossible to bridge sometimes. Blithely, we ignore what our culture sits atop. Our indifference defines policy, determines what will literally survive. Bare Hill, or any number of unknown sites, loaded with significance, become, through ignorance, easily dispensable. The real estate of memory is not immediately profitable, except as it supports tourism.

Hand in hand here: an "I love New York" tourist ad on the radio, a hygienic-voiced male urging Americans to visit "the same lakes and waterways that the Seneca Indians were attracted to hundreds of years ago"—as if it were a matter of attraction. And as I listen, dumbfounded, a truck goes by on the railroad tracks, two men directing gigantic sprayers on each side, spilling defoliant out at the trees and underbrush that have encroached on the tracks, spraying it out past the tracks onto the road, and out, in a blast, onto the hood of my car.

To be in a place that was dwelled in so felicitously, with troves of associations, and to see it mistreated pains me. A weak sense of the past encourages a weak sense of place. When people are attached to their forebears, they want to remain close to where they lived, continue their traditions, tend their graves, embody their hopes. Many may remain where they were born out of habit or spiritual duty, but the staying itself is conducive to life because the lived-in land then becomes an extension of the self, the family and group; to endanger the land is to wound one's collective body.

Lacking that connection, as most of us do now, how do we come to feel loyal to a place? What makes it *feel* like a place at all? I've been hunting down stories so that the land rings for me. I've been looking for the play between land and people, for coherence, a sense of conscious choices in design, evidence of the past left visible in the present. I want a place where work, pleasure, and the spiritual can casually coexist, a place where children feel them-selves in community. I want to be in a place where people feel they genuinely belong, where the life lived and its location coincide with a kind of inevitability and fruitfulness, where life is not being lived, as Lawrence Durrell puts it, at "right angles to the land." It's what I experienced in Ireland, but perhaps that's the sense of place of a vanishing era, no longer to be found. I won't find it easily here, especially in the town of Geneva itself. I've given up my illusions about that. But something about this land, this fifty-mile radius of central New York, comfortably encompassing the contemporary worldliness of Ithaca along with Ganondagan, Letchworth, and the still-burning hearth of the Iroquois, continues to tempt me with hope.

On our happiest days, out walking, Zoe announcing each small event we pass—"Squirrel eating a nut!"—and layers of other voices in my head joining the shuffle of leaves and finches, I glimpse what a grounded life here could be. As with Jemison, the freedom to go elsewhere is becoming a moot point.

I've found festering wounds beneath fine scenery here, an

angular discomfort. But I've found as well a palimpsest of lives by which I might patch together an understanding, a kind of poultice for my own placelessness. This place's traditions are not my own, but I can perhaps attach myself to them. It will take an act of deliberate adoption, a willed transplant. Having a sense of place may by now require a continual act of imagination.

III

DWELLING

Oh the lark in the morning
She rises from her nest
And she comes home in the evening
With the jewel in her breast
—Irish folk song

The word "DWELL" has a complicated past. We think of it as implying permanence, continuity in a place. But at root it means to pause, to linger or delay. We dwell on a subject, but eventually give it up. How long do we have to stay somewhere to say we dwell there? J. B. Jackson takes on the question, but doesn't try to answer in months or years. Instead, he speaks of habits, of a place becoming customary. Habits are acquired, they form over time. With disuse they are forgotten. To dwell in a place rather than simply exist in it seems to hinge on allowing adaptive habits to form, the act of accommodation.

It used to be easier. A home and its land were once widely understood as belonging to a family forever. Even today, most people in the world are born and die within a radius of a few miles. Our much-talked-about casual mobility in this country is an exception. Twenty to thirty percent of Americans move each year; the average American moves fourteen times over a lifetime. Permanent residence is at odds with our notion of property—property as commodity, as route to profit, rather than something attained to keep. The American dream requires that you own your home, but Americans rarely stay in a house longer than five years. Remaining in a home and passing it on to your children is a "certifiable" oddity—in Michigan, houses occupied by the same family for one hundred years or more carry a plaque designating them "Centennial Homes."

American mobility rates have remained fairly constant over the past hundred years, but the *distance* of the moves has increased considerably. To change not just your town, but the region of the country you live in, is understood as a way to change your life, and we aim to do that often. Numerous milestones—college, marriage, birth of children, a new job, divorce, retirement—almost require a change of location. In fact, to stay in one place for life is usually interpreted as being unambitious, unadventurous—a negation of American values. Big cities like New York are perhaps the greatest exception to this rule; there is so much potential mobility within them, and cities can be so addictively stimulating, that many would refuse to move elsewhere no matter what the opportunity. But for most of the rest of the country, moving up in the world means moving on, and often that means moving from the rural to the urban and ultimately the suburban. To stay while others move on may be to feel left out, condemned: "Many people prefer moving to staying around and saying good-by to everyone else," reports the wife of an oft-transferred businessman.

The easy replacement of home ignores its emotional charge for us, ignores how important familiarity is in the constitution of home. The need for a stable, orienting place is deemed by many to be essential to cognitive development and psychic health. However often and successfully we manage it, moving is wrenching, especially to children. Psychiatrist Harold Searles has found that among his schizophrenic patients, a large percentage had experienced numerous changes of residence during childhood. "I have repeatedly seen these patients struggling to remember where they lived, at what age, struggling in a way which indicated that it was very important for their own sense of personal identity, of personal integration, to be able to establish such a continuity of experience in their memory." Among schizophrenics this struggle may be pronounced, but it is a groping for order, for a clear organization of experience, that's familiar to many of us.

Frequent dislocation, or the sudden destruction of a known

environment, can be fundamentally deranging. It means the loss of personal landmarks—which embody the past—and the disintegration of a communal pattern of identity. Home is where we know and are known—through accumulated experience. People relocated from condemned slums often suffer terribly no matter how much more "attractive" the new housing provided. The interconnection between the physical facts of a place and the life lived there is indissoluble.

Eliminated townscapes may remain powerfully alive in people's memories, as vividly illustrated in Vasco Pratolini's novel *Il Quartiere*, where Florentines walking a razed section of their city continue to follow the paths of its former streets rather than cutting diagonally across the space where buildings once stood. It's easy to understand their tribute, feel the tingling impossibility of walking into newly cleared air—a sense of taboo for those who want to believe in the solid dependability of the physical world.

When an entire place or landscape is destroyed, the sense of betrayal and disorientation is acute. Harvey Cox recounts the shattering story of a Holocaust survivor from the Czech village of Lidice, which shows such loss in the extreme:

> The Germans had arbitrarily picked this hamlet to be the example of what would happen to other villages. . . . They came into the town, shot all the men over twelve, then shipped the wives to one concentration camp and the children to another. They burned the village completely, destroyed all the trees and foliage and plowed up the ground. Significantly they demanded that on all maps of Czechoslovakia the town of Lidice must be erased. The woman survivor confessed to me that despite the loss of her husband and the extended separation from her children, the most

shocking blow of all was to return to the crest of the hill overlooking Lidice at the end of the war—and to find nothing there, not even ruins.

English poet John Clare felt similarly violated by the Enclosure Act, which, in the late eighteenth and early nineteenth centuries, vigorously transformed the common open-field system of rural England into private holdings in the name of efficiency. Instead of the long strips and winding trails of the old communal arrangement, small square fields and straight, connecting roads were rapidly imposed on the land, virtually erasing its prior boundaries and landmarks. Even streams were diverted to fit the plan. The landscape was reconfigured on a blank map; what people had lived in for generations became unrecognizable.

Inevitably, such a rapid transformation of landscape had profound personal and social consequences. Previously, a parish had been circular in conception, its village at the center of a ring of three or four large, shared fields around which crops and cattle were rotated. That was *Landschaft*, from which the word "landscape" derives, and it meant more than just a way to organize space. It stood for an ideal of habitation, of people's obligations to one another and the land. A community had to cooperate and follow traditional customs in order to survive—in the common-field system, for example, harvesting of crops had to occur at the same time so that everyone's cattle could then safely be let in to graze the stubble. The entire field, of course, had to be sown with the same crop, at the same time; there was no place for personal idiosyncrasy or procrastination in such a world. Observes John Barrell, "This obligatory submission to the ancient and customary was no doubt part of what made open-field parishes—thus turned in upon themselves—so mysterious to the improver, and so closed to the traveller; and the effect of enclosure was of course to destroy the sense of place which the old topography expressed, as it destroyed that topography itself." After enclosure, the communal sense of place and identity was divided into numerous fenced and hedged private loyalties; a parish became little more than an intersection of roads on the way to the next parish.

John Clare and others like him who had rarely been outside their own parishes were caught in a moment of violent physical and social transformation. Removed from Helpston where his family had farmed for generations, Clare suffered catastrophically from the loss of familiars and the location of his memories; he left an eloquent record of his pain.

> Ive left mine own old home of homes
> Green fields and every pleasant place
> The summer like a stranger comes
> I pause and hardly know her face

The disorientation of removal for Clare was such that even the dependable sun "seems to lose its way / Nor knows the quarter it is in." Outside Helpston "the very wild flowers seemed to forget me"—as if it had been the known landscape that confirmed his existence.

Unable to write about his love of nature in general terms, Clare lost, with his displacement, the crucial particulars that gave his voice a body. Over the following few years, his connection to the external world increasingly slipped. He spent the last twenty-seven years of his life in an asylum writing such lines as "I am—yet what I am, none cares or knows."

When Clare's publisher visited Helpston, he was perplexed by Clare's devotion to it, his mourning of its alteration—it looked so boring a place to a Londoner. It comes as a shock, too, to read that the strange land Clare was exiled to was but three miles from home.

All over Europe, from the Renaissance on, the landscape was increasingly divided as in England, places visibly defined in small units. A side effect was the increased prizing of "shapeliness" in the land, regarding the landscape as a work of art. *Landschaft* had become *landschap* in the hands of Dutch and Italian painters. Landscape painting reflected the growing visual preference for a landscape composed of balanced parts, while at the same time it helped to disseminate that as an ideal. Some claim people only learned to see landscapes by learning to appreciate landscape painting. At its most extreme, says Samuel Monk, "Nature was scarcely seen at all, for the lover of the picturesque was bent upon discovering not the world as it is, but the world as it might have been had the Creator been an Italian artist of the seventeenth century." Our view is still controlled to some extent by that aesthetic norm—highway planners provide us with scenic overlooks that command us to admire the land from a carefully contrived viewpoint.

Though enclosure was largely economic and agricultural in motive, it of course had aesthetic implications, too. And it made social distinctions more visible—between rich and poor, between places for work and leisure. It was in this landscape that the great English gardens were created—by, as Raymond Williams puts it, "a self-conscious observer [who] was very specifically the self-conscious owner" of a pleasing stretch of land. It was in this landscape that private property provided both topographical and social place rather than one's place being communally defined.

The notion of place in which one owns and cares for a plot of land still exerts enormous influence on contemporary Americans. The extent and condition of our property, and our choice of style in dwelling, create a powerful emblem of our identity and status.

At the same time, though, we are awash in a landscape of mobility that eschews connections to particular plots, has no need or desire for great distinction between places, and is essentially utilitarian about the land, often lacking environmental conscience. Place has come more to mean proximity to high-ways, shopping, and year-round recreation, rather than natural situation or indigenous character. In some ways, that's been liberating. In the hierarchy of landowners, admission to place is hard won and restricted; in the landscape of mobility, new communities—be they townhouse tracts or trailer parks—can crop up on the spot and rapidly assimilate new members. Yet we remain caught between nostalgia for place in its traditional sense and cool detachment, between a sense of responsibility for the land and the freedom of indifference.

We've been told we live in a global village, which sounds a little like a *Landschaft*, but in truth, the technologically shrunken world has left us without much of a foothold. "Homelessness," warned Heidegger, "is becoming a world fate." And now we watch it literally and figuratively all around us.

Numerous modern writers have applauded the condition of "perpetual exile" as ethically healthy, a necessary severance from the sentimentalities of nationalism, for example. Others, though, prominently Simone Weil, have argued for attachment: "To be rooted is perhaps the most important and least recognized need of the human soul. . . . A human being has roots by virtue of his real, active, and natural participation in the life of a community, which preserves in living shape certain particular treasures of the past and certain particular expectations for the future."

Given how often I've moved, my community is widely scattered. I have close friends all over the world; none of them knows each other. We have only our own brief intensities of common experience to bind us, our telephone calls and letters. Friendship is tethered to loss, dependent on mental reconstruction instead of daily enactment. Despite my growing number of friends here, I sometimes feel stranded at the center of a frag-mented orb, my life divided into a series of experiences and places that can never be brought together—except in the solitude of memory. My family too is deposited all over the continent. Crucial junctures in our lives take place in hospital hallways or over bad coffee in airports.

In many ways our upbringings prepare us for this essential solitude. The obsessive privacy of the typical American home molds us in an image of separateness, turns us of necessity inward. Nowhere else in the world has isolation been such a common pattern of settlement as in America, especially historically in rural America. As settlers moved out onto the rectangular grids the country was carved into, their farmhouses were almost invariably set toward the middle of the plot, very rarely clustered at the corners near adjoining blocks of land so as to provide proximity to other families. In Quebec, by contrast, farm plots were made long and narrow so that houses could be set side by side along a road. Congress, debating the Land Ordinance Act, briefly worried about the lack of any central focus in the grids. Congressmen from New England believed the lack of a central meetinghouse would lead the settlers into sin. No gathering of towns or villages was conceived of in the grand design; each family went it alone out on the grid. The itinerant merchant materialized, and the mobile library; social life atrophied. These settlers were people who'd primarily come from urban centers in Europe. Their survival in such extreme solitude became an anticommunal American ideal.

Individualism and mobility are at the core of American identity. I'm admittedly the observer and writer I am in part because of the freedom to wander I've had. I did spend five years experiencing what it meant to stay put in a small place with a vital, rooted culture, but mobility is what got me to Ireland and back and what then led me through the experience of several American cities. Mobility is, for many of us, essential to personal and economic development. "Mobility is always the weapon of the underdog," says Harvey Cox. Yi-Fu Tuan, too, reminds us that rootlessness goes hand in hand with American ideals we tend to admire—social mobility and optimism about the future: "To be tied to place is also to be bound to one's station in life, with little hope of betterment. Space symbolizes hope; place, achievement and stability." A fixed place can obviously be seen as a trap, home to drudgery and hopelessness. "Roots are ruts," complains a rising young executive. "To be rooted is the property of vegetables," scoffs geographer David Sopher. To Sopher's mind, the prevailing "domicentric" bias in our thinking has turned "rootless" into the stigmatizing image of the shifty vagabond and made all wandering peoples suspicious—gypsies, tinkers, the Wandering Jew. When people are seen as lacking loyalty to a place, lacking perhaps even the ability to be loyal to places, it is easy to persecute them, see them as threatening to communal stability. The privileged and unadventurous may rightly fear that mobility threatens established traditions, and so they exaggerate the healthy attachment to place into rigid exclusivity and sentimentality. For the underprivileged or disaffected, though, mobility may represent a lifesaving escape, the eluding of oppressive inherited values and the stranglehold of tradition. For a phase of one's life, at the very least, it is a great relief to be free of the influences and expectations that a home place holds, just as one often needs to escape the clutches of one's family in order to mature. ("As for relatives," Stieglitz responded to Dove's plaint of being inundated by them in Geneva, "everything is relative except one's relatives & they are absolute.") Place requires "encounters and obligations," summarizes James Houston; it means accepting certain limitations. Space, on the other hand, is "the arena of freedom that has no accountability."

As a national ideal carried to an extreme, mobility has unfortunately created the circumstances for widespread fragmentation and damage—to people, communities, and the land. The deliberate avoidance of ties to a place, which take years to build, removes constraints, allows us to be indifferent to our towns and cities, to ignore their human and environmental plights, to say *but this isn't mine.* To cling to the right of mobility with all the freedoms it bestows is ultimately to contribute to destruction.

In other traditions, a balance between wandering and staying is aspired to, the understanding that a full life involves both venturing out and returning. (It is like the balance the poet seeks in a traditionally metered poem between the security of a repeated pattern and the surprise of variation.) In the allegorical world of mythical and religious journeys, the greatest challenge of the journey is to return home, to share the lessons of one's experience, to incorporate the journey into its place of origin and help others toward one's insight. Or, as T. S. Eliot has it:

> We shall not cease from exploration
> And the end of all our exploring
> Will be to arrive where we started
> And know the place for the first time.

In Buddhist tradition, the cherished figure of the bodhisattva is the enlightened one who chooses to return home after his spiritual journey, to delay entering nirvana in order to share his insights with others. While remaining in a single place can indeed be imprisoning, to wander compulsively makes one a noncitizen. There is a delicate dialectic to play out. "Before any choice," says French geographer Eric Dardel, "there is this place which we have not chosen, where the very foundation of our earthly existence and human condition establishes itself. We can change places, move, but this is still to look for a place, for this we need as a base to set down Being and to realise our possibilities—a *here* from which the world discloses itself, a *there* to which we can go." Or as poet Richard Hugo puts it, "If you are in Chicago you can go to Rome. If you ain't no place you can't go nowhere."

When we lack a here, our wanderings are full of longing and

confusion. With no abiding sense of home to get back to, all my travels have had a certain restlessness in them, a neediness. Rather than simply browsing the postmodern menu of the world, like many of my generation, I keep trying to fall in love, find "it," the ultimate place I can imagine spending my life in. Writers travel in idiosyncratic ways, and the record of their journeys can tell us much. For Alastair Reid, for instance, traveling has always been an "away from" a firm "here," his native Scotland, a desire for the keenness of being perpetually foreign. Lawrence Durrell, on the other hand, preferred to be called a "residence-writer," not a travel writer, his books delving into, testing the perfection of the places he alighted in, whole-heartedly taking on their coloration. "Why should we take such an odd pleasure in being taken for a different nationality from our own?" asks Reid. "Perhaps because we have succeeded in getting away with an impersonation. . . ." Or perhaps, as Durrell might have it, we have succeeded in pasting on a truer identity than the one we were circumstantially given or molded into, have found the truer stage for ourselves, the truer home of our imaginations. Given the thin gruel of my series of childhood homes, my own searchings have been driven by Durrell's kind of longing.

———

Out on the edge of Geneva, large rolled carpets of hay, like big jelly-roll mounds erected in a field, a haphazard pattern of circular straw sculptures. They are so weirdly evocative in the August sun that I stop to study them, consider them, find their place in my memory. And strangely enough the echo they strike is of Carnac in Brittany—that field of granite monuments, eleven long avenues of more than three thousand standing stones, huge to tombstone-sized, unexplained, of an age with Stonehenge.

Years ago, I wandered to Carnac in the midst of a vague

pilgrimage. I'd decided to go to the Breton coast to visit the setting of Eleanor Clark's moving book *The Oysters of Locmariaquer*, a work she describes as "a journey of interrogation" into the famous French oyster and the people who raise it. Mine was a journey of writerly admiration and appetite. I checked into an inn, ritualistically ate a plateful of the storied oysters with good white wine, then set out walking near dusk toward the edge of town where a sign announced "Dolmen." There I found a field of rolling mounds and fallen stones with just one dolmen left intact—a bridge of boulders, not as stark and tall as those burial sculptures I'd known in Ireland, doorways in open air, but wonderfully cavelike, still partly covered with earth, its huge slabs of rock set upright into the earth and roofed with a plate of stone thousands of years ago. The quiet of a distant intention hung over the enclosed, designated space. Someone's bones housed here. Twilight gathered, I stood beneath the cross stone, extending myself . . . and then I heard a chirping, a piping, a song or calling . . . I heard . . . something, and it was rising out of the ground just beyond the field. Trembly, I headed in its direction. Flutelike first, the music grew, added a drum, maybe a lute. It wandered as I followed, hopping tree to tree, distancing itself from my approach. It was almost dark. I despaired of finding the melody, its source and reason.

Then I saw fire between the trees, a big gash of it, and froze. The music seemed to be coming from the flames, the sky above orange and alive. What in the world had I stumbled on? I pushed forward, and abruptly I was out of the trees and into a clearing, standing before a huge bonfire being danced around by hundreds of costumed women, men, and children. A five-woman electric band was playing old Breton folk tunes on a hilltop beside them, and glasses of brandy were lined up on a table for the taking. A bacchanalia, a fest, and suddenly I remembered that it was the eve of the summer solstice, remembered years of bonfires on mountaintops in Ireland, the drinking and singing—a pagan rite kept alive by Celts. I hung at the edge—this was theirs, not for outsiders or tourists—but the old women soon beckoned me toward the brandy, and enlivened by it I let my feet follow the ancient folk dances ringing the fire, let myself be warmed and spun. The trees swayed, the sky clarified. As much as I loved that this ritual had persisted, I loved how it had been adapted: that was no lute I'd heard, but a synthesizer, and Orpheus was a woman, blond hair flung over a shoulder, lipsticked, smiling. I floated back to the inn.

Next morning I drove to Carnac, parked away from the beach and creperies, and faced the astonishing forest of stones—gnarled weather-beaten steles, unpolished, untamed. Stonehenge hundreds of times over. Nearby were the tallest, high as thirteen feet, and some of the carved ones, indecipherable. Farther on the stones get smaller, plainer, are gorse choked and lichen painted. I stared down the lines, groping for a logic to their arrangement. All I could feel was the force of their existence. That they were probably erected more than six thousand years ago was enough to keep me staring. The vastness of the project stunned too—the incalculable labor required to cut, move, carve, and arrange three thousand large stones.

For those who believe in the spaceships of gods, Carnac's stones are imagined to be navigational beacons, patterned runway guides, or even energy-storage cylinders that a plane could beam in on. "Theories have proliferated in abundance over the centuries and range from suggestions that the stones are immense plugholes that prevent vast underground springs from bubbling up and inundating the land, to the perennial, and universal, folktale that the upright pillars are the bodies of soldiers turned to stone through magical powers by someone they were pursuing. Concurrent with the latter belief is the familiar legend that at certain times the stones return to life and hold dances, go to the nearby spring for water, etc."

Evidence of the astronomical knowledge behind the stones'

arrangement is strong—each group seems to have a specific solar orientation. Lengthy research by Alexander Thom suggests that Carnac was a kind of laboratory for testing and refining observations of sun, moon, and stars. There are as well numerous fertility and agricultural symbols engraved on some of the stones—plows, wheat, ox horns, axes, snakes. But whatever the intention of the design and symbols, Carnac is a cemetery too, and one people may have brought bodies to from many places, the remains of several races having been unearthed there.

The big strung-out field held a taut silence. I walked the rows in and out, up and down, their mystery drawing me as compellingly as last night's wild music had. I wove them; I touched them; I held out my wings and found a landing strip. I was already late to meet friends back in Locmariaquer. And then the solstice festival of the night before reerupted—a dozen couples, clownishly dressed, suddenly appeared and began to play a carnival game among the stones, the men stuffed into baby carriages, the women, hobbled, racing them along a balloon-festooned obstacle course, cheered by onlookers, accompanied by a band of pipes and drums. What could this mean? Some invisible finish line was reached, the cheers rose, and the players collapsed in hilarity, their ritual fulfilled. The sun, the sun of the year, shone down swaggeringly on the old silence and granite gray. Carnac was suddenly aflame, the band taking off down the main avenue, piping the air into dance, clowns shimmering in ruddy clusters, still laughing, the music and light and unspoken meaning of the place gathering into one of the rarest celebrations of place I've been fortunate enough to witness.

Inexplicable Carnac has been called "the skeleton of a dead place," whose meaning has withered. But these raucous carnivalists wouldn't agree—even though they were now climbing back into their Ford Escorts, trailing ribbons and prizes, to head for a drink in town. They had come, they had played, they had paid some kind of obeisance.

—Around 1880, not far from Carnac, people who had been married for several years and not had children, came, when the moon was full, to a menhir; they removed their clothes and the woman began to run around the stone, trying to escape from her husband's pursuit; their relations kept watch all round. . . .

—Women used to come and sit on the cromlech of Cruez-Moquem with their dresses tucked up; a cross was set upon the stone precisely in order to put an end to this practice. . . .

—Kings and clerics in the Middle Ages were constantly forbidding the cult of stones, and in particular the practice of seminal emission in front of stones.

They still visit, in broad daylight.

———

I am back in a Geneva hay field, not dancing or being chased, feeling a little self-indulgent. There's no mystery-laden pattern here, just stacks of grain randomly thrown out by a machine. Still, it has kept me looking, remembering. It has, true enough, transported me somewhere else by association, but now this place holds that place, like an envelope, and my feelings for the two are intertwined. We do bring our experiences home, finally.

I thought I saw Carnac again, once, on the road between Geneva and Waterloo. It was astonishing, but there under the full moon I saw the silvery spikes of it rising out of a scrubby field, row after row, calm and empty. I kept blinking my eyes, unnerved. Then I saw the sign: the "Seneca Drive-In Theater," defunct, the poles of its sound system left erect in the gravelly, weed-choked graveyard of drive-in movie days, left to glint in the moonlight, an electronic alignment, musicless.

Once a Carnac is glimpsed, there's the understandable desire to return or to find it elsewhere, to experience again the shock of a whole, richly layered place. It drives me still to travel. I still half think I'm going to find *the* place for me, for us.

I come from a people in diaspora who only lightly touch the place on earth they happen to be living. My grandparents fled the pogroms of Russia and Eastern Europe, lost the coherence of their villages, reestablished it, to some extent, in the immigrant streets of New York. Then their children, my parents, fled the city for an American-dream suburban life, severed from the intimate communities of their childhood. None of the many homes my parents made for me and my sister approached what they had come from—their goal was to get as far from that life, with its poverty and ghetto narrowness, as possible. Suburbia may have offered a new form of community to them, but it was more truthfully a series of stepping-stones to status. The streets outside our increasingly pricey homes, though, looked exactly the same to me—mass-produced and bare, something for us to buy into, move on from.

Housing developments still grieve me. Not only are they interchangeable and ubiquitous, but they are also such an ominously forced form of neighborhood—house colors legislated to a single shade, or choice of similar three, landscaping controlled by the neighborhood association. Even the street names have in recent years been reduced, strangled into intimacy— moving beyond earlier schemes based on a theme (trees, race-tracks) or a letter (my Levittown development was stuck together on the letter "f"); newer developments often choose a single name and cram together, say, a Windsor Court with a Windsor Mews, a Windsor Drive, Road, Avenue, Lane, and Place. A friend tells me how visiting his mother, having forgotten what Windsor she was living on, and all the houses an identical rosy beige, he drove around desperately in her car, pressing the garage-door opener, waiting to see which door would open to welcome in her car.

It's no wonder we return from these visits "home" dispirited. The developments many of our parents retire into have no connection to childhood for us. Even if our families remain in our hometown, the place is often so drastically altered that our landmarks are as completely obliterated as John Clare's. We're left disoriented, unable to find our way to old haunts. Most of the fields and woods are probably gone anyway, and to see a building or a business in American suburbia that has survived intact a twenty- or thirty-year lapse is a rarity. It's a tissue-paper world, ripping before our eyes, even more temporary than we are.

Because we've been left so little to rely on, we're forced into self-protective amnesia. If our places change so radically, so quickly, what do the lives we lived in them mean? The rhythm of change and persistence, the balance of past and present, has been warped. We ourselves have been thrown out.

Maybe my persistent yearning for a full-fledged home derives more from my Jewish background than I've allowed. Most American Jews come from irretrievably lost places. We remain half-at-home here, alert enough to pack in a hurry if need be, the ghost of the Holocaust too close for comfort. To not belong, to imagine constantly an elsewhere, becomes a chronic unease. It does not compel, or perhaps even allow, loyalty to one's present place, the making of a solid home. That is the resistance I'm trying to overcome here finally. When the landscapes we find ourselves in are not diffused with *our* meanings, our history or community, it's not easy to attach ourselves to them. It cannot be a natural connection, but must be a forged one. It is easier to turn inward from a strange land than to attempt to bridge the gap.

Historically, the physical life of Jews in diaspora, in ghettos, was cramped and oppressive, often literally cut off from the cultures that surrounded and ruled them. In compensation, think some, the temporal dimension of Jews' lives—their history—gained disproportionate importance. "Their spatial existence was always a tenuous and painful reminder of their isolation from the surrounding world," says critic Stephen Kern, "and was far less important to them than their existence in time. Thus the Wandering Jew is at home only in time." Cultural identity had to be internalized, kept abstract, free of attachment to its physical setting. Yiddish is said to be the only folk language in the world that has no base in nature—its vocabulary is bereft of plants and animals, almost the entire natural world.

Jews have perhaps had a complicated, ambivalent relation to nature from the start. Though natural symbols survive in ritual, Judaism is the religion that by and large defused the tradition of sacred place. This is the religion that imaginatively placed divinity *outside* nature, the religion in which God, instead of existing *as* nature, used the forces of nature as punishment (plagues of locusts, floods). Harvey Cox finds it revealing that the Hebrew concept of God "arose in the social context of a nomadic, essentially homeless people." The pagan gods the early Jews set out to overthrow were the numerous place-defined, local nature deities. For Jews, holy places were not crucial, because their single God was a spirit who could be worshiped anywhere. "Anywhere" meant that the where of one's life faded in significance. Identity depended on human community and common belief, not on a shared location.

That tendency toward placelessness helped define the thinking and writing of numerous artists and intellectuals this century who remain highly influential. Proust is an interesting literary example, a writer for whom the meaning of places depends entirely on their personal associations: "The places that we have known belong now only to the little world of space on which we map them for our own convenience. None of them was ever more than a thin slice held between the contiguous impressions that composed our life at that time; remembrance for a particular form is but regret for a particular moment, and houses, roads, avenues, are as fugitive, alas, as the years."

His plaint is close to my own on occasion, close to the fact of quickly vanishing landscapes. But for Proust, the implications are more extreme. Says Kern: "If there is a single illusion that Proust most wanted to dispel it is that life takes place primarily in space. The spaces in which we live close about us and disappear like the waters of the sea after a ship passes through. To look for the essence of life in space is like trying to look for the path of the ship in the water: it only exists as a memory of the flow of its uninterrupted movement in time. The places where we happen to be are ephemeral and fortuitous settings for our life in time, and to try to recapture them is impossible." Places are ephemeral when they are treated as dispensable, when we are not embraced by their traditions or when the traditions have drained away. Even for exiled modernist James Joyce, Dublin is what solidly persists when chronological time breaks down in his work and fantasy takes over. Place is the concrete, time the fluid. For most of us this century, it is the reverse. "Most individuals feel almost naked without their wristwatches," notes Wilbur Zelinsky, "but how many carry compasses, maps, or field glasses. . . . ?" We continuously, unconsciously, transform space into time, say a city is four hours away rather than two hundred miles.

E. V. Walter, a sociologist specializing in the study of place, points to Freud as another figure whose temperamental affiliation with time rather than space has had a crucial influence on our thinking. "Freud moved theory of the mind away from grounded experience and helped to build the couch as a vehicle abstracting patient from place. Despite his own existential recognition of the inner need that yearns for place, Freud's psychology never integrated personal identity with the sense of belonging, and the real power of places." The mind, for Freud, is very much conceived of as "its own place."

Tellingly, Walter points out, Freud even rejects the rich spatial metaphor he invents in *Civilization and Its Discontents* to explain the mind. There, Freud asks us to imagine the city of Rome with its past entirely visible alongside the present, relics from previous periods occupying the same space as contemporary buildings. But just as we construct such a Rome in our minds, Freud abruptly dismisses the notion—because it's physically impossible. The Rome Freud suggests, though, where Renaissance palaces, ancient walls, temples, and modern office buildings would vie for our attention, is exactly the kind of place the willing visitor creates with tourist manuals and an open mind. In Rome, more than in most other places, it's possible to experience a vivid sense of the continuity of human generations in a place.

David, Zoe, and I spent several months in 1985 in an apartment on a downtown Roman street whose semicircular curve derived from the ancient Theater of Pompey. In the deep basement of a neighborhood restaurant, one could glimpse remnants of the theater wall. The piazza we looked out over, home to operatic arguments over garbage and the price of bread, was the site of Caesar's assassination. For me, his imagined cry, sifted through Shakespeare, indelibly mingled there with the screeches of children and the roar of motorbikes. Around the corner, inside the scaffolding and green netting that swathed landmark buildings on nearly every block, I listened as renovating workmen remonstrated with each other, bickering theatrically about tools and strategies. There, too, I distinctly heard other men, from the days of the empire through the Renaissance and baroque, having the same conversations about these very same buildings—"No, not there, blockhead, the column goes here." It was to feel aloud the palimpsest of Roman streets, just as Freud proposed, an evocative clutter that seems remarkably analogous to the workings of a lively mind. Rome's an ideal metaphor, in truth, for the landscape of fantasy and memory—

everything seeming to exist simultaneously, having equal weight and sway. A biographer of Freud concurs that "Today, archeological relics seem quite appropriate as symbols of psychoanalytic procedure and its results."

But while Freud uses archaeological metaphors freely elsewhere in his writing, describing the "unearthing" of his patients' pasts and the "relics" of their experiences, he allies the cacophonous mental experience of places with hysteria. The mnemonic symbols of cities, for instance—monuments and memorials— are seen as comparable to irrepressible memories of traumatic experience: "Every hysteric and neurotic behaves like a Londoner who might pause in deep melancholy before the memorial of Queen Eleanor's funeral, instead of going about his business, or who might shed tears before the monument that recalls the ashes of the metropolis, although it has long since risen again in far greater brilliance. Hysterical patients suffer from reminiscences." Although it may be a matter of degree, Freud's line of reasoning, asserts historian Joseph Rykwert, rests on the analogy that "close attention to the city's monuments . . . suggests a sick citizenship." Instead of recognizing that the symbols and memories of a place are the way people can integrate themselves with a culture, Freud thinks of them as a curable disease. "It seems almost as if he were advocating an indifference to one's environment," Rykwert says.

Given this stance, Freudian psychology perhaps helped intensify our separation from place. Harold Searles laments that the entire nonhuman environment is virtually ignored by Freud and his successors because of their intense focus on the human personality and human relationships—"as though the human race were alone in the universe, pursuing individual and collective destinies in a homogenized matrix of nothingness, a background devoid of form, color and substance."

This is our inherited thinking, an essential severance from place true for many of us, not just those historically in diaspora.

We have been taught to live consciously in time rather than place, with our lives divided into well-defined passages. Without the continuity of place, our sense of time is exaggerated, becomes an omnipresent drama. Wendell Berry, too, wishes psychotherapy were more conscious about restoring our connection to places—"The lost identity would find itself by recognizing physical landmarks, by connecting itself responsibly to practical circumstances; it would learn to stay put in the body to which it belongs and in the place to which preference or history or accident has brought it. . . ." But that is not, typically, how nowadays we "find" ourselves.

We almost cannot when the stage sets on which we play out our lives are struck with each act, ditched. We only have the plot. The where of our immediate past is often unrecognizable, our further past unlocatable. Many of us are unable to trace back our ancestry beyond a generation or two. Even if we can, we have little idea, really, of *what* we've come from, what places and experiences have unbeknownst to us filtered into our personalities, helped shape our values and temperaments.

In my case, because my father was orphaned when young, he wasn't even sure exactly where his parents had come from. My mother's family wandered restlessly around Europe and back and forth across the Atlantic so that it's impossible to know what they thought of as home, if indeed they thought about it at all. No one in my family spoke much about the past. My father, particularly, eschewed it with a tight-lipped shrug— his shattered childhood was no doubt too painful to retrieve. It was only when he died that we found a shoe box of souvenirs he'd kept, his infant boots and family photos, a galaxy of ghosts we didn't know we had, faces formally posed at what look like Coney Island booths, or studio portraits from back in Russia, people whose identities we could only guess—these two must be sisters, see how alike they are, and this their mother, perhaps our great-aunt. Though a few pictures are scribbled on in loose

Cyrillic, and some framed with Hebrew "Happy New Year," none is dated, none located, none shows the background of a lived-in place. These my ancestors preferred to be remembered beside a cardboard ivied casement or on a fake park bench, some ideal of gentility that befit their dressed-up notion of themselves. They are all serious, alert but unsmiling. Had they ever felt at home?

I had always wanted to find them. But the closest I came was to learn Russian, to prepare for pilgrimage. And now, unused, even that has been forgotten, and the past dwindles further away.

Reaching back to those faraway ghosts isn't going to help me here. The only way I'll ever feel at home now will be by making a home for myself with the help of local ghosts. By force of circumstances I must do it here, in upstate New York, where for the foreseeable future we are going to stay.

With the birth of our second daughter, Clea, we are increasingly homebound. Our trip to Italy will likely be our last out of the country for a while. My pilgrimages are of necessity local now, my adventures in lively conversation and in books, after the kids are asleep. I often read about the pilgrimages of others, anxiously wondering if I can continue to make life-altering discoveries by staying home, pressing more deeply into a single place. I read with fascination about the Hindus in India who are frequently on pilgrimage, who compose their sense of place through their wandering obeisance, and wonder if my more circumscribed wanderings here are somehow comparable.

Millions of Hindus routinely set off hundreds or thousands of miles on pilgrimage. They journey to the country's cardinal points, to twelve sacred "lingas of light" where Siva split through the earth, to thousands of "footprints" of the gods set in stone, to places where great rivers join. The whole of India, in fact, is understood as the body of the divine—the literal body of Sati. She is the mother goddess born into the shape of a woman, the beloved of Siva, who burned herself to death after an insult. In his grief, Siva danced insanely all over India with her corpse in his arms. To relieve him, the other gods followed behind, cutting off bits of Sati's body until she was finally gone. Places where her body parts fell became the worshiped "seats" of the goddess also known as Devi, Kali, or Durga. Fifty-one body places, in some traditions 108, are held sacred. Her skull is enshrined in Calcutta. Her tongue is worshiped in the Punjab, her navel in Puri. Pilgrims often walk for weeks, barefoot, to pay homage to her—though nowadays they can also buy a bus ticket for an "official, government-promoted 'All-India Pilgrimage' to one or more of her discrete body parts." There are as well Mother India temples with no image or relic of the goddess at all, but rather a marble map of India itself that pilgrims can circumambulate. Such rituals have been an important means of coalescing numerous distinct regions into a nation. Indeed, Surinder Mohan Bhardwaj dedicates his book on Hindu pilgrimage to "the countless dedicated pilgrims whose footprints have given meaning to India as a cultural entity." Because of this sacralized national identity, the partitions of India that created Bangladesh and Pakistan were painfully protested by religious Hindus as a "vivisection" of the body of Bharat Mata, Mother India.

A mythological system of this kind, suggests scholar Diana Eck, composes the landscape and is just as orienting as other forms of geography—it creates centers and axes, it defines peripheries, it maps. By the act of ritualistic pilgrimage, mythology becomes a "living geography," guided by inherent features in the natural landscape as well as places imaginatively sanctified by the deeds of gods. Mass-produced maps of India show these marks of the gods as prominently as railroad stations and post offices.

Even with such a firm sense of sacred place, though, most Indians, especially in the north, do not have a sense of place about their home landscapes akin to ours. "To emphasize the physical properties of place and the individual's unique experience of these creates a peculiarly Western mystique of place that is not at home in India," explains David Sopher. Further, the fundamental notion of maya in Hindu thought, the transitoriness of the material world, demands an ultimate detachment from place. Unlike other cultures where geopiety arises from staying with one's buried ancestors, the Hindu "seeks death far from home, beside a river that will sweep away forever one's ashes after cremation"—a desire to be free of earthly place in favor of cosmic identification. Thus, landscape in India, as for the aborigines of Australia, lends itself most easily to symbol, abode of the divine. The average Indian doesn't expect to leave an individual mark on the landscape, doesn't expect that significant moments in one's own life constitute the sites for later, personal pilgrimage.

My own pilgrimages, up to now, have been of that less lofty sort, for the most part literary or autobiographical. A book got me to Britanny. Paris I negotiated first while reading Hemingway's *A Moveable Feast,* finding the *lieux* of his reminiscences as a way to begin to take in the city as a lived-in place rather than as spectacle. Now, it's become stirring to revisit places I've experienced as powerfully layered with meaning—like Carnac or the west of Ireland—or even locally, semicomically, to relive Clea's near-birth in the back seat of our car, two miles from the hospital on Border City Road. Whenever I drive there now, whenever I go over the huge bump of the potholed railroad crossing that tore me up that day, I cringe, I laugh. Ugly as it is, there by the electricity substation and the propane company's stack of empty tanks, it has joined my own collection of meaningful landscapes, the places by which I assimilate and chart my experiences on earth. No Mecca, no navel of Devi, no Jerusalem, but one of the places that tie my life together, that tie me here—my lovely baby forever associated with eighteenth-

century wrangling over borders and twentieth-century urban
waste, the terrifying thrill of her emergency birth flitting
through my mind every time I pass there in the midst of daily
chores. To achieve the attachment I hope for here, I need more
places like this—my life set down before my eyes, the landscape
vividly holding my personal past as well as the communal, much
as it does for the Apache. But the truth is, there are few enough
obvious common places to hold dear in this landscape.

The official local mecca, the touristic jewel of the Finger
Lakes, which I've avoided for years and must finally make a
small pilgrimage to, is the Rose Hill mansion. Touted in maga-
zines that devote themselves to American antiquities, it is osten-
tatiously perched on a hill over the northeastern corner of
Seneca Lake.

The two faces of Geneva: this national historic landmark, a
bright white, cupolaed, Ionic-columned mansion, "one of the
finest examples of Greek-Revival style in America . . . idealistic,
exuberant and vital"; and just over the left-hand border of the
photograph, the lived-in, tumbledown shack, its weed-strewn
yard populated by kerosene tanks and a broken washing machine, its boarded-up front porch brandishing a handmade
"Beware of Dog" sign, a rusted-out Chevy in the driveway right
beside where the tourist buses pull in.

The shack was the place lit by a kitchen lamp when I drove
past at 4:30 in the morning once on my way to an early plane.
The yard was an eerie gray-green pool of rubble, the lake two
stone's throws away but invisible. Rose Hill was wearing a
floodlit pallor, staring down the dark; downtown Geneva was
only a gold mercuric glow around the rim of the lake. I remembered that Sullivan's army camped on this hill on the eve of his
attack on Ganundasaga.

At night when the streets of your cities and villages are silent and you think them deserted, they

will throng with the returning hosts that once filled
them and still love this beautiful land. The white man
will never be alone.

How often we think we're alone, in a field, in a car, in the
dark, breathing. I'm unable to look at Rose Hill without clouds
of blood and sweat settling into its whitewash.

The mansion was built in 1839. It's named for Robert Rose,
the Virginian who emigrated in 1802 and settled on this site
with his large group of slaves. The farm's early plantation
life-style fell apart after the emancipation of New York State
slaves in 1827. It became a notable farm midcentury, though,
under the energetic Robert Swan. Swan's father-in-law, John
Johnston, whose farm was contiguous to Rose Hill, was the first
farmer in America to lay a tile drainage system—sixteen miles
long—having imported molds for the ceramic tiles from his
native Scotland. So successful was his work that he complained
that he'd made his land "too rich for wheat." Robert Swan had
come to study farming with Johnston and fell in love with his
daughter. His own father bought him Rose Hill as a wedding
present. And there the better-remembered Swan outdid his
father-in-law, laying sixty-one miles of ceramic tiles to drain the
estate's wetlands, increasing his yield from five bushels of wheat
per acre to fifty. Swan won numerous awards for his agricultural
successes and was influential in founding the state agricultural
experiment station in Geneva. Downtown on Exchange Street,
Thomas D. Burrall was inventing a threshing machine, a grain
reaper, and numerous other tools that contributed to the advance of American agriculture and Geneva's renown.

On the day I visit Rose Hill, Geneva's place in agricultural
history is again confirmed with the first release on open American land of a genetically altered virus—designed to kill the
cabbage looper—in a field not far from the Seneca burial
mound.

The original Rose Hill estate ran as far as the eye could see from the upstairs eastern bedrooms. Today, at twenty acres, its boundary is visible, as are two Mennonite girls driving up, improbably, in an old Buick to check on things—their family now farms part of the old estate. Bonneted in white netting, frocked in full-length flowered cotton, they are not so far in grace from the women who once lived here, though far in means. An early photo of the mansion shows staid, gowned women seated on the portico watching their petticoated daughters politely play croquet on the sloping front lawn. Their view of the lake is mine recaptured at this moment—columned, set beyond balustrade, pleasingly framed.

For a time, evidently, the grand life got lived here. But by the end of the nineteenth century, the estate had changed hands numerous times, and its new owners couldn't maintain its extensive grounds. It became a nursing home, a restaurant, eventually a glorious ruin. It wasn't until the 1960s that it was bought by Robert Swan's grandson, renovated, and transformed into a landmark.

What's worth saving and admiring in this building? Why does it matter?

> Other lives were lived here:
> mostly un-articulate
>
> yet someone left her creamy signature
> in the trail of rusticated
>
> narcissus straggling up . . .
> —*Adrienne Rich*

I am caught between a keen desire for the land to remain marked by the lives that have been lived on it and intolerance for our sentimentalities about the past elite. Nothing much distinguishes the families of Rose Hill except their wealth and Swan's vanished tiles. I'm unmoved by the carefully selected Empire-period furnishings and expertly restored moldings. Instead, walking through the place in a surly frame of mind, I find myself unexpectedly touched by things rarely pictured or mentioned: the children's playroom with its piled blocks and a doll dozing in a tiny hammock; the gold-leaf bedroom suite that was built by prisoners in the Auburn jail; the double-wedding-ring quilt with its central oval—the space where the monograms of the couple and date of marriage were meant to be set—in this case a blank field of white: a prepared-for wedding that never took place. Here is the nanny's room with its cradle for the mistress's newborns, and the kitchen, which the lady of the house probably saw only a few times in her life, the mansion's hidden hub with its solid maple rolling pins, coal steam irons, and big kettles patinaed by the hands of generations of slaves and hired girls. To touch these things is to sense a life.

Pablo Neruda advises:

> It is well, at certain hours of the day and night, to look closely at the world of objects at rest. Wheels that have crossed long, dusty distances with their mineral and vegetable burdens, sacks from the coal-bins, barrels and baskets, handles and hafts for the carpenter's tool chest. From them flow the contacts of man with the earth. . . .

Neruda made startling poetry from such close looking, poetry "impregnated with sweat and smoke," as Irish poet Seamus Heaney describes it, similarly drawn to the artifacts of the ordinary: "It could even be maintained that objects thus seasoned by human contact possess a kind of moral force. They insist upon human solidarity and suggest obligations to the generations who have been silenced, drawing us into some covenant with them." The solidity of that covenant—the weight of the rolling pin in my hands.

I want, like other writers, to bind such mementos to the

present through the connective tissue of language. I'll even pay to see them, hungry for a time when the utilitarian and the beautiful were not so divided, consoled to stroke a time when objects still dependably outlived their users. But the tour is moving on to the banquet room. My fellow tourists have paid for grandiose gestures, and that's what we get in the well-preserved dining hall, which I'm now being impatiently herded toward.

When did we become so worshipful of an idealized, prettified past? Until relatively recently, vestiges of history have been allowed to decay or disappear without much concern. I'll never forget the story of the easygoing Irish work crew instructed by the tourist board to build a stone wall around the ruins of an early church: they dismantled the church and used its stones to build the wall. Colonial Americans were, as a matter of principle, indifferent, or even hostile, to the past. Liberation from the oppressive aspects of tradition they'd left behind in Europe was an essential ingredient of the American spirit. In drastic opposition to the Indians' sense of their ancestors, for instance, Thomas Jefferson announced that "the dead have no rights. They are nothing; and nothing cannot own something. . . ." To inherit was a form of tyranny. Emerson disdained stone houses as lasting too long.

Even a hundred years into our own official history, on the occasion of the centennial of the Declaration of Independence, the celebratory exhibition in Philadelphia showed remarkably little regard for the American past it supposedly saluted. Only one small log cabin tried to reproduce the revolutionary period. According to J. B. Jackson, "There had been a proposal for a demonstration of Colonial farming techniques, contrasting them with those of 1876, but nothing came of it." Instead, the focus was on "the marvels of the present and the promise of the future."

Indeed, as a nineteenth-century German traveler famously

put it, "Americans *love* their country, not . . . *as it is,* but *as it will be.* They do not love the land of their fathers; but are sincerely attached to that which their children are destined to inherit." Instead of depending on a communal past for our identity, we largely define ourselves by our hope for the future. It is apparent on a daily basis. The new gadget readily replaces the old tool; what's old is old-fashioned, headed for the landfill. Says Wendell Berry: "All our implements—automobiles, tractors, kitchen utensils, etc.—have always been conceived by the modern mind as in a kind of progress or pilgrimage toward their future forms. The automobile-of-the-future, the kitchen-of-the-future, the classroom-of-the-future have long figured more actively in our imaginations, plans, and desires than whatever versions of these things we may currently have." While, at their best, our ambitions lead to genuine human progress, in the trivial material realm, the habit of impermanence and the chronic transfer of loyalty beyond the immediate devalues the landscape of the present and permits its throwaway consumption. The religious ideals of early settlers must have helped shape us in this—when the *hereafter* figures more strongly than the *here,* it's easy to justify using up land and resources now. We look forward and take whatever we want. Tocqueville noted with astonishment that as ground was broken to build Washington, D.C., men had "already rooted up trees for ten miles around lest they should interfere with the future citizens of this imaginary metropolis."

In the late nineteenth century, though, under the threat of increasing immigration from unfamiliar countries, there began a shift that encouraged Americans to passionately assert their values, to look back proudly at their own small, accumulated past, and to canonize the founding fathers and their artifacts. Where Grainne and Diarmait and the Hindu gods had slept, George Washington now spent the night.

Locally, by 1929, Sullivan's founding raid on Geneva ("severe but salutary") was a proud enough memory to merit an

enormous sesquicentennial bash—"A Historical Pageant of Decision—Why the Republic Westward Grew." The pageant
drew between 50,000 and 75,000 people to Geneva, more than
any other occasion before or since. On the sloped lawns of
White Springs Farm (site of a former Seneca village wiped out
by smallpox, plundered of hundreds of skeletons, pots, and
trinkets), a five-acre natural stage was set. For four hours, a cast
of 2,500 re-created Sullivan's devastating march and its political
payoff as represented in an epilogue—"Washington's Dream
Comes True." Cannons boomed, hundreds of horses, cows,
squealing pigs, and honking geese did their bit, Indians "died,"
and a hundred girls performed a minuet.

Here as elsewhere, a WASP heritage was now something to
flaunt. The past quickly became commodity; colonial relics
provided a palpable connection to the nation's origins and
carried status as increasing demand outstripped supply. By the
time of the bicentennial, we were firmly in the grip of nostalgia.

Nostalgia has a revealing history. The word was coined in
1678 for the disease of homesickness. Its symptoms included
insomnia, anorexia, palpitations, stupor, and the persistent
thinking of home. Nostalgia was described in European medical
encyclopedias up until the nineteenth century as fatal. The
illness progressed from "a sad, melancholy appearance, a
bemused look, . . . an indifference toward everything" to "the
near impossibility of getting out of bed, an obstinate silence, the
rejection of food and drink; emaciation, marasmus and death."
Prognosis was said to depend entirely on whether or not the
patient could be sent home. Victims of nostalgia probably died
of meningitis, gastroenteritis, and tuberculosis, but "because
everyone believed nostalgia fatal, it so became." To travel far or
long from home was to risk your life. Armies were frequently
beset by the malady, leading one Russian general in 1733 to
announce that "any soldier incapacitated by nostalgia would be
buried alive." Two or three burials put an end to that particular

epidemic. French officers, more compassionately, allowed their soldiers convalescent home leave. Prophylactically, Swiss soldiers were forbidden to play, sing, or whistle alpine melodies, whose effect was known to be swift and disastrous. Remarkably, the U.S. surgeon general still recognized nostalgia as a contagious disorder in army induction centers during World War II.

Young women of the eighteenth and nineteenth centuries were also frequently struck with nostalgia, especially girls sent away from home as servants. Homesickness was a plausible explanation for the fires such miserable girls sometimes set in their employers' homes, or even for murder, as in the case of a nursemaid "who killed her four-year-old charge one night and calmly admitted the crime the following morning. Her only motive . . . was that she felt she could go home if she killed the child." The effects of displacement were keenly acknowledged in such cases.

The meaning of nostalgia shifted in the nineteenth century, though, from being primarily a geographical disease to a psychological one rooted in time. Rather than the loss of home, it came to indicate a yearning for the past, especially for childhood. Freud turned it into regression. The importance of place had already eroded, overtaken by consciousness of time. "The decline of the theory of nostalgia coincided with the decline of particularism in the provinces," says Jean Starobinski—the decline of local rituals and social structures.

For us, nostalgia inevitably suggests sentimentality, a useless longing for something no longer possible. But we might consider it as part and parcel of our rootlessness, our feeling of not particularly belonging where we happen to be. The oft-quoted "Where are the snows of yesteryear?" implies, as Robert Heilman comments, that the snows have been moved somewhere else, a place we might, with luck, find. Nostalgia is built of dislocation, discontinuity. It is a response to the disquiet of upheaval. "Asian villagers living for generations in one place would be baffled by nostalgia," says Russell Baker. "It is an affliction of traveling races who do not like where they have arrived and have no taste for the next destination."

We are so habitually nostalgic by now that we anticipate looking back in the midst of enjoyment, look forward to watching the videos we're taking of our children even as we make them. "Make every moment a memory," demands the photographer's studio. "I am looking to the future with nostalgia," the elder Mayor Daley once told Chicagoans.

Yet only very choice images or sites in the landscape attract our nostalgic instinct to preserve. The American past is either neglected, actively destroyed, or selectively museumed, rarely lived in or understood as a whole. It is "fenced off in a preserve called History," says David Lowenthal. "It is always in quotation marks and fancy dress." And it is rarely seen as something whose meaning adheres to its location—you don't necessarily find the past where it occurred, but where it's convenient to tourists (like Mary Jemison's cabin hauled out of the gorge). That someone's home should retain meaning as visual biography when moved a hundred miles closer to the interstate shows how little regard for environment we really have and what a convenient, thoughtless nostalgia we indulge in.

(What brought tears to my eyes in the room where Keats died in Rome was not anything preserved inside, but the view out his window, perched over the Spanish Steps, raucous with lives going on—knowing he gazed out at that perpetual, lively bustle as he lay dying.)

So little is saved anymore, I end up feeling grudgingly grateful for Rose Hill—which at least values its setting and has no one prancing around in a period costume making canned speeches. There are so few sites commemorated in the region. Nearby, in the Syracuse area, the book *Architecture Worth Saving in Onondaga County* became obsolete a decade after it was published—so many of the pinpointed buildings were destroyed between the mid-sixties and mid-seventies.

Geneva itself has just lost an unlikely but evocative landmark—the Agway Tower, a white concrete grain silo set smack in the middle of the downtown. To many it was an eyesore, a blight against the lake and sky view. But since its demolition to make way for new lakefront development, it's been oddly missed. The 190-foot-high tower was built in 1937—a stark, slim rectangle rising ambitiously from a squat base. It was so sturdily made that when it came time to destroy it, the wrecker's ball bounced playfully off the walls for days.

The Agway Tower had been a controversial building from the start—it was the first commercial building to compete with Geneva's skyline of church spires. The worry of the pious was not altogether unsound. My friend Marvin tells the story of how his young daughter always figured that because God was much too tall to crouch down inside a human house, his earthly shelters were necessarily inside church spires—and the Agway Tower. Arthur Dove made the tower secularly sacred by painting it over and over, first as the stark white industrial building it was, in *Cereal Mill,* and then as *Building Moving Past a Sky,* a tumultuous dark oil full of cold fronts and the impermanence of towns. Later he turned it into *Flour Mill Abstraction,* the tower lifting off its base, surrounded by whimsical, flattened, Miró-like shapes and colors—a calligraphic fancy. Never has Geneva looked so purple, turquoise, and burgundy, recognizable only by that signal tower. Dove was getting rapidly bored with his exile here.

Even though for many the Agway Tower was associated with all-night grueling labor during harvest season, its absence has been registered by those who once worked there, brought their grain, joked and drank coffee there, or simply used it daily to gauge distance and the day's visibility. Their sense of loss is dismissed by those who applaud the removal of the odd-looking building and the land it freed up for envisioned tourists.

For me it was the landmark I sleepily aimed the car toward each morning, and it was, too, a pleasing reminder of Dove, a concrete memento of the play of the imagination, a vision of buildings moving past skies. For future generations, Dove's vision will be all that remains of the tower. They might see those paintings and even fail to identify them with Geneva. A piece of the place's definition has broken loose. Even for a newcomer like me, Geneva is less anchored without that high beacon. Its commercial arteries and development plans swell, but as its land is rearranged, its highway moved to make room for a hotel, the commonest part of its past is eliminated and it loses its distinction. A one-of-a-kind building, born of the local economy, will be replaced with the imported design of a chain hotel. Tourism, based on the distinctions in places, so frequently requires, to sustain itself, the elimination of those very distinctions.

Given our technology, whole landscapes can be cleared in a day. A familiar stretch of land can readily disappear beneath a parking lot or reservoir. Warfare annihilates vegetation and terrain; deep plowing alters land as previous forms of cultivation and grazing could not; industrial pollution, landfills, mass tourism—all are culpable, and so too, sometimes, is our zeal for knowledge: "The most ancient living tree ever found—a bristlecone pine 4,900 years old—was cut down to determine its age."

To belong to the land again in a vital way, we have to preserve enough to walk out into and recognize.

IV

THE CENTER OF THE WORLD—I OWN IT

———

> But it wasn't a dream, it was a place.
> —*Dorothy, on returning from Oz*

DIGGING IN THE GARDEN, cutting worms and centipedes in two, finding glass shards and tin cans, chips of tile, medicine bottles, cold-cream jars—their mouths crammed with dirt—a chair from a child's dollhouse, the rim of a china cup. Deeper: a Seneca arrowhead, a strip of berry-colored cloth. My yard is a patch of history I dig up, push seeds into, and then stand back from with hubris when it erupts in neat rows of green. I am, more than anywhere else in the landscape, a creature of the garden, happy to invest my sweat here, to watch daily for nearly invisible increments of growth in our lettuce or green beans and breathe the mingled scents of herbs. Here I can feel the active love of attachment, the work of place making.

Before we had children, we followed the example of many of our colleagues by leaving each summer, traveling abroad or situating ourselves in a city, staying away from Geneva as long as possible to absorb other worlds and store them for the long winter. We left, ironically, during the most beautiful months of the year, almost entirely missing the region's short period of plenitude. It was only when our annual travel plans were thwarted by Zoe's and Clea's quite different needs that we spent our first summer here, put in the first garden I'd grown since Ireland, and connected ourselves to another season and rhythm of the place. We've stayed every summer since.

As much as I love the lush summers, I am, I have to come clean, violently allergic to most of the natural world. Put me in a hay field and I'll be gasping for air within minutes, staggering home for asthma sprays. Treks through woods are itchy affairs.

I was fortunate in Ireland, in retrospect, to live among bare rock, ocean, and bog. Here I'm always at risk. This explains my love, I guess, of odor- and pollen-free vistas, the color play of distant woods and mountains, even the view from the scenic overlook or the picture window. My natural world is not, for the most part, hands-on; it is, rather, in the shape of things—the old sense of landscape. But the vegetable garden is a tolerable risk, especially if I let David do most of the weeding. I'll do more than sing to it (I have a friend whose interest is confined to walking behind her gardening partner crooning, "Plant a radish, get a radish"). In fact I look forward to the feel of soil in my hands, love to sow and pamper plants, to harvest them, or simply to squat in the sun at the edge of the garden after two days of torrential rain, listening to the bluster of the nearby creek. I let a barn swallow swoop close to my ear, hear gulls squawking on the lake. I rub mint between my fingers, absorb heat. I wonder if the truest way to belong to this place might simply be by patient work.

Our garden, though large enough to keep us busy all sum-mer, is a minute patch among the acres of fields that surround us. We live close to Kendaia now, on the eastern side of the lake—a shift of perspective after nearly five years. Our cliff-top rented house on the western shore was reclaimed by its owners; we had to move. It was a sorrow, a panic at first. But surviving the transplant, I've found that my sense of place here is not housebound or overly specific—it has been flung out into the wider landscape so that though our new rented house is twenty miles from where we were (four by goose flight over the lake), we are very much in a known landscape, equally loved. Our mailing address is now Geneva, though we're ten miles from downtown and in a different county, telephone exchange, and school district from the town. Boundaries crisscross and blur out here, snagged in history.

Our house is a small white dot in the cleared land of the

military tracts. One whole horizon is corn. The lake is a flicker between trees, a short stroll down, sunset instead of sunrise on the water. This house sits more firmly on the land than the first one, into which the lake beckoned at all hours, a constant invitation to voyage. Here, with few trees left, among pedestrian hardworking fields of corn, alfalfa, wheat, and hay, I finally feel more grounded, more like a settler. With the lake at arm's length, and pickups and tractors meandering past on East Lake Road, there can be no illusion of being islanded. We are firmly in the wide world and can't ignore the land's broad, rolling insistence.

Our own little clearing is under constant attack from the hay field it recently was, which it still is a few yards to the north. As Horace said, "You may drive out Nature with a pitchfork, yet she still will hurry back." We have chosen not to be earnest about our garden and have been fairly lucky. Only once has a deer buckleapt through and toppled tomatoes. Rabbits and woodchucks have failed to find us. What we lose to insects we accept as nature's annual cut—the usual ten or fifteen percent. When I'm spading a row and see a swirl of yellow jackets over a hole at the end, angrily declaring the territory their own, I'm happy enough to desist, end the row a foot early.

Those days that I'm indifferent and watch the weeds accumulate, I content myself with the Seneca explanation: "If you do not feel like working in your garden, someone has passed a spell on you. To counteract it, burn tobacco and tell the spell to go back where it originated. 'Go there to whoever hired you and get in their way.' " Well, I'm allergic to smoke, too, so I surrender to my spell.

I'm especially happy to be spellbound when it's time to mow the lawn. The lawns out here are enormous, comically estatelike in proportion to the puny ranch houses and trailers. Our neighbors patrol theirs on the backs of tractor mowers, never letting the grass get long enough to nod. We, on the other hand, put off mowing till the last possible moment—when we're eliciting stern glances from passing cars.

Lawns are unquestioned in America, so "normal" a fact of the landscape that we can't quite imagine living without them. But attachment to our manicured yards seems absurd alongside our typical treatment of the land. Notes J. B. Jackson: "The slightest excuse is enough for us to strip an entire countryside. And yet—there is the front yard with its tenderly cared-for Chinese elms, the picnic ground in the shadow of the pines. . . ."

The tender care is rather haphazard at our place. Two hundred years ago, we wouldn't have gotten away with it. There were laws here, against allowing the Canadian thistle to grow on your land, for instance. "Once in each of the following months—May, June, July, August, and September and any owner or occupant of any lands in the Town of Seneca who shall neglect or refuse to cut the Canada Thistle, he shall forfeit and pay for each month he shall so neglect. . . ." The thistle was ranked second only to the redroot in its "evil influences," a leading player in the moral drama of domesticated land.

I do occasionally fantasize about a more perfect garden, usually early in the season when it's still catalog lovely. I especially ponder how I'd frame it, protect it, set it off from the ragged lawn. I think I'd surround it, first of all, with a stone wall, the kind so common in Ireland, made of the stones unearthed in the opening of the land, added to every time you dig deeper. A waist-high gray sculpture of a wall. "Garden" does derive from the old German word for "enclosure." And as Michael Pollan wisely meditates on it, a garden is a place "that is at once of nature and unapologetically set against it." So I think about walls and boundaries, the inherited habit of setting off the places we love—

In the night, when all is silence,
In the night, when all is darkness,

When the Spirit of Sleep, Nepahwin,
Shuts the doors of all the wigwams,
So that not an ear can hear you,
So that not an eye can see you,
Rise up from your bed in silence,
Lay aside your garments wholly,
Walk around the fields you planted,
Round the borders of the corn-fields,
Covered by your tresses only,
Robed with darkness as a garment.
Thus the fields shall be more fruitful,
And the passing of your footsteps
Draw a magic circle round them,
So that neither blight nor mildew,
Neither burrowing worm nor insect,
Shall pass o'er the magic circle

Longfellow claims to have gotten this from early settlers' reports of the local Indians. In his notes to "Hiawatha," he describes the belief in the magic circle as being authentic:

A singular proof of this belief, in both sexes, of the mysterious influence of the steps of a woman on the vegetable and insect creation, is found in an ancient custom, which was related to me, respecting corn-planting. It was the practice of the hunter's wife, when the field of corn had been planted, to choose the first dark or overclouded evening to perform a secret circuit, *sans habilement,* around the field. For this purpose she slipped out of the lodge in the evening, unobserved, to some obscure nook, where she completely disrobed. Then, taking her matchecota, or principal garment, in one hand, she dragged it around the field. This was thought to insure a prolific crop, and to prevent the assaults of insects and worms upon the grain. It was supposed they could not creep over the charmed line.

There are numerous hints that Iroquois women did on occasion plant or attend their gardens ritualistically naked, particularly those who were "demonstrably fertile," symbolically contributing their fertility to the ground. Contemporary farming on Iroquois reservations, though, observes taboos against menstruating women doing the planting, and even advises against pregnant women walking through the fields. So the tradition, as elsewhere, is ambivalent. Mircea Eliade describes East Prussian women sowing peas while naked, and women in Finland sprinkling furrows with breast milk. The object of such practices, he says, "is certainly to make the crop thrive, but also to protect it against the evil eye or the depredations of rabbits." Pliny mockingly reports ancient Roman rituals similar to what Longfellow describes: "Another method, too, of preventing caterpillars, is to make a woman . . . go around each tree, barefooted and ungirth . . . an absurd notion. . . ." Absurd or not, I wouldn't mind dancing the borders of our plot naked in the full moon. Whatever about caterpillars, it would create a memorable boundary in my own vision of the place. And who would dare cross me?!

The desire to make a magic circle abides in ritual and play, expressing our need to create a symbolic center. Groups as well as individuals seem to require a marked center from which to observe the rest of the world. On both cosmological and geographical maps, of course, people almost invariably place themselves at the center. Countless holy places—like Stonehenge—enclose a circle, create a navel. Numerous cultures fix the mythic center of the world at an omphalos. Even nomads carry the means of a center with them; they erect it—as a fire, for example—when they set up camp. And the artist often lays claim to the world aesthetically from a chosen vantage point. "About an hour this side of Albany is the Center of the World—I own it," declared painter Frederick Church in the tradition of self-conscious observer-landowners. A defined circle gives people a sense of power and confidence, akin to the extraordinary strength of animals in their home territory. Our own weak encirclements in open space, our mowed lawns setting us off from the chaos of forests, are crucial to our sense of security and self.

Up until the sixteenth century, Europeans confidently believed themselves to be at the center of the universe, stars and sun whirling around at a respectful distance. Copernicus's assertion of a heliocentric system, moving earth to the periphery, was truly unbalancing, fundamentally disturbing to the human sense of placement. Because the planet itself lacks obvious reference points for the placing of a center, symbolic centers are of necessity self-made, local.

The making of such a center is typically accompanied by elaborate ritual. In ancient Rome, for example, a new town had to be physically marked out first, cut off from the chaotic space around it. Several forms of augury preceded even the selection of the site. Intense care was essential because the founding of a town was seen as in some sense equivalent to the founding of the world, and the setting of its center was the crucial first step. "That is why," says Joseph Rykwert, "the place on which it is built cannot arbitrarily or even 'rationally' be chosen by the builders, it must be 'discovered' through the revelation of some divine agency." The literal physical circle of Roman settlements was created first by a plow. So charmed and charged with power was this cutting of the boundary that when the plow reached the location for the town's obligatory three gates, it was lifted, carried across the land (a portage for the porta) to leave open an unsanctified space through which daily life could flow. The walls followed the cut line.

Despite the animation of the boundary by human or animal sacrifice, the charm of its walls and standing stones did need to be periodically reinforced, and so communities annually paraded around their borders, visiting holy stones and groves along the way. These ritualistic perambulations live on in the Christian era, transformed into Rogationtide, the "beating of the parish bounds." Still widely practiced in rural England each spring, the procession is used both to symbolically confirm parish borders and to seek God's blessing for the newly planted crops. Though organized by the Church, Rogationtide remains very much a local pagan festival at heart, ritualistically enacting the definition of place. In the days before surveyors and deeds, such a tradition was no doubt essential for passing down crucial information—circling the bounds was a geography lesson, especially for the young.

When the ritual was less casual and merry, when stones were still believed powerful, participants would cut wood wands with which to strike and "reenergize" them, and children would be beaten at important landmarks and thrown into ditches—perhaps a remnant of human sacrifice, or simply a way to enhance their memory of the stones' locations. Perambulations were also performed in times of crisis—such as a siege or an epidemic—to strengthen the enclosure's defenses.

Because boundaries are essentially protective, the punishment for violating them was extreme. Crossing a boundary without authorization was a desecration, a threat to the place's defensive shield, and was typically punished by death. For leaping the city wall, Remus got killed by Romulus. The Bible and folktales from all over the world testify to the extreme danger of tampering with landmark stones: "Cursed be he that removes his neighbor's landmark." In Swedish legend, Jack-o'-Lantern was a mover of landmarks and therefore doomed to wander the night, haunting boundary lines, forever. Lighting a sinister-faced pumpkin each Halloween is an unconscious reminder of the ancient injunctions of defined place.

In secular terms, boundaries are potent because political

stability depends on an ordered, respected landscape. Observed boundaries reduce conflict. ("Good fences make good neighbors.") Boundaries enforce the social order, too. In early New England villages, hierarchically arranged outward from their centers, trespass was construed as a crime not only against property, but against social rank. We continue to honor borders—from fences to frontiers—with a sense of prohibition equal in intensity to the authority of the religious. Ownership for us, private property, has taken on the taboos of the holy.

Eliade argues that a completely secular experience of the landscape is really impossible. Secular people tend to replace sacred, ritualized places not just with private property, but with individual privileged places—the sacred places of one's private universe—and set them off imaginatively as hallowed: for instance one's birthplace, the first foreign city ever visited, the scenes of first love, of life-altering decisions or events. Like Carnac and Border City Road for me, these are our version of landmarks. In common usage, landmarks are more often the names of banks and gas stations we jot down on a scrap of paper while taking directions to an unknown destination. They are mundane, impermanent. You tell people to turn right by the Gulf station, and overnight it's turned into a Sunoco. But even unlikely landmarks can become charged, as with some San Francisco gang members who dedicated parking spaces in their neighborhoods as memorials to dead comrades. " 'Keep Out' was painted in one shrine to honor a slain gang member who had customarily parked there. Police say a motorist who ignored the warning was shot and killed."

There's sacred place—reduced to where we customarily park. Of course in earlier traditions, hallowed places could not be created by personal resonance, but only by their association with a god. For the Romans, the spirit of the place, the *genius loci*, meant literally the *begetter* of the place. A temple built at a sacred place was meant to "locate" the divinity, and was understood as an extension of the god's presence in the land. In this country, one could create a sacred grove by cutting down trees in the middle of the woods and having a revival meeting. But for the ancients, the holiness of the place came first, the shrine after, in response. *Nemos* was the name used in ancient Greece for a sacred, enclosed tract of land; its inherent power, its protective goddess, was Nemesis—the avenger of trespass by those not properly prepared for the sacred. We've secularized nemesis into that which we can't best—an ungrounded abstraction. The concept of *moira* suffered the same displacement; we translate it as "fate," but it was first literally an "allotted portion"—the place individual gods were assigned to rule in accordance with how their characteristics matched the landscape. "The original conception of moira," Erich Isaac explains, "thus turns out to be spatial rather than temporal. We are to think of a system of provinces, coexisting side by side, with clearly marked boundaries." To better understand the Greek gods, suggests Paula Philippson, we'd do well to examine their assigned landscapes.

———

Whose assigned landscape is Seneca Lake? In dead of winter, early morning, huge columns of mist erupt from the warmish surface of the water, rise into the icy air, and let sunlight prism through them, become dancing rainbowed goddesses, subject only to the building heat of the sun. By afternoon they've vanished. The lake is turbulent, sullen. And now the trees are hypnotized by sudden snow, a lake-effect squall, black clouds blasting across the water and dumping themselves on the eastern shore, an inch in minutes. A hard west wind sends gusts of snow chasing across fields. I chase after, dazed by the sudden blankness, the closing down of the sky, as if a god had stamped its foot, turned its back, and let the world turn a terrifying, unbound white, shelterless. Where can we turn?

For the Seneca, local spirits could be found everywhere—

underground, in rocks, riding the lake. If you believed and were courteous, you could hear them. One, the Talking Stone, could tell the story of everything that had ever happened here. *This happened in the time when men and animals lived as brothers and could understand each other's language. Listen!* This happened in the time when people could understand the language of stones. I stop in the woods as the snow thins out, let it accumulate quietly on my hair and gloves. The trees creak. The stones are dumb, hidden. How far down am I willing to listen?

One August night, shortly after moving to East Lake Road, we were sitting, content in the quiet, when suddenly there was a boom, an explosive shudder in the windowpanes, our shoddy bookshelves swaying. We looked up, startled. A plane crashing at the depot? Or, God forbid . . . David laughed—here by Kendaia, at virtual ground zero, we wouldn't even have time to look up. Back in 1941, in response to local fears of the possibility of explosions in storage igloos at the depot, a Colonel Parker confidently declared that "other than a loud noise, a rattle of windowpanes, and a subsequent ringing in the ears, there would be no injury." What do they think they'd get away with telling us these days? Another boom. Maybe thunder. But no, the sky was clear and calm. Maybe we'd just heard the lake's spirit-owner speak—the legendary lake gun.

Lake guns, or death drums of the Seneca, are the periodic booms reported by lakeside residents for centuries, an eerie phenomenon out of history and myth that persists. The guns boom unpredictably, often on sultry summer evenings, sometimes on icy mornings; they sound like distant cannons.

The supposed Seneca explanation was floridly recorded by George Conover:

> Among the braves of the tribe there was one, straight as an arrow whose regal form towered above all others. Agayentah. One day, out hunting, he took

shelter from an impending storm under a large tree on the bank of the lake. Amid a roaring of thunder and a hurricane of wind there came a death-winged shaft of lightning that dealt both tree and warrior a fatal blow. The tempest hurled the two lifeless trunks down the embankment and into the water.

The next morning, while the Seneca braves were filling the land with lamentation, there appeared on the surface of the water something like the trunk of a tree standing erect, protruding about two feet. With the next storm it began its ceaseless wandering, sometimes against the wind, sometimes with the wind, sometimes disappearing for a period, and then reappearing and resuming its ceaseless march. The "Wandering Jew" the white man came to call it, though it was known to the Indians as the "Wandering Chief."

It is said that strange noises presage the advance of the "Wandering Jew" and that during the quiet and death-like stillness that precedes an approaching tempest, and at evening also, whenever the setting sun covers the water with bloody tints, may be distinctly heard, as symbolic of the tragic events we have related, those wonderful sounds familiarly known as the "Lake guns of the Seneca." Agayentah is on the march.

It would be nice to assign those watery exclamations to the inexplicable, imagine them the sighs of a rootless wanderer, cousin to myself. But science hypothesizes that the booms are small gas explosions, and the marching trees the result of a strong undertow. My colleague Bill Ahrnsbrak says it's more than a coincidence that reports of the guns have diminished since gas fields were opened on the lakeshore. Poking holes provided another outlet for the gas—a kind of antacid, he jokes, to keep the lake from burping.

A local man claimed to *see* the lake burp once back in 1905: a large flattish dome rising out of the water, fifteen to twenty feet across, three or four feet high, suddenly popping. It's hard not to mystify or personify the earth's powers at such moments, not to feel overawed by how little we finally know of it, how in its sway we are when it decides to act up or quake.

It was under the spell of the Irish landscape that I first let awe lead me to study primitive and mystical conceptions of the earth. I was reading William Irwin Thompson's book, *Passages About Earth*, about power points, the notion that lines of energy surround the earth and that where they intersect we find particularly charged, resonant places on the planet. In ancient cultures, people known for their spiritual abilities slept on identified power points. These were the places early temples were built.

The idea had personal resonance, for Thompson tells the story of St. Colman, the outlawed, esoteric early Christian who, forced to flee the holy centers at the power points of Lindisfarne and Iona, ended up building a monastery on my obscure Irish island in 667 A.D.—a holy refuge I passed the ruins of daily. Colman and his monks practiced an ecstatic brand of Christianity close to nature—St. Cuthbert of Lindisfarne prayed while standing in the sea surrounded by animals and birds. The places these monks gravitated to were deemed to have unusual natural powers. If Lindisfarne and Iona were acknowledged power points, so then, I figured, must my island be, chosen by Colman as sanctuary. The idea jibed well with the intensity of my experience of the place. And my education in poetry made me susceptible to the notion too, for, as Thompson explains, it was this archaic heritage of sacred place that was "resurrected by the romantic poets, especially Wordsworth, who tried to show that

there was a special affinity between altered states of consciousness and unusual points in the landscape." It had certainly been
my experience that particular places on the island—hillsides,
caves, and beaches—could draw me out of the ordinary and
provoke poems the way Wordsworth's landscape provoked him:

> The anchor of my purest thoughts, the nurse,
> The guide, the guardian of my heart, and soul
> Of all my moral being

Out of the blue Marvin mentions to me that this area of the
Finger Lakes rests within a "sacred triangle" marked by three
power points, a landscape long recognized as particularly fertile
spiritually. The same kind of power points as Thompson talks
about? Have I by some fluke stumbled onto another spiritually
resonant place? Where are these points, I ask him, and what has
happened here to suggest their power? Marvin points to the
Iroquois longhouse line, old trees and springs he visits, covens
near Ithaca. He has a living map in his mind.

Power points, lines of power, and fields of benevolent force
are ideas held by a number of cultures, notably the Chinese,
who, "since at least the 2nd century BC, have regarded the earth
as a living organism, comparable with other organisms such as
the human body. Just as the human body incorporates channels
along which its life blood pulsates, so it was thought that the
earth included similar channels, sometimes described as 'the
veins of the earth.' . . . Parts of the earth which are favorably
sited lie at points where such channels converge. . . ." As in the
Chinese practice of acupuncture, these earthly channels must be
left unblocked in order for energy—the life force of ch'i, which
links spirit and substance—to circulate freely. Ch'i is often
visualized as a dragon, its body and even its arteries outlined in
the curves of mountains and rivers. Maxine Hong Kingston's
fictional woman warrior is mythologically tutored in the forces
of the dragon in order to gain her supernatural strength:

"You have to infer the whole dragon from the parts you can see and touch," the old people would say. . . . Dragons are so immense, I would never see one in its entirety. But I could explore the mountains, which are the tip of its head. . . . When climbing the slopes, I could understand that I was a bug riding on a dragon's forehead as it roams through space. . . . In quarries I could see its strata, the dragon's veins and muscles; the minerals its teeth and bone. . . . I had worked the soil, which is its flesh, and harvested the plants and climbed the trees, which are its hairs. I could listen to its voice in the thunder and feel its breathing in the winds, see its breathing in the clouds. . . . In the spring when the dragon awakes, I watched its turnings in the river.

But it is not only in myth that the Chinese pay their respects to the dragon. Site selection for temples and even houses depends on the recognition of and alignment with the channels of ch'i, for human health is seen as intimately related to terrestrial health. The idea is applied even to the dead. Chinese graveyards were for centuries laid out by a geomancer, an adept using the elaborate science of *feng-shui*—literally "wind and water." The geomancer sees in the lay of the land—the arrangement of hills, valleys, rivers, and a sensation of what lies between and beneath them—the presence of benevolence or danger. Assuring the right location for an ancestor's bones is regarded as crucial to a family's future. "Even the slightest shift in the skull's location or the excavation for a rival grave nearby could adversely affect this delicate relationship between living and dead. . . . Whole lineages were said to have declined or even disappeared because of interference with the ancestral bones."

Because the siting of virtually all buildings traditionally depended on its principles, the practice of *feng-shui* had a profound influence on shaping China's landscapes and cities. In fact, it's been seen, less mystically, as a kind of town-and-country planning responsible for the notable beauty and harmony of the Chinese landscape. *Feng-shui* principles even determined the layout of the Great Wall. And they often worked, until recently, to preserve the Chinese landscape from extensive development. As John Michell explains it, when Europeans arrived to industrialize the country, "they were informed that their railways and factories could not take certain routes or occupy certain positions. The reasons given were impossible to understand, for they had no relevance, economic, social or political, to the problem of laying out an industrial network. The Europeans were told that a certain range of hills was a terrestrial dragon and that no cutting could be made through its tail." It amazed the Chinese, Michell says, that materially advanced Europeans could actually be ignorant of geomancy, "so culturally retarded that they could see no further than the visible surface of the landscape." Another researcher, Paul Devereux, thinks of the geomancer's sensitivity to the land as an unusual environmental consciousness. He wonders whether conditions like radon concentrations, for example, are what the geomancer recognizes as "bad breath" at a site.

Unlike other forms of Chinese divination, which depend on the interpretation of random patterns, geomancy asserts that the qualities of a site derive from forces that exist inherently in the earth. Just as with James Lovelock's Gaia hypothesis—which regards the planet as self-regulating—for the traditional Chinese the earth is unquestionably a living system. Lovelock has said, "I find that country people still living close to the earth often seem puzzled that anyone should need to make a formal proposition as obvious as the Gaia hypothesis. For them it is true and always has been."

In England, there's been an explosion of interest in these

ideas since the early seventies. English writers speak of channels
of energy as ley lines, a term derived from Alfred Watkins's 1925
book, *The Old Straight Track*. Watkins had exhaustively charted
Stone Age tombs, mounds, standing stones, dolmens, and
notches cut into hills and was startled to discover an uncanny
tendency for them to occur in lines of many miles' length.
Pre-Reformation churches, built on earlier holy sites, also fit
into the alignments. Watkins was unsure of the meaning of the
lines he discovered; he speculated that they might be ancient
trackways.

We know now that "lines" on the land occur in a number
of places. They exist in this country in California and in the
Southwest, lines dozens of miles long etched by the early Indians. In South America, lines, geometric designs, and animal
figures, such as the famous Nazca geoglyphs of Peru, can be seen
clearly from the air. The Nazca lines cover an area about sixty
miles long and several miles wide and were made, probably in
the sixth century, by removing stones from the lighter colored
sand and gravel beneath. The lines rise over precipitous hills,
without seeming destination, useless as paths. They are, rather,
pattern: a set of lengths systematically recurs; some lines evidently mark solstice and equinoctial points and the constella-
tions. Prior to their rediscovery in the forties, they had been
ignored by the local inhabitants for centuries, their significance
a source of bewilderment.

Radiating lines found at an Incan site in Cuzco, Peru, seem,
from early explorers' comments, to have been ritually used by
the emperor. Devereux speculates on a possible connection
between such lines and kingship, pointing out that the Proto-
Indo-European root *reg* meant "movement along a straight line."
From that root we derive words like "rex," "regent," "reign," as
well as "right," "regiment," and "regular." The modern English
word "ruler" is of course both a leader and a straight edge for

making a line. Straight lines may thus, in hierarchical societies, have been associated with the movement of the king, who literally "ruled the land."

Lines on the land may, then, be political or religious in origin or, as for the Australian aborigines, part of a mythic system or, akin to the Chinese notion, mark the route of powers inherent in the land itself. John Michell has been a leading voice in taking up that last idea. Along with others in the last fifteen years, he has hypothesized that clusters of British megalithic sites and their alignments may signal the routes of natural powers that megalithic builders were actually aware of and marked with their monuments. He looks to such traditions as the fairy tracks that still abide in Irish folklore: "These paths, sometimes visible as old roads, sometimes preserved only in local memory, were said to be the routes of seasonal processions. On a certain day the fairies passed through the land, and anyone who stood in their way might be struck dead or be taken off never to return. A man whose house happened to be situated on a fairy path must on that day leave his front and back door open, for it was unwise to obstruct the fairy parade." There is even a story of a man being advised to cut off the corner of his house after years of bad luck—it was in the way of a path. He complied. An Irish seer explains the paths as "lines of some kind of magnetic current, whose exact nature had lately been forgotten." However fanciful such talk might sound, there does seem to be, as Devereux asserts, "a worldwide blank in the human record concerning straight lines in the landscape."

Recent research identifies many of the lines and early monuments as occurring in fault zones. The Great Serpent Mound in Ohio—that quarter-mile-long earth-sculpted snake—is built over an unusually compressed area of intensive faulting. Carnac is hemmed by fault systems and sits atop France's most volatile tectonic region. The geological forces that lie behind faults, jumbling many minerals near the earth's surface, can cause anomalies in electromagnetic currents, alteration in groundwater levels, and variations in gravity and radiation. Fault lines may thus help explain leys and dragon lines.

In the Chinese practice of *feng-shui*, straight lines are in fact feared because energy travels too quickly along them. This is combated by making winding paths (which show up via Chinese influence in nineteenth-century English gardens). Another protective measure is to build a "spirit wall" in front of the entrance to a building, creating, in Nigel Pennick's words, "a corner unnegotiable by straight-line fliers." For the same reason, the eaves of Chinese houses were set at different heights from those of their neighbors—to discourage too strong a current passing across them. Explains Michell: "The lines of the dragon current run straight across country, but locally their course should be modified by a series of gentle curves."

It's imagined by investigators of ley lines that Britain's Stone Age builders were more like surveyors, attuned enough with the earth to have recognized these channels and have marked them with mounds, stones, clumps of trees on hilltops, and notches cut into ridges. Their purpose, unlike the curve-cautious Chinese, might have been to harness energy.

When writer Eleanor Munro stumbled on an alignment of hills and circles of standing stones in the Hebrides, she described feeling as if she'd "strayed across a connection as live as a high tension wire, and my mind flickered with the shock of it." Indeed, less metaphorically, a number of researchers have reported electric shocks and being thrown back from stones while investigating them. Unusual magnetic conditions have often been noted, compasses spinning out of control in the vicinity of some sites. At Carnac, the stones seem to divide a stable geomagnetic field from a zone of disturbed magnetism. Ultrasound readings at stone circles have shown irregular, high activity around particular stones and "holes" of unusually low activity within circles. Researchers speculate whether such

anomalies could have been perceived by the builders of megalithic monuments.

There is one way, at least, the earth's energy can manifest
itself visibly—in light. The phenomenon of earth lights has
been noted for centuries. Early miners used the appearance of
balls of light near the ground as means of locating veins of
copper and tin. Lights are also well documented as appearing
along fault lines—they are sometimes associated with earth-
quakes and may at other times be indicative of lower levels of
tectonic disturbance. Such lights are described as multicolored,
variously shaped, and mobile. They sometimes singe the vegetation around which they hover. They sound surprisingly like
descriptions of UFOs. And indeed what previous societies may
have interpreted as earth spirits, as entrances to an underground
world, or as evidence of telluric energy, we, given our estrange-
ment from the land, are inclined to view as extraterrestrial.

One researcher, Michael Persinger, working with the assumption that earth lights manifest disruptions in the electromagnetic field, has observed in the laboratory the effects on the
brain in proximity to such disruptions. Subjects report visions,
the feeling of floating, loss of their sense of time, the hearing of
externalized voices, erotic sensations—all typical of the descriptions people report of close encounters with supposed UFOs.
It may be that proximity to earth lights causes an altered state
of consciousness. And it could be that this altered state was
valued by earlier cultures as part of religious ritual, and that the
sites of its occurrence were marked and hallowed.

Recent research has revived interest, too, in the way megalithic sites may have been celestially keyed. Repeatedly, as at
Carnac, observers find signs that megalithic stones mark the
solstices, equinoxes, and the transits of the moon and stars. The
accuracy of the placement of stones has stunned those who have
investigated them. Evidence at the sites indicates that they were
redesigned numerous times, over generations, Stonehenge at

least five times. There may have been an experimental process at work, refinements in design. In this view, stone circles may have been used as part of an elemental science involving natural energies best generated under certain astronomical conditions.

In England, ley hunters scour the countryside, tracking down the invisible. They have remapped the British landscape, crisscrossed it with lines. Where the leys intersect, they often find mounds or stones to mark the spot. And they often find animals standing on them—those natural adepts at recognizing energies we may have lost the simplicity to feel.

———

Although there is a mound on a farm up the road where cows loiter, I don't expect the invisible geography of this place to reveal itself to me so readily. No dowser I—more often a doubter.

I drive back to the mound at Ganundasaga. It remains low, tamed, distracted by traffic. It shows no light. I know it has as its ancestors the larger monuments of Native American Mound Builders, several of which have been found within a few miles of where Mary Jemison lived. Maybe they mean more than burial. Maybe they're as resonantly placed as Carnac or Jemison's tract. One, in Newark, Ohio, is a startling sculptural array of circles, squares, and octagons built of earth, covering four square miles. The intricate design is dissected now by downtown modern Newark, and the octagon and its surrounding flattopped mounds have been handily transformed into a golf course. To shouts of "Fore!" one might try to discover why such monuments were made there, how they were used, but it wouldn't be easy.

The closest thing to ley lines we might be able to discern now are those airline-route maps found in your seat pocket—the ambitious webbing of the planet, shortest distance between two points. Or more concretely, our interstate system, etchings of highways and cloverleafs cut indifferently through mountains and the centers of cities, a new form of the power of intersection. Or perhaps the tradition is kept alive by contemporary earth artists who emulate megalithic monuments and Native American mounds by building large effigies, ramps, and geometric structures out in the western deserts. Sometimes these earthworks align with the stars; sometimes they make patterns to view from the air. In part, they are meant to forge an aesthetic connection to pre-Columbian culture and to reassert the power of nature, and for those reasons they intrigue me. But in cases in which land is bulldozed, carved, and rearranged, these pieces also clearly mar the environments in which they're built, which poses a dilemma. Robert Smithson, creator of the famous *Spiral Jetty* in Utah, boasted that for him the *"disruption* of the earth's crust is compelling." That sounds suspiciously like the architect of Mount Rushmore, Gutzon Borglum, who proclaimed that American achievements should be "built into, cut into, the crust of this earth."

If there are spirit lines here, I won't find them marked by such displays, but perhaps in something as subtle as the inadvertently beautiful patterns of plowed and planted fields. I like to think that even my garden making is an exercise in learning the secrets of this slice of earth, a way to keep my ear intelligently, respectfully to the ground.

One summer morning, the shock of seeing the ground speak: I'd wondered why a small triangular corner of the flower bed behind the house was flourishing while the rest of the bed was barren. It's a long strip of land ripped up when the house needed repairs, and rather than reseed it with grass, I'd naively strewn seeds at it from a package I picked up at the drugstore called Instant English Meadow, pictured as a wonderfully ragged collection of wildflowers, a patch of pure countryside, importable. All I got was mud. Except for the one corner, which was struggling into flower. Why? Not until I was up before dawn one morning, sitting out back with the first birds, did I see the reason. The midsummer sun, rising nearly in the northeast, was angling its way around the north wall of the house for the first half hour or so of its ascent, casting a bright triangle of light on the usually shaded bed, corresponding exactly to the budding corner of the English meadow.

At work in the garden, I've learned to look more closely and to listen for the voices of the Seneca, who once farmed this same piece of land, to come a step closer to penetrating the place's silences.

—*When to plant: When the first oak leaves of spring are as big as a red squirrel's foot.*

—*Plant peas during a full moon, corn three days before one.*

—*Plant nothing when the east wind is blowing.*

Listening, I feel close in spirit, though not in efficiency, to the women who farmed here. They would go out with their babies on their backs, toddlers scampering beside them, while the men, never much involved in Iroquois agriculture, hunted. Today, four-year-old Zoe is trailing me with a half-handled hoe, and baby Clea is babbling from the edge in her stroller. When I stoop to pull a row of knee-high weeds, Zoe shrieks to stop me from destroying some Queen Anne's lace. "It's so beautiful, why are you pulling it out?" I earnestly explain how our beans won't grow if they're choked by weeds, how we can't even see them to harvest at the moment.

"But this isn't a weed, it's a flower. What's a weed?"

That's a larger question than I can manage just now. "You like this flower, don't you?"

"Yes, I want to keep it. Look! It has seeds sprinkling out. I'm going to plant them so it will grow again. Not *in* the garden, Mama, but right over here *near* the garden so we can look at it while we're picking beans, okay?"

Sure. We strike a deal. Momentarily excited by her project, she's busy at work, and I return to my sacrilege weeding, but soon she's in need of another way to help.

"What can I do now? I want to plant more."

I stand up, try to imagine Seneca children tossing corn seeds around a field, and decide to risk sowing chaos. I hand her a package of red-leaf lettuce seeds and hover, trying not to restrict, though the instructions on the packet unnerve me. I watch her fling the seeds down in piles. I wish them luck and turn away. When they come up a couple of weeks later in dense bunches, I let her thin them by fistfuls, leaving big gaps between the coppery clumps, and, teeth gritted, decide we'll manage with whatever late-summer lettuce survives her learning.

To be a greedy gardener seems somehow offensive. What I get from the garden I like to regard as a gift. Nature and I have cooperated. Though when we have summers of drought, then summers when it rains daily for six weeks and the garden is a swamp, I feel angry, cheated. Who's cooperating here? This is my garden! Not my chief source of food, it's true, but the food I most covet and hoard in the deep freeze for the worst of winter nights, an essential ingredient of the life we've made for ourselves here. (Thirty plastic sacks of frozen green beans last summer, why only eighteen this year?) I have no gods to explain the failures of the weather, no fertility goddess to cede possession of my garden to. I've found no ley lines, made no magic circles. I may have begun to feel centered here at last, I may pay my rent promptly, but what in the end does that entitle me to?

For the Iroquois, entitlement to the land was unfraught by anxieties like mine. An individual never owned land—a nation did—and decisions on its use were made by the group. The constitution of the Iroquois League declares, "The soil of the earth from one end of the land to the other, is the property of the people who inhabit it." The Iroquois understood that inhabitation changed, too—if a tribe moved from an area, its claim on it ceased, and another tribe could then take it up. Furthermore, as Onondaga faithkeeper Oren Lyons puts it, "Land doesn't belong to the nation as much as it belongs to the future," a principle that makes people see themselves as caretakers, accountable "unto the seventh generation" to follow. Such a viewpoint helps us understand the outrage caused by the selling or ceding of land to the colonists.

"Father!" Cornplanter cried to George Washington,

> You have compelled us to do that which has made us ashamed. We have nothing to answer to the children of the brothers of our fathers. . . . For they ask continually: "Where is the Land which our children, and their children after them are to lie upon?"

Among the Seneca, the treaties giving up land provoked such fury that prophet Handsome Lake, in his code for the revived Longhouse Religion, made the selling of land a cardinal sin. He consigned Red Jacket, key negotiator for the disastrous Fort Stanwix Treaty, to "a special hell in which he would be forced to carry dirt in a wheelbarrow for eternity." A Dantesque sentence!

Just as Europeans were bewildered by Chinese geomancy, so they had no understanding of the Native American vision of the land they happened on. They thought of the newly discovered continent as virgin, as wilderness, not recognizing its fertility as the outcome of centuries of ecological management. Says Lisa Aug: "The unequaled monument of the pre-Columbian American civilization was one European settlers could neither see nor understand: a carefully maintained environment capable of sustaining itself and future generations indefinitely." To fail to recognize that made it easier to claim a supposedly unclaimed land. Says Christopher Vecsey: "The virgin land rhetoric may have been more of a ploy by whites to take land occupied and developed by millennia of Indians, than a description of actual conditions." It's easy to ignore reality. (The Saudi cleric who declared it a sin for women to drive also ruled that the earth is flat.)

One might say, as Aug does, that "more than bullets, more than disease, what destroyed the self-sustaining, ecologically sound Native American civilization was the European attack on the land itself." Remember Sullivan and his "warfare against vegetables"? Beginning in colonial New England, the new Americans vigorously assaulted forests, animals, and the soil itself, abandoning it when it failed them. They indifferently erected dams for mills that disrupted the spawning patterns of fish the Indians depended upon. Beavers were all but wiped out for the sake of fur hats, but by then silk hats had become the fashion in Europe anyway. Later, the extermination of the buffalo— over three and a half million killed between 1872 and 1874 alone, just for their hides, meat left to rot on the ground— ensured the destruction of the Plains Indians.

The Indians, in contrast, conserved plants and animals by taking only what was needed and wasting nothing. Plains Indians had close to a hundred uses for each buffalo they killed—for food, clothing, tepees, bedding, fuel, tools, shields, boats, coffins, bowstrings, glue, spoons, paint, hair grease, needles, decorative and religious objects. In the Northeast, deadwood was burned rather than live trees cut down, and fields periodically lay fallow so that used land was allowed to restore itself. Native American scholar John Mohawk says:

> The real historical Indian was far, far more capable and in lots of ways applied a lot more energy and intelligence to managing the environment than people imagine that he did. He spent a lot of time studying how the water interacted with the land and how the weather worked and how everything came together and which plants grew. He gave incredible

attention to detail. The average Indian in the fifteenth or sixteenth century in the northeast probably knew more about the local botany than your professional botanist today, and he probably had a much wider variety of stuff to look at than you do now.

More than two hundred medicinal herbs were well known. And plants were described in breathtaking detail: the Tewa, for instance, are said to have forty names for different parts of each leaf. Oren Lyons asserts: "Indians have another reality, and we have a lot of experience with that reality. Comes from being in one place for 15,000 years, and working with it, celebrating it, teaching the next generation."

Nature was above all viewed as kin. The rain was called Grandfather, the sun Uncle. Lyons says that if the rain is acid and the sun gives you skin cancer, it's as if your family has turned on you. Before, everyone got along. Animals and human beings were kin too; in many Seneca myths they were seen as identical, only becoming outwardly distinguished over time. Thus, the hunter empathized with his victim's suffering. Apology and thanksgiving accompanied all hunting:

> I am very sorry I had to kill thee, little brother, but I had need of thy meat. My children were hungry and crying for food. Forgive me, little brother. I honor thy courage, thy strength, and thy beauty. Each time I pass this place I will remember thee and do honor to thy spirit. Forgive me, little brother. See, I smoke to thy memory.

Each time I pass this place I will remember . . . because I have stayed. The site of road kills, ditched woodchucks and skunks, the midroad splattered wingspan of a hawk—a record known and remembered. Where a sun-reddened buck once stood amid the young corn, hugely antlered, his silhouette possessing the skyline there forever after—places marked on the map I carry behind my eyes now, a new cartography that resists the forgetfulness I was reared on.

Each time I pass . . . Sprawled across the right lane, her long blond hair flung out from her shoulder. I slam on the brakes, skid to a halt. I recognize her as a neighbor. She has gotten up, staggered toward the ditch at the side of the road. Then she slips, crumples. I rush from the car, leave Clea crying in her car seat, cradle the woman's bloodied head in my hands, tell her to hold on, I'll get an ambulance, please hold on—and then the dream is broken by Clea's real morning cry from the crib. I stumble from bed and stagger across the hall.

Driving past there again, no blood on the road, no sign of disturbance. Instead, the tiger lilies have opened—marvelous flung gestures of orange, open eared for my lamentation and gratitude.

Because I've stayed, the land feels attentive, full of reciprocal energy. The Iroquois call that energy in nature *orenda*—a power inhabiting all living things, sometimes described as a kind of voltage or static electricity that can be accumulated through ritual and then used. It touches all things equally.

Clea making her morning round of greetings, burbling "Hi" to us, to Zoe, the dog, her toys, her breakfast . . .

Children begin with a primitive view of the world, and if they're Western, they correct it; Native American children's conception grows stronger the farther from white influence they are raised.

In town, a video arcade—the largest game displays a pristine Adirondack landscape, a forest-circled bright blue lake and cloudless sky with blips of deer fleeing through the trees; opposite sits a child armed with a computerized gun. It's called Shoot Away.

It is the association of the Indians with nature that may best explain their destruction—they were simply treated the way

Europeans treated the land and its wildlife, as something that could be casually abused. Not surprisingly, the rationale for usurping Indian land was that whites believed they could better utilize it—occupy it more densely, cultivate it more intensely, build upon it more enduringly. Peter Thomas explains that "In the minds of European immigrants, their Old World agrarian pattern with its diverse crops and domestic animals was so superior to native American horticultural practices that propagandists and colonists alike used the issue to justify the dispossession of American native populations. It was maintained that the Indians had simply not 'improved' the land." The Indians' seasonal shifts of settlement, and their dependence on hunting rather than domestic herds, placed them on a lower rung of agricultural development as far as Europeans were concerned. Although ethnographers have shown that in fact both colonists and Native Americans used comparable amounts of cultivated land to support a small village, the "land utilization" argument became conventional wisdom among the colonists. "These people must die out," editorialized Horace Greeley, "there is no help for them. God has given this earth to those who will subdue and cultivate it, and it is vain to struggle against His righteous decree."

Behind this kind of self-justification lay the obvious immigrant terror of the so-called wilderness and hatred of its inhabitants and their ways. As Vecsey describes it, the Puritans believed that the religion of the Indians "affirmed the satanic quality of the wilderness, just as the devilish quality of wilderness proved the evil of Indians." Indians were variously called pagans (etymologically of the countryside rather than the village), heathens (of wild, uninhabited places), and savages (of the forest)—all of which endorses the view of nature as that which is irreligious, unable to be civilized. In the Western tradition, to be civilized is to rise above nature, to protect yourself from it and use it. Such an antagonistic stance inevitably led to both environmental destruction and racism, "especially toward people who were seen as nature folk, whose religions recognized and valued relations with nature."

The same association between land and women has also had disastrous implications in Western hands. According to Carolyn Merchant, when the image of earth as mother still abided in Europe, it "carried with it subtle ethical controls and restraints"—"One does not readily slay a mother, dig into her entrails for gold or mutilate her body, although commercial mining would soon require that. As long as the earth was considered to be alive and sensitive, it could be considered a breach of human ethical behavior to carry out destructive acts against it." But with the decline of the matriarchy, with nature seen as generically female and culture as male, the land was forced to be as submissive as women were. Nature's association with the female justified viewing it as inferior.

The scientific revolution did away with any remaining restraints by depersonifying nature into "natural resources," a term that, significantly, appeared around 1500, concurrent with the European discovery of the New World. The disenchantment and degodding of the natural world into a mechanical, secular planet was a necessary prerequisite for the development of science and industrialization. Just as conquering a people requires destroying their landscape—their literal land or their pattern on it—scientific progress required destroying the old predominant worldview of nature.

The vigorous European advance into the American continent carried a similar revolution of values. Says Lisa Aug: "Not only did Europeans harbor the incredible notion that land could be owned, paid for with lifeless bits of metal or paper, but they treated it with an implacable violence unmatched even by their treatment of native tribes. The European's apparent hatred of all other living things was so utterly foreign to people for whom the earth was the source of all life, that communication on the subject seemed impossible."

———

> We know the sap which courses through the
> trees as we know the blood that courses through our
> veins. We are part of the earth and it is part of us. The
> perfumed flowers are our sisters. The bear, the deer,
> the great eagle, these are our brothers. The rocky
> crests, the juices in the meadow, the body heat of the
> pony, and man, all belong to the same family. . . .

When I first read that passage, attributed to Chief Seattle, I was lyrically aroused. The metaphor of family aptly evokes a dutiful, emotional tie to the natural world, which I aspire to. But having discovered that those words derive from a 1971 TV film on ecology—meant to capture the Native American spirit—I know how much of my own longing I was projecting, how much we as a society in the past twenty years have looked to the Indians (out of both despair and guilt) for a model by which to live in nature. Chief Seattle's fictional letter to President Millard Filmore is now a standard text of environmental consciousness and as such articulates an idealistic solution to the problems we are preoccupied with. But it is too easy to make a cliché of Native American culture, to use some watered-down version of its ideas for our own current crises. Indian cultures themselves are various and distinct; they don't share a single vision of the earth but are very much products of particular locales. It is in those local distinctions that we can learn a great deal about how to live in our own places.

V

HOMEGROWN

———

Across the entire breadth of York State, undeviating, a hilly strip scarcely twenty-five miles wide invites the world's wonder.

—*Carl Carmer*

Everywhere I go now I see things no one else does. Ghosts on the road, secret signs. I am like Freud's hysteric, populating the landscape with a visible, beckoning past, searching for what can't show itself plain. One eye on the road, one eye on the invisible, I straddle the here and there, the now and then, and feel surprisingly at home—at home in what's both here and not here anymore.

Without enough time to walk and muse much, except in the summers, I've learned how to contemplate while driving. Though protectively encased as I cover tens of miles, I am feelingly in the landscape. I notice and know because I've worked to make this my place. I introduce Zoe, commuting with me to a kindergarten in Geneva instead of going to the army-base district out here. We stop to visit some newborn colts, notice the wind shifting south, a softening, shy breeze. The wind of the fawn in Seneca lore, Zoe remembers me telling her.

The road we daily commute, Routes 5 & 20, is no mere four-lane highway where heat sways or snow sifts in bannered gusts. It is, for me now, palpably the longhouse line, macadamless, an idea stretching midair, but also earthbound and practical—the Iroquois' admirable capacity for holding the symbolic and daily in one image. Their astuteness about this land seems to have been as honed as the Chinese's. Here is a route so judiciously chosen that even sophisticated surveys have found no better location for a cross-state road. It is, as Morgan asserted, "one of the great natural highways of the continent." It even divides the weather, "north of the Thruway" being a familiar phrase of weather forecasts: while lake-effect snow routinely pummels the area just south of Lake Ontario, snowfall invariably diminishes right around the New York Thruway, making it more reliably passable, as the Iroquois no doubt observed. The current Thruway, along with Route 20, mirrors the longhouse line almost exactly; it salutes the Iroquois only in the names of its service areas—which house not hearths but Burger Kings. Nearly all major upstate cities and towns lie shoulder to shoulder along this old alignment.

As I drive farther out into the land, I discover more of the tales that have housed themselves here. I circle the lake, weave the hills, visit neighboring lakes and counties, journey to places where I've learned others have come and paused to dwell, then try to reconstruct them and map the landscape with their presence, discern a pattern. The most evident form of spiritual energy I'm likely to find in this land is in the lives of its people, past and present.

Two miles south of our first house, I find a woman standing by the western edge of Seneca Lake surrounded by a crowd, waves lapping the toes of her black boots and the hem of her long cape. A question seems to hover in the air: Can she walk on water? "Do ye have faith?" she exhorts. "Do ye believe that I can do this thing?" She's never failed to stir a crowd. "Do ye have faith?" she demands again. "We believe," they chorus, "we believe." "Good," she declares, and coolly turns to depart the shore. "If ye have faith ye need no other evidence."

She is Jemima Wilkinson, known to her followers as the Publick Universal Friend, and this apocryphal event takes place in the late eighteenth century at the site of Dresden, about twelve miles south of Geneva.

Jemima Wilkinson is the least well known of the important religious innovators of that period. Unlike Ann Lee of the Shakers and John Murray, founder of Universalism, she was American-born, the first American-born woman to found a religious society. Like Ann Lee, she was originally Quaker, emphasized celibacy, equality of men and women and of black and white. She preached old-fashioned moral values and the coming of the millennium.

She had predicted the new millennium would arrive in early April 1780. That April passed uneventfully, but several weeks later, southern New England, the early center of her ministry, experienced the so-called Dark Day—"For several days before the mysterious event the atmosphere was smoky, but on the nineteenth of May, 1780, at about ten in the morning, the sun was blotted out and it became as dark as night. The strange darkness was not an eclipse of the sun. Combined with a smoky smell and copper red or yellow clouds, it lasted until about two o'clock in the afternoon and was a terrifying experience. . . ." Wilkinson's prediction, to some, seemed fulfilled.

As a young woman of twenty-four in Cumberland, Rhode Island, she had suffered a hallucinatory fever. Upon recovering, she claimed to have actually died, been inhabited by a new spirit, and immediately began to preach the visions she'd seen. Though she hadn't appeared to have died to those attending her, the story nevertheless developed that she had lain in a deathlike trance for hours, or even days. On rising, she refused to answer to her name but henceforth called herself the Publick Universal Friend, believing her new identity and mission to have been sent by God. Whatever its origin, her sense of mission gave her, by all accounts, striking self-confidence, eloquence, and determination. She was said to have an extraordinary memory—she could neither read nor write, but had memorized the entire Bible from hearing it read to her. Though completely inexperienced in public life, she was soon preaching in crowded churches before local farmers, and soon after to the wealthy, to scholars, and to Indians. Her theological ideas were unoriginal, but her presence was emotionally compelling: "She preaches up Terror very alarming."

164/ FROM WHERE WE STAND

About ten years into her ministry she began to plan a
community dwelling, a "wilderness sanctuary." Scouts were sent
to explore the Genesee Country in 1785. First reports were
enthusiastic. But a second scout was so bogged down in snow
that it took him five days to wade from Elmira to Geneva. He
warned of the hostility of the few Indians who'd returned
post-Sullivan, which made it "too soon to enter the sad, dark,
land of the lakes." Nevertheless, a group set out to pick a site
and resolved that it be on Seneca Lake (despite the more
favorable impression one scout had of the Genesee River, where
he'd met Mary Jemison). In the spring of 1788, the first group
settled near Dresden, the site of the Keuka outlet into Seneca
Lake, where a waterfall provided the possibility of a mill.

Despite uncertainties about title, the community cleared the
land and stayed, thus becoming the first group of settlers to
winter west of Cayuga Lake, the first whites to farm here. They
built the first mill and helped feed new settlers brought in by
Charles Williamson. Wilkinson herself arrived in 1790, at
which time her community contained 260 people, by far the
largest settlement in western New York, two and a half times
the size of Geneva. For her role in helping new farmers get
started, preventing the famines that took place elsewhere, she
has been called the patron saint of early white agriculture in
western New York. She was also respected and treated gener-
ously by the remaining Indians. When six hundred Iroquois
passed through on their way to Canandaigua to negotiate the
Pickering Treaty, they camped on her land and listened to her
preach. She followed them up to the meeting and spoke on their
behalf.

The Dresden community was doomed, though, by title
complications and the escalating value of the land as it was
tossed back and forth between speculators. Wilkinson's group
was finally driven west of the Preemption line to site its New
Jerusalem, this time by Keuka Lake. There they settled in a

township near Penn Yan that is still today called Jerusalem. But as the years passed, the group's unity and reputation staggered under defections (the birth of a child was plain evidence of disobedience) and gossip about Wilkinson's financial dealings and alleged manipulation of her followers. Even as it lost its spiritual cohesion, however, the community remained a colorful oddity to outsiders, a tourist attraction described as "the second wonder of the western country," an obligatory detour for those on the grand tour to Niagara Falls.

When the Universal Friend died, or "left time," as she preferred to call it, her body was taken by night to a secret grave, as she'd requested. Only the descendants of the undertakers, living still in Penn Yan, are said to know the grave's location. A mystique continues to surround her; her surviving effects—a gilded saddle and carriage, a beaver hat and black cape—are on display in a small museum in Penn Yan.

At the opposite end of Keuka Lake, a contemporary eccentric draws away my attention. "They took my name and heritage but they didn't get my goat." A portrait of the goat smiles from the elaborate label of a wine bottle—its name is Guilt Free. The label is signed Walter S. █████ , Baron of Bully Hill, King of the Goats—the blanked-out last name looking like the smudge of a censor's stamp. And therein lies the story.

It's been a crime for Walter Taylor to print his name on a bottle of wine since the Taylor Wine Company was bought by Coca-Cola in the mid-seventies. The drama began before that when, at a wine makers' conference in San Francisco in 1970, Walter Taylor denounced New York State wineries for diluting their grape juices with water and mixing them with cheap California or imported wines—low-grade "tank car" wines. Styling himself as the "conscience of the wine industry," Taylor protested that the executives of the big companies that had taken over the family wineries didn't care about wine quality or about the vineyards—they "didn't want to be in touch with the

plants." Walter Taylor and his father had been very much in
touch with them, experimenting through the sixties with grafts
of French varieties at Bully Hill, the original Taylor family
vineyard, founded in 1878 and passed on through five generations. The new hybrids, Taylor claimed, made it unnecessary to
cut the harsher flavor of the New York labrusca grapes—the
only type previously thought suitable for New York's cooler
weather. The hybrids created European-quality wines.

Two weeks after the San Francisco speech, suddenly accused of misusing company funds, Walter Taylor was fired by
the Taylor Wine Company. Starting over at the family vineyard,
he hired purists to create the new Bully Hill wine—100 percent
New York with only two "universally used" chemical additives
instead of the sixty allowed by state law. He listed all ingredients
on his labels, even the names of the local grape growers ("I'm
a freedom fighter against anonymity"). Fighting his own anonymity, he slung a guitar over his shoulder and went on the road
to promote his new wine. It took off.

The Taylor Company ignored him until he began bragging
about how his wine was the original, real Taylor, and then they
successfully sued him for copyright infringement and unfair
competition. Taylor had to remove his name from his wine
labels; he couldn't even sign his own paintings that adorned
them. "They have stolen my birthright," he proclaimed on the
courthouse steps. But he quickly capitalized on the affront. He
handed out Magic Markers to his staff and a bunch of eager
customers and had them black out the word "Taylor" wherever
it occurred on his bottles of wine. The deleted name became the
trademark he still uses, a way to keep alive his outrage.

The Coca-Cola Company was not amused. They sued
again, and Walter Taylor was found in contempt of court. His
reputation was by now made—a David battling the corporate
Goliath. Courting the press, he used each new legal setback to
his own advantage, and business boomed—sales of Bully Hill

wine rose from $650,000 to $2 million during the two-year court battle.

Walter Taylor inspired a new generation of small vineyard owners to begin making their own wines instead of selling their grapes to the Taylor conglomerate. These small independents have been dubbed the "Upstate Upstarts" by the wine industry, but because of them New York State wine sales have doubled in the past fifteen years.

Until an accident in 1990 left him paralyzed, Taylor was a great showman whom tourists flocked to see at his vineyard wine tastings. He's explicitly spiritual about his work: "A product is an extension of a person's soul." And he has a vividly paranoid imagination, claiming there are hidden submarine routes beneath the lakes, electron towers and launchpads secreted on nearby mountaintops. His life firmly embedded in the local landscape, he distributes maps of the area marking the sites of his personal mythology—like the cave where he says he was rescued from Coca-Cola by guilt-free goats—as well as spots like Nightmare Alley near Hammondsport: "Possible view of unloading railroad wine tank cars and liquid corn syrup (cheap, adulterated and not taxed). Bring your camera."

———

Taylor is, to my mind, a direct descendant of Jemima Wilkinson in his reformational passion, and between the two of them is to be found a long line of nineteenth-century revivalists, utopians, and spiritualists, including, most memorably, Joseph Smith standing with his Book of Mormon atop a hill in Palmyra, just west of Geneva down the longhouse line. What is it in Bully Hill and the hills of Palmyra that sets people preaching, remaking their neighbors? "Something about the land," muses Paul Horgan, "induces people to arise and prophesy and cock their ears toward the invisible powers."

Some still do it, or at least come watch it. Every summer

they come to Palmyra to see a cast of six hundred lavishly costumed volunteers, twenty-five multilevel stages, "grand illusions and special effects including ethereal water curtains," explosions, real fire, lasers, and, of course, a digital sound track by the Mormon Tabernacle Choir. "The music rises dramatically. Spotlights search for the star of the show—and find him suspended in mid-air fifty feet above the stage." It is America's oldest and most elaborate religious spectacle, the Hill Cumorah Pageant, the Mormons' annual outdoor staging of the tales of the Book of Mormon and Smith's discovery of their source, the golden tablets, on that very hill, culminating with the descent of Christ into the crowd. For more than fifty years, tens of thousands have gathered in the summer dusk to be moved to or confirmed in faith. "We're trying to reach audiences used to rock concerts, spectacular light shows and sixty-minute television programs," says a promoter. "Our target audience is eighteen to thirty-five-year-old non-Mormons. We want those people to get the message that the events portrayed on this hillside actually did happen." The special-effects coordinator of the show is a veteran of *Robocop* and *Rambo III*.

What must we do to be saved? Blond Mormon youth stay in the uncharacteristically tame college dorms for two weeks each summer. The boys wear ties to dinner, unprecedented on campus except during pledge season. I still have trouble placing them here. But the pattern is becoming clear. As Whitney Cross, author of *The Burned-Over District*, describes it, "Across the rolling hills of western New York and along the line of De Witt Clinton's famed canal, there stretched in the second quarter of the nineteenth century a 'psychic highway.' Upon this broad belt of land congregated a people extraordinarily given to unusual religious beliefs, particularly devoted to crusades aimed at the perfection of mankind and the attainment of millennial happiness."

Today's devotees have been drawn back down the well-known canal / highway / longhouse line that grows more deeply etched on my mental map the more I learn. The line was, of course, the literal turnpike west for migrating New Englanders; it could become a psychic highway only because this area was historically a funnel through which thousands of westbound emigrants passed. It was because of them and their spiritual fervor that central New York was dubbed "The Burned-Over District," not for any recollection of the scorchings of Sullivan. The area's rapid growth, and a continuing stream of rebellious, often skeptical emigrants, fueled social and spiritual upheavals, spawned numerous religious communities, and made the careers of more than a few evangelists. Alongside the Shakers, the Publick Universal Friend, and Joseph Smith, there were the Millerites, who left their crops unharvested the summer of 1844 awaiting the end of the world, and there was itinerant preacher Charles Finney, the nation's first professional evangelist, who fomented self-redemptive revivals in village churches all over upstate New York. There was John Humphrey Noyes's utopian Oneida Community, a thriving experiment in socialism notorious for its institution of group marriage. There were oddities like the séancing Fox sisters and the agnostic Robert G. Ingersoll, born, ironically, in Wilkinson's Dresden, a notable proselytizer on such subjects as "Some Mistakes of Moses." The people these preachers and reformers worked among were argumentative and extremist.

Their radicalism extended to secular matters too—they were dedicated fighters for abolition, temperance, and, later, feminism. Women were an important element of all the area's movements. Unlike in New England, here women frequently preached and composed the majorities of the churches; they dominated revivals and prayer meetings, perhaps helping to pave the way for the women's movement. It was in Seneca Falls, ten miles east of Geneva on the longhouse line, that Elizabeth Cady Stanton lived, wrote, and organized the first women's rights convention in 1848. Amelia Bloomer invented the liberating pants that bear her name on a sewing machine on South Main Street in Geneva. Susan B. Anthony, Frederick Douglass, and Lewis Henry Morgan were all contemporaries in Rochester. The women's movement's most radical leader, the scholarly and charismatic Matilda Joslyn Gage, lived in Fayetteville, just south of Syracuse.

Resisting the area's intense religiosity, Gage was fiercely opposed to the Church, counting it as one element of women's "four-fold bondage" along with the state, capitalism, and the home. Women's suffrage was, to her mind, but a first step in a long revolution. Unfortunately, Matilda Gage was largely written out of the history of the women's movement because of Susan Anthony's conservative turn in 1889, when she overthrew Gage's leadership and suppressed her threatening politics for the sake of an alliance with the temperance movement. Now that Gage's work has come to light, it's interesting to discover that she was one of the few in the movement who also turned her attention and pen to the plight of the Iroquois. For her efforts, she was made an honorary member of their Council of Matrons. She also wrote frequently about the matriarchy and goddess worship, which she firmly believed preceded the patriarchy—a vision that waited a hundred years before being taken up again by contemporary feminists.

This area's passion for new religious and political ideas earned Syracuse the nickname "the City of Isms," so frequent were the conventions of abolitionists and other reformers. New "sciences," like phrenology, flourished. The populace was innovative in the practical realm, too—patent records show that inventors worked with unusual concentration along this same midstate line, most notably creating a great variety of agricultural equipment. Their earlier, unequaled zeal for classical place-names is seen by Wilbur Zelinsky as the beginning of a pattern in which the area was a testing ground for "exotica"—"When the cultural geography of this area receives the attention it deserves, it will be found to have spawned a number of other significant American innovations," innovations that represent "the extroverted buoyancy and expansiveness of spirit that many observers identify as American." Zelinsky's assertion that this area has been important in forming the nation's character affirms my own fascination. And its long history of radicalism is perhaps why my own thinking feels somewhat at home here—in some of those "isms," there are strands of tradition I can attach myself to.

Curiously, though, most of those revolutionary nineteenth-century New Yorkers did not see themselves as adventurous radicals (and "radical" is the last word they'd use to describe themselves today). They were mostly middle-class, middle-aged people whose moderate success, perhaps, caused them guilt and anxiety. Their inclination toward self-improvement, though, made this area the stage for the most intense religiosity in the country's history. Instead of "burned," some called it "the infected district." But New Yorkers regarded the burned-over epithet proudly. They considered their moral intensity their most admirable quality.

The family of Joseph Smith was typical. Poor farmers, slightly educated, interested in the supernatural, they had emigrated from Vermont to western New York in 1816, when Joseph was ten years old, after an infamously frigid, crop-withering summer dubbed "eighteen hundred and froze to death." The senior Smith's farming was less than vigorous—he preferred to daydream. Neighbors remembered young Smith, too, as a loafer and "money digger," a supposed diviner who used a "peeping stone" to sight and dig for treasure. Smith claimed he was guided to his greatest find—the revelatory golden plates—by an angel. The Book of Mormon is said to derive from the history provided on the plates, though it also clearly partakes of local legends about the Mound Builders, whom Smith portrays as Hebrew descendants, and contemporary religious and political controversies, especially anti-Masonry.

Whitney Cross claims that Smith's ascension as prophet "might have happened to almost anyone of Joseph's fellow Yankee migrants." Thomas O'Dea, too, says it was "accepted and expected" in the area that new religious groups would arise "based upon novel claims." Mormonism can be seen then, says Cross, as "the first original product of the common circumstances which would breed a train of successors. . . ."

By the end of the movement, mid-century, the Fox sisters of Newark (neighbor of Palmyra) had captured the loyalties of thousands with their table-rapping séances. Rather than being regarded as eccentric occultism, their noisy sessions fit well the prevailing religious fervor. Enthusiasm for the manipulated young sisters spread so far that even Emerson felt compelled to rail against the "rat-revelation, the gospel that comes by taps in the walls, and thumps in the table-drawer." And as far as Thoreau was concerned, "The hooting of owls, the croaking of frogs, is celestial wisdom in comparison."

The enthusiastic still flock to Hill Cumorah—for a cinematic version of the sacred in this culturally burned-out district. I'd almost welcome a return to the reformational passions of that lost era, some sign of life, which in its more serious manifestations showed genuine nonconformity and utopian idealism. Little of all that is fondly remembered here. The early women's movement is commemorated in ambivalent Seneca Falls by a triangular slice of park smaller than our front lawn. The only traces of the period's spiritual idealism are perhaps in Walter Taylor's religion of the pure grape, or the utopian farming and craft-making commune of the Rochester Folk Art Guild, located near Bare Hill, or in the growing numbers of Mennonites settling here.

Though one can explain the emigration of the Mennonites from the Lancaster, Pennsylvania, area by the overcrowding and rising costs there, and by the cheap land available here as local farms fail, I suspect this region is attractive to them for more reasons than that. They must know something of its history, its literal and spiritual fertility, its likely tolerance of their unconventionality. After some initial jitters, the community has indeed been hospitable. Penn Yan has even built a special parking lot downtown beside the drive-in bank with hitching posts for their horses and buggies. Deer-warning and cow-warning signs on the highway have been joined by silhouettes of carriages.

Mennonites began coming to the area in 1974. Within ten years, there were eighty families around Penn Yan, and now a new cluster of farms has spread east of Seneca Lake. Young Mennonite women have come off the land to work in produce shops in town, bringing fresh bread and pies to sell. Out at the roadside stands by their farms, the barely educated girls often have trouble making change, but in town they operate cash registers, wear sneakers beneath their traditional dresses. Contact with the outside world has modified them, but the conservative structure and rigor of their community remain. Whether they work in town, in the fields, or in the kitchen, they work relentlessly, at all hours.

Mennonite farmer John Wagner called us at five in the morning. David picked up the phone and repeated to me, "Rhode Island Reds or bantams?" It sounded like a nonsense refrain in the zany dream I was in the middle of. I replied, "Rhode Island Reds or bantams."

"*Pick* one," he said.

We'd gone to visit the large Wagner farm the week before to look into buying some chickens. The Mennonites raise them naturally, of course, and as I was pregnant with Zoe at the time, I wanted to avoid the hormones in commercial meat. The Wagners slaughtered their older hens each spring and would sell us fifty at a good price; we had found someone to split the bounty with. Wagner said he'd call the day of the butchering.

The phone rang again at six. Did we want them dressed? Dressed up? No, plucked and cleaned. Definitely. "That will be twenty-five cents extra per chicken." That's all? "That's fine." "You can come get them this evening."

Five daughters working for hours for twenty-five cents times fifty chickens. Gathered round the table in the oil-lamp-lit kitchen that night, a nineteenth-century softness, their heads bent over bowls of chicken livers, bowls of hearts, the fifty shining birds. They'd asked us to bring plastic bags, and now they set about packing everything up for us. Shy and gentle faced, they peeked at me and my obvious belly, flashed a timid smile. They'd been at it since five in the morning, and dozens of other chores had been done too. A quilt was spread on a table, half-made. Bread and pies were stacked for the morning. Laundry was soaking in a basin, the cows had been milked, cream was rising in a pail. Not since Ireland had I seen so much work going on, and the memory of it in my own hands warmed me, though the distance I'd come from it in ten years was jarring—loading the bagged chickens into the car, driving them back to the deep freeze, back to washing machine, word processor, and take-out dinner. I was glad, at least, to have those honest chickens to cook, though whichever breed it was I picked that morning, I must have picked wrong—the meat was hopelessly tough, only edible when boiled hours into soup.

Perhaps in their quiet way, the Mennonites have picked up the thread of this region's religious character, made and remade in waves of influence and experimentation aimed at ultimate simplicities. To see them in their Sunday best, playing volleyball of an afternoon, flowered dresses brushing the grasses, is to be stopped in one's tracks a moment, thoughtfully cast back. Whether or not they influence our spiritual lives, they certainly provide a wholesome model of agriculture. While modern farms are failing all over the state, the unmechanized farms of the Mennonites are flourishing. The number of New York dairy farms dropped by twenty-five percent during the eighties; but in Mennonite-settled Yates County, the number doubled.

The state advises failing dairy farmers to convert to such products as snow peas and kiwi fruit for the upscale market—an idea as disconcerting as the llama ranches that have cropped up among horse farms between here and Canandaigua. Those long, shaggy necks, glimpsed from 5 & 20, turn the land into zoo. The Mennonite farms, in contrast, feel indigenous.

———

Officially, the enduring contributions of the burned-over era are the Mormon church, several Adventist denominations, two species of Methodism, and a sprinkling of spiritualist groups. Enduring too, though, is the sense, among some, of this territory's unusual energies.

Enough traces of sanctity remain that even those usually indifferent to such matters have had to pay heed. When state officials put together a proposal to site the planned super collider up in Wayne County, north of the Thruway, they discovered that the fifty-three-mile circular tunnel would go right under Hill Cumorah. They knew enough not to suggest that, but then the next version had the tunnel going through the Sacred Grove, where Joseph Smith claimed to be visited by God and Christ in 1820. After a brief attempt to pass that off, the planners moved on again. "We have been dodging and weaving like a football halfback . . . bumping off Indian reservations and sacred hills. . . ." The tunnel was in the end awarded to Texas, and the national commission's report noted that more letters of protest about the project had come from Wayne County, New York, than from any other proposed site.

The land has recently won out over development elsewhere too—at Bare Hill. The Seneca's sacred birth hill has been temporarily bought by the Trust for Public Land, which will hold it until the appropriate public agency can get funding. It's hoped the hilltop will eventually be used by the Department of Parks and Recreation to expand its Native American educational program begun at Ganondagan.

Most intriguing to me in the saving of Bare Hill over the past couple of years has been the active role of non–Native Americans in the fight. Surprisingly, longtime Canandaiguans profess a spiritual connection to the hill not unlike the Seneca's: "Bare Hill is one of those special places that nourish the spirit." "There's a certain energy up there, a power that deserved to be treated with more respect. We just felt it needed to be undisturbed." "A spirit . . . pervades the whole place and affects everybody who goes up there." Their unity with the Seneca in their attachment to the hill has been a striking milestone in relations between the two cultures here.

Hundreds of local people show up for the annual anniversary festival commemorating the dedication of Ganondagan. There's a craft show, native corn soup and hash, buffalo meat, and the lively Allegany River Indian Dancers. They do dances of friendship, of the rabbit and the fish, and a dance for the passenger pigeon—though the bird is extinct, the dance, wonderfully, remains extant: chanted, foot stomped, drummed, belled. Close up, a whiff of mildew on the ceremonial robes of the dancers, taken out of storage for the occasion. "Yes, we eat pizza and play video games, but we also have this very rich culture." Peter Jemison and his son join in. Children young as four. And octogenarian, local historian Sheldon Fisher is there. Fisher spent decades working to preserve Ganondagan, one of a touching series of men I've discovered who've devoted themselves to the study and protection of the Iroquois.

I can't help but think back fondly to those scholars and activists at moments like this, watching Fisher watch this dance. There was first of all, most famously, Lewis Henry Morgan, that Father of American Anthropology, who began as a boy enthusiast for the Cayuga tribe, which had inhabited the area around his Aurora home. He studied the Iroquois for more than ten years, chiefly on the Seneca's Tonawanda reservation. The resulting book, *The League of the Hodenosaunee*, published in 1851, remains the classic source of ethnographic information on the Iroquois.

Morgan's original interest in the Iroquois may have been merely to acquire authentic rites for his club, the Grand Order of the Iroquois, a group of young white men presumptuous enough to have imagined itself heir to the "dying" Iroquois League. The club itself died out within a decade. Morgan did unapologetically borrow elements from the ceremonies he'd been privileged to observe. But he also, as a lawyer, lobbied on behalf of the Seneca when their reservations were threatened with reduction, and so earned their respect. He was adopted by the tribe and named Tayadaokuh—Bridge—a link between the cultures.

Morgan was guided in his research by Seneca chief Ely S. Parker. Parker was just sixteen when Morgan took him under his wing and got him into a private school. Unable to become a lawyer as he wished, because he wasn't a U.S. citizen, Parker instead became an engineer and ultimately a U.S. general and Ulysses Grant's personal secretary (he was present at Appomattox, having drafted the terms for Lee's surrender). Later, he was the first Native American to be appointed commissioner of Indian Affairs. It was Parker who wrote the eloquent letter trying to protect the Ganundasaga burial mound. And it was Parker who took Morgan to Tonawanda, gained him entrée to the tribe's rituals, and explained what Morgan observed. Parker was as much a "bridge" as Morgan, a liminal figure who was vital in accomplishing the coherent translation of a huge body of knowledge. Indeed, Morgan dedicated his book to Parker, referring to their "joint researches."

Morgan moved on from his original research to study comparative kinship systems and to write three more books, including the widely read *Ancient Society*, which has been called "the most catalytic book in the history of anthropology." Karl Marx, deeply impressed by it, took extensive notes and planned to write about Morgan's theories of family, government, and evolutionary "stages" of human progress. But he died before he could write the planned work, and it was Frederick Engels who took up what he thought of as a bequest and wrote *The Origin of the Family, Private Property and the State in the Light of the Researches of Lewis H. Morgan*. Engels claimed Morgan's book was "one of the few epoch-making works of our time." His "rediscovery of the primitive matriarchal gens as the earlier stage of the patriarchal gens of civilized people has the same import for anthropology as Darwin's theory of evolution has for biology and Marx's theory of surplus values has for political economy." It was among the Iroquois that Morgan first got the idea. Maybe Matilda Gage got it from them too . . .

Engels also marveled at the League of the Iroquois—with its democratic council of sachems (chiefs) selected by the women (and they had the right to unseat a chosen chief), its requirement of unanimous consent in all decisions, its lack of a single leader, and its inability to convene itself except by the initiation of a member tribe—a perfect example, he said, of "a society which still has no *state.*"

After spending his working life in Rochester, Morgan retired to his birthplace on the eastern shore of Cayuga Lake. There he was the talkative proprietor of the Aurora Inn. And it's said (though not in any biography) that Longfellow once wandered in to stay the night. Late, over drinks, Longfellow asks—Are there any good stories from around here, Indian legends or epics? So Morgan happily sits down and tells him the tale of the founding of the Iroquois League, the woe of Hiawatha, the condolence ritual, and so on. Presto—"The Song of Hiawatha."

> Should you ask me, whence these stories? . . . I should
> answer, I should tell you,
> From the forests and the prairies . . . I repeat them as
> I heard them
> From the lips of Nawadaha,
> The musician, the sweet singer.

Actually, Longfellow sculpted the tale from Ojibwa myths, but for some reason chose the Iroquois name for his hero.

Morgan's work, important as it is, was preceded by the little-acknowledged research of a native Iroquois writer, Tuscarora David Cusick. *Sketches of Ancient History of the Six Nations* was published in 1827, a generation before Morgan, and details the history, culture, and lore of the Iroquois from a native intimacy, but with admirable ethnographic skill. It's unclear whether or not Morgan was aware of the book. Russell Judkins believes that, "This work, which clearly pre-dates the development of Euro-American anthropology, . . . has special significance as an intellectual endeavor, and as an anticipatory work contributing to—as well as being an early contribution of—Native American scholarship and anthropological perspective. . . . In fact, based on the example of this case, one might suspect that the Native American mind has had more to do with the invention and the development of anthropological understanding than Euro-American versions of intellectual history have generally been willing to see and to admit." What a riveting idea—that Iroquois self-reflectiveness contributed to the evolution of ethnography.

The role of Ely Parker, as well as of Cusick, clearly points to a remarkable degree of Iroquois self-awareness about their social, political, and religious organization. Judkins believes that Parker may have been the truly "catalytic" figure in Morgan's work, the one with the initial insights, and Morgan a receptive transcriber able to organize what Parker told him into a theory.

That same self-reflectiveness is exemplified by the career of Ely Parker's grandnephew, Arthur Caswell Parker, who was a tireless archaeologist, interpreter of Iroquois culture, and long-time director of the Rochester Museum and Science Center. Half-Seneca, he moved easily between the two cultures, was admitted to secret ceremonies non-native writers were barred from, wrote numerous monographs and studies, and built a significant collection during his two decades at the museum. He confessed that he was "vain enough to hope [I] will out-Morgan Morgan," and on several topics he did. His study of maize and its uses was pioneering; contemporary Iroquois specialist William Fenton claims it "set a standard for such studies and was used as a model for similar work on the Plains Indians and in the American southwest."

Sheldon Fisher speaks Arthur Parker's name with awe. He proudly tells me that he studied archaeology with Parker from the time he was a boy—another boy, like Morgan, enamored of the tales in his native bailiwick. Fisher ultimately worked with Parker to help build the museum collection. Later, Fisher created his own museum, Valentown, a lovely old two-story wooden building just across the highway from the enormous, unlovely East View Mall. Funny enough, Valentown itself was originally a kind of mini-mall—a cobbler, a baker, and a miscellany of others housed under one roof, huddled expectantly where the railroad line was aimed. But the line never got that far, and the businesses failed. Fisher has on display hundreds of never-worn antique shoes from the shop, along with numerous Iroquois artifacts—jewelry, rattles, corn-husk dolls, a huge bark canoe perched amid piles of old tools—the whole place jammed with his excitements. Unorganized, untidy, it is an idiosyncratic one-man operation. Admission is $1.25, but 25 cents extra at night—the cost of turning on the lights. Fisher personally escorts each guest nimbly up and down the long stairways like a man half his age.

The day I visit him there, he wants to tell me everything he knows to help my search for the land's stories. He boasts that he's been to longhouse ceremonies, says he could tell me secrets. I say please don't. He says he knows the burial site of Jikonhsaseh at Ganondagan—Arthur Parker showed it to him; he says he's shown it to Peter Jemison so someone will continue to know. Can this be true? Halfway through my tour he discloses that he's got three False Face masks over in his house—he took them off display out of respect for Seneca wishes because the masks are sacred, regarded as alive, are even traditionally fed porridge. Fisher, though, thinks his masks must be dead; they haven't been back to council for so long. So he invites me to see them, and this I don't turn down.

His house is more cluttered than the museum, books and papers competing with Iroquois and colonial paraphernalia. He searches for an old cardboard box on the floor, newspapers crumpled inside, lifts out his own Seneca hat of turkey feathers, one eagle feather on top, pointing back, and then hauls out three breathtaking basswood masks. I hold them in my hands, meet face-to-face the fierce gritted teeth and puckered lips of the Wind Blower, stroke his horse-tail hair. Child of museums, I'm used to seeing these two-dimensionally, high on walls, behind glass. Up close, there's no doubt, they look live enough to feed. How they might appear on the heads of dancers in the longhouse smoke is beyond my imagining.

Honored for his primary role in the forty-two-year campaign that led to the dedication of Ganondagan, Sheldon Fisher was adopted by the Heron Clan of the Seneca, given the name of Hiawasees, the Eagle Who Gathers News and History.

Today at Ganondagan, wearing his clan necklace, he stands back with pride gazing at his work—a dedicated space, its celebration. The corn-burning French and colonial Americans are gone; so are the revivalists. Seneca music, fleetingly, is back. Coming to Ganondagan is, repeatedly, a vital act of reorientation for me, a respite. It is one of the few places here one can reliably feel the presence of the Seneca.

I drive back through Canandaigua, pass its welcome sign emblazoned "The Chosen Place"—its Seneca meaning become a tourist slogan. New plazas and townhouses are sprouting up amid loosestrife and goldenrod, Canandaigua become so over-developed you can barely glimpse the lake from town. But there is at the same time this countermovement of feeling—a new grant of land to expand Ganondagan, the saving of Bare Hill.

The Seneca plan a ceremony to restore the spirit of the land atop Bare Hill. But apparently, in spite of litter and a lapse of more than a hundred years in ceremonies, the spirit of that place has in fact survived, and won converts.

———

This area is the only place in the Northeast I've felt the precariousness of the whole American enterprise. Out amid the rotting barns and wide-open fields, I sometimes feel it could all crumble in a minute. Tear down the electric poles, a few factories and stores, and we're gone. Take a piece of lakeshore land near Kendaia, turn it into a navy boot camp, finish with it, give it to the air force for a while, and when they don't need it anymore, throw up your hands, give it to the state, tear down the buildings, make it a park, call it Sampson, let it be a place for swimming and picnics, let it be, and it becomes . . . part of the package being negotiated for the Cayuga land-claim settlement. Though it's in traditional Seneca territory, it's close to original Cayuga land, and a convenient place for the state to give up. Just a few miles down the road from where we're living, the Cayuga might well be returning.

What lies behind such a possibility? The Cayuga, alone

among the Iroquois, ended up with no reservation in New York State. Their efforts to regain their land have been going on almost continually since 1795 when chiefs sold sixty thousand acres to New York State for $1,800 and a small annuity. Within six months, the state resold the land to settlers for $292,000 (much of it became the military tracts). The Cayuga have pointed out repeatedly that the state violated federal law in negotiating and implementing the treaties and that the treaties were never ratified by Congress as required. All that remains of the annuity is a box of muslin sent annually by the U.S. government via UPS—every Cayuga receives a yard and a half of cloth.

Many Cayuga went to Canada or Oklahoma; a small number remain in New York as guests of the Seneca on their reservation near Buffalo. They live there as second-class citizens, without a vote or the right to inherit land. No matter how long they stay, their situation can't improve. Tribal membership passes matrilineally. If a Seneca man marries a Cayuga woman, their children are Cayuga, and when the Seneca father dies, the Cayuga children have no right to stay on the land they were raised on. The tensions of modern reservation life have led to incivilities very much at odds with the spirit of the League. Previously, intermarriage between tribes was an ideal—marrying "across the fire" was seen as a way to perpetually reknit the League's alliance. At the end of each condolence ceremony, in fact, the League is symbolically rebound by the women crossing over to dance with men of their opposite moiety. Now there are cases of Cayuga widows being cast out of their Seneca homes.

The situation of the Cayuga worsens whenever there's a crisis over Seneca land. And since World War II, there's been an almost continual sense of crisis on Iroquois reservations in New York. A dam project ate up part of the Onondaga reservation south of Syracuse in the late forties; the St. Lawrence Seaway project in the fifties devoured Mohawk land and destroyed their fishing industry. The Niagara Power Project, orchestrated by Robert Moses, claimed an eighth of the Tuscarora reserve north of Buffalo. And most shockingly, the Kinzua Dam flooded the entire Cornplanter Tract of the Seneca's Allegany reservation in southwestern New York—a full third of the reservation.

The Kinzua project was first dreamed up in 1927 as a means of flood control along the Allegheny, downriver in Pennsylvania. It was authorized by Congress in 1941, put on hold, then taken up again in the mid-fifties by the Army Corps of Engineers. The Seneca argued that the plan was a direct violation of the Canandaigua Treaty of 1794, which had established the reservation as Seneca property and promised that "the United States will never claim the same, nor disturb the Seneca Nation, nor any of the Six Nations, or of their Indian friends residing thereon and united with them, in the free use and enjoyment thereof. . . ." Seneca president George Heron testified before Congress that "the truth of the matter is that my people really believe that George Washington read the 1794 Treaty before he signed it, and that he meant exactly what he wrote."

Nevertheless, a series of court decisions, culminating in a 1959 Supreme Court ruling, upheld the government's right to condemn a section of the reservation by eminent domain. The flooding problems and power needs of Pennsylvania residents were to be solved by flooding the most fertile bottomlands of the reservation.

The project had a kind of momentum hard to stop in this country. Once it was a line item in a budget, once so many hours had been invested in its design, not even TVA expert Arthur Morgan's testimony that in fact another location for the reservoir would be more economical, and would avoid taking Seneca land, could brake it. Most of the planning had gone on under Eisenhower, but it was Kennedy who wrote to the Seneca in 1961 that it was "not possible to halt the construction of Kinzua Dam."

The prospect of the land loss had hung over the heads of two generations. Completed in 1965, the reservoir submerged the homes of 130 families (one-third of the reservation's population) as well as the Cold Spring Longhouse, religious center of the reservation. The families were relocated from their rural homes to two dense, suburban-style housing tracts. The longhouse fire was moved in a nine-hour ceremony. But the floodwater permanently obliterated the reservation's cemetery, its monument to Cornplanter—first in the nation dedicated to an Indian—and the sacred places where prophet Handsome Lake had had his visions and begun to preach, revitalizing the Longhouse Religion during the agonizing early days of reservation life.

An ominous rider on the bill authorizing Kinzua also established a committee to meet with the Bureau of Indian Affairs to "think ahead to termination"—the ultimate dismantling of the reservation. Most believe that the loss of the land base would mean the end of the Seneca as a nation. Laurence Hauptman wrote in 1986 that "Even today, more than twenty years after the flooding of their homeland began, Seneca elders have difficulty speaking of this modern time of troubles. Going against Iroquois customary decorum, Seneca elders break down and cry, expressing their anguish in recalling the years 1957 to 1964. To them, the relocation and removal of Seneca families from the 'take area' was their second 'Trail of Tears.' . . ."

The displacement of Native Americans is catastrophic in a way white Americans don't fully understand, because as well as the usual emotional attachments to home, and the dependence of traditional Indians on a known environment for healing herbs and food, there is a strong religious dimension in their relation to their place. The dislocation from sacred space—from where revelations occurred and where ancestors are buried—profoundly damages spiritual life. The effects on Navajo following recent forced relocations near Big Mountain, Arizona, have been poignantly documented. "Relocation is a word that does not exist in the Navajo language," explains an elder. "To be relocated is to disappear and never be seen again." The displacement of spiritually rooted communities like the Navajo and Seneca "is about the worst thing you can do to a people short of killing them," says Thayer Scudder. "Judges and members of Congress—as highly educated and mobile individuals—are probably almost totally unaware of the impact. . . ."

There's no consolation for the Navajo in the new homes some have been given, as there wasn't for the Seneca in the new buildings that $15 million in compensation money made possible. And then there were suggestions like turning part of the Allegany reservation into a living museum of Iroquoia. Perhaps such a notion lingers behind the reservations in general. We've created them to the proper scale—two out of three are smaller than Disney World.

The experience of Kinzua radicalized a generation of young Iroquois and made them leaders in the Red Power movement. Their militancy, along with the continual diminishment of the reservations and the pressing need for more land, led to the assertive revival of Iroquois land claims in the seventies.

The Oneida pressed their case first and won a Supreme Court ruling in 1974 giving them the right to sue in federal court. The Cayuga quickly followed suit. The Seneca challenged their initial treaties and won an $8 million settlement. The Cayuga, though, are determined to settle only for land.

Their renewed quest to regain their territory was at first met with incredulity or indifference. Later, as the case was treated seriously by the Carter administration, much of the local population reacted with alarm and vehement racism. People said they thought they'd gotten rid of the Indians once before—why were they coming back with this "surprise attack"? Eleven thousand property owners were in the claimed area. From the start, though, the Cayuga made it clear they wanted to negotiate a settlement rather than sue and that they were prepared to accept parcels of public land rather than displace home owners. But local hysteria at having a reservation anywhere in the area unraveled a modest settlement that made it all the way to the floor of Congress in 1980. It would have given the Cayuga Sampson State Park and a grazing area farther down the lake, 5,400 acres in all, and a few million dollars. After the collapse of the agreement, the Cayuga filed suit in U.S. district court for the return of more than 64,000 acres of land and $350 million in trespass damages. The claimed land flanks Cayuga Lake and cuts a wide swath up the state from Pennsylvania to Lake Ontario— the whole of traditional Cayuga territory. It includes the city of Ithaca and prosperous small towns like Seneca Falls and Lewis Henry Morgan's hometown of Aurora, as well as numerous farms and resort cottages.

A second settlement, proposed in 1984, would give the Cayuga nearly 8,500 acres of public land and considerably more money than the first offer. Local recalcitrance continues to stall that plan ("I'd rather have a nuclear power plant there than Indians," declared one angry town councilman). Meanwhile, the legal process slowly but surely strengthens the Cayuga's case. The original treaties have now been declared invalid by the courts, and the objections that the Cayuga had abandoned the land before selling it (when chased off by Sullivan and Clinton), and that they'd waited too long before trying to reclaim it, have also been dismissed. Lawyers are advising the counties to settle.

There are only four hundred registered Cayuga remaining in New York State. With their families, they constitute about a thousand people. Chief Frank Bonamie, spokesman for the tribe and long involved in the claims case, lives in Ithaca at the south end of Cayuga Lake, the only registered Cayuga living in native territory. He thinks about two or three hundred people from the tribe would immediately settle on a new reservation. Several industries are poised to locate there too. The biggest factor for the families who would choose to come is having their own school and preserving their language. When I ask him if his own grown children would settle there, he confesses they can't— their mother isn't a Cayuga. There's a sad irony in that—in the desire to preserve the matrilineal tradition, many people of passionate commitment must be excluded.

The thought of a reservation at Sampson, so near my own front door, is pleasing. It would in some small way put things right, let us make our peace, even more so than Ganondagan, which, though evocative, is not a lived-in community. With the local natives back approximately in their place, we could together concentrate on the crucial matter of preserving this local environment, a concern embedded in Iroquois principles.

Despite their principles, New York's Iroquois reservations have hardly been spared environmental degradation, and the Cayuga reservation would be at the front door of the Seneca Army Depot, a less-than-desirable location being all anyone is even half-willing to cede. Iroquois reservations, in fact, seem to have been targeted for pollution. The Environmental Protection Agency is currently trying to clean up a twenty-five-acre dump on the Onondaga reservation that has been discovered to contain more than a thousand barrels of toxic chemicals and a tract the size of a football field eight feet deep in medical waste. Conditions at the Mohawk's Akwesasne (St. Regis) reservation up on the St. Lawrence Seaway are even more appalling. Alcoa has had a factory a few miles west of the reservation since 1903. By the early thirties, serious pollution problems were already evident. After the seaway opened, Reynold's opened an aluminum plant one mile from Akwesasne and began dumping fluorides into the air at the rate of three hundred pounds per hour. Cattle promptly fell ill. The livestock industry has been virtually wiped out. General Motors subsequently set up a facility fewer than a thousand yards from several Mohawk homes and used the river shoreline to dispose of PCB-laced sludge. That dump, separated from the reservation by only a chain-link fence, is now on the Superfund cleanup list. Investigators of local wildlife turned up the highest level of PCB contamination ever found in a mammal—11,522 parts per million in a shrew (3 parts per million is deemed unfit for human consumption). It's now unadvisable for the Mohawk to eat anything locally grown or caught.

The most ironic emblem of the desecration of the reservation is that local turtles have become unwitting monitors of toxic contamination. For the Iroquois and many other American tribes, the turtle represents the very foundation of the planet— the earth is mythically Turtle Island, perched on the turtle's reliably sturdy back. From the scientist's point of view, the turtle's being omnivorous, relatively sedentary, and long-lived means that the toxins in its tissues are a good indicator of local conditions. The turtles captured and analyzed at Akwesasne were so riddled with PCBs, insecticides, and other contaminants that their flesh qualified as toxic waste. In Iroquois mythology, when the turtle dies, the world dies.

Conditions like these have inevitably led to despair and internal division on the reservations. With their traditional subsistence economy destroyed, residents have had to turn instead to marketing their tax-free advantage, selling gas and cigarettes to the white population ("We Scalp Prices, Not People"). Most divisively, they've also opened gambling halls, an issue of such controversy among the Mohawk that it's often flared in violence. Among the Oneida, infighting has meant that in spite of legal victories, they still haven't progressed toward establishing their own reservation. The Cayuga settlement won't come easily either. Long centuries of damage have perniciously accumulated.

There's a prayer of eulogy sung as the Iroquois gather for

the condolence ceremony after a chief's death. Its environmental metaphors almost seem to have foretold where things were headed:

> Woe! Hearken! We are diminished.
> The cleared land becomes a thicket
> The clear places are deserted!
>
> Alas! Woe! Woe!
> They are in their graves,
> They who established it,
> They who established the Great League.
>
> Yet they declared
> That the Great League
> Would endure forever. . . .
>
> But woe!
> The League has grown old.
> Thus are we miserable.

What is sung for each dead chief can now be sung for the League as a whole. They are all in their graves—generations of Cayuga and Seneca as well as revivalists and first feminists—but their voices filter through. Arising out of this same soil as they did, they mingle for me in a poignant fugue I'd hear nowhere but here.

VI

SUNG LAND

———

An unsung land is a dead land.
—*Bruce Chatwin,*
of the Australian aborigines

WELCOME (AGAIN) TO GENEVA—"Lake Trout Capital of the World." A leaping blue fish bedecks our local welcome sign, the sign that peddles the image of locale, the commodity of place. All over the country, communities keen to mark their importance grasp for distinction and inflate their heroes in what's perhaps the country's most visible remaining evidence of a sense of place. "Nanaimo, the Bathtub Capital of the World." "Yale, Oklahoma—Home of Tami Noble, 1985 National All-Around Cowgirl." Towns even trade on past infamy. Salem, Massachusetts, promotes itself as "The Witch City—you would not have liked being here in 1692, but you really ought to experience it now. Stop by for a spell."

The need to assert the distinctiveness of one's place must derive from the fear that little distinction in fact exists. "It is a form of reassurance, a hopeful declaration that we are truly precious, somehow unique, and that the world will ignore us at its peril," says Wilbur Zelinsky. Perhaps there's been a trace of that in my own drive to sanctify this place; one must always beware of foolish hubris. I remember chuckling over a tiny French village, glimpsed from a train, its two competing hotels with signs aimed at the tracks—"Hotel des Nations" and "Hotel de l'Univers." It is the small place that most often resorts to boastful roadside, or trackside, claims—the large city needn't bother; it has a recognized character. Local Boy or Cowgirl Makes Good implies that someone from out there has recognized the quality of here. Robert Heilman remarks that you'll never find a sign declaring "Metropolitan Boy Makes Good."

For the small place, rather, "hereness has triumphed elsewhere," "there justifies here." The fear of living nowhere, in an un-validated no place, or in an indistinct clone town, is a very real one, and the welcoming sign is probably directed less at the passing traveler than at the community itself. There is no need to flaunt your identity, says Zelinsky, "if you are already convinced of your place in the cosmos, like the British, who have not yet shaken the habit of regarding England, or Greenwich, as the alpha point of our terrestrial globe." But for those of us on the so-called peripheries, it's only by investing pride and concern in what's immediate that we can feel situated, in place.

Despite its occasionally obnoxious manifestations, the celebration of the local is a healthy impulse, a resistance to homogenization, an attempt to define and center ourselves where we are, and consequently to value and preserve our local landscapes. Of course, as Yi-Fu Tuan points out, such geopiety is akin to patriotism, so it follows that it has its sentimental, xenophobic side. Still, "remove its exogenous imperial cloak and patriotism is compassion for the vulnerability of one's native soil." That vulnerability is evident in the self-deprecating humor of many on the periphery. "You Are Entering the Loneliest Town on the Loneliest Road in America"—Eureka, Nevada. "Humility" and "humor" are both linked etymologically to "humus"—the soil, the earth—and to the human being, who is at root, linguistically, an earthling. "The soil is man's intelligence," says Wallace Stevens. "The poetry of earth is never dead"—Keats. The poetry of place learns from the earth, is humble and good-humored before it.

After all my exploring I return to the poetry of this place. There's a story for everything. The stories tell the land:

> In the beginning, mother earth had twin sons—
> one good, peaceful, and patient; the other evil, rest-
> less, vicious. The good twin made deer, the evil one

the mountain lion to kill it. The good twin made berries; the evil made briars and poisons like the suicide root.

All over the land the good brother planted mountains, and in the valleys he made hills to protect the rivers and keep them straight. He set forests on the high hills, and on the low plains fruit trees and vines.

But the evil brother hurled the mountains apart, drove the hills into the valleys, bending the rivers as he hunted them down. He gnarled the forests, made monsters who loved the sea, but caged them in the rivers where they writhed. He herded hurricanes through the sky, chasing the sun and stars.

In the end, the good brother caught his twin and cast him off the edge of the earth. Yet, somewhere under the world, the evil brother still lives. When the sun rises and travels across the sky dome, which rests like a great upside-down cup on the saucer of the earth, people are in the daylight realm of the good brother. But when the sun sets and the dome lifts to let it escape into the west, people are in the realm of night and the evil brother. They both keep an eye on the world.

Tell these stories when you shouldn't and the bees will come and sting your lips, your tongue will swell and fill your mouth, snakes will crawl into your bed while you sleep and choke you . . . then you will desist from forbidden talk. Have I transgressed?

Certain stories weren't told by the Seneca during the summer because they could offend the "little people," the magical helpers of fruits and vegetables. Tale-telling was so powerful it could unbalance the seasons—creatures might become entranced by tales, wander dazed through forests and forget to go to their winter homes. "To listen to stories made the birds forget to fly to the south lands when winter came," Arthur Parker explains, "it made the animals neglect to store up winter provisions. . . ." Even plants would cross a threshold to hear a story. "All the world stops when a good story is told."

The story of deer: black silhouettes on warning signs, shot up for practice, for kicks, preseason; drunks in pickups (stay out of the woods now); viewing stands in the crotches of trees; a stiffened carcass mauled by dogs. Deer won't go near human hair—if you want to protect young plants, drape them with your hair. A woman who lost hers to chemotherapy told me this. How do you meet a deer?

The story of deer: when deer come near the house, they are like ambassadors from another realm, willing, for a moment, to flirt at the border. A listening pause. She holds. I stare, rigid lest I spook her. She is just outside my study window. But the span between us is an abyss neither of us can cross. It allows only our gaze, our alert meeting, a summit between two sovereigns with everything to negotiate, conducted in silence. I stress the need for compromise. But she is the first to turn, give up, leave, while I strain for the final white whip of her tail and am left empty-handed.

The story of poetry: thinking the conversation with the deer matters. Not simply, romantically, reading her as a sign, an outward sign of inward grace. Not superstitiously in the old magical way requiring divination, action. But as world to be attended to, silenced by, and recorded—even if I risk misreading her and myself. For this is the all, the only, the unavoidable *is.* It will assert itself despite us, inevitable as weather.

The story of the weather: six months of the year, gelid distances, land, sky, and lake a single off-white, trees scratched in as afterthought. The gables of houses fringed with icicles, waves frozen in place by the shore. Ten or twenty below sometimes, creak of boots on the tamped-down fields, our frozen breath making a canopy of mist. Sumac poised like fatted turkeys, ready to flee. Severity tearing at the heart, but nothing will yield in such cold, thought itself held ransom till spring.

The story of weather: knocks us out of the normal, deranges our highways and plans. The best we can do is try to predict it. We listen to forecasts compulsively, study color maps in motion. And still it catches us unawares, eludes detection, floods us out, ices the road. It is the stuff of our small talk. It demands our regard—or should one say "awe"?

Arthur Dove: "This is a beautiful day. Am tempted to go out looking. . . . Weather shouldn't be so important to a modern painter—maybe we're still 'too human.' "

Insulated from all but the worst of weather, we are obsessed with measuring it. My neighbors have thermometers that track the day's high and low, can definitively say, "It went down to twelve below last night," reading a red metal arrow. They record rainfall and snowfall in tubes in their gardens. They chart the movements of birds, the numbers, the dates, the species that visit their feeders. They have decades' worth of first-frost dates, last snow, first crocus. Spectators and gatherers of information, they think of themselves as "outdoorsy," nature lovers. They tell their stories in numbers.

> They are a wonderful people. They have divided the day into hours, like the moons of the year. In fact, they measure everything. Not one of them would let so much as a turnip go from his field unless he received full value for it.

One spring: so cold and interminably wet that the dogwood never bloomed and the peonies disappeared before they could flower. Fierce storms—wind that would be gale force at sea, the lake slamming and moaning. The trees crying, a kind of keening, low and constant, unintelligible. They look to me like banished women, heads forlornly hung, arms sweeping toward earth in the whoosh of each wind blast. What are they grieving?

Story of the earth: Zoe wants to know if the earth is alive. I tell her yes. She wants to know why. I start thinking about Gaia, *orenda*, about the old myths in which women were turned into birds and trees, but she says, "I know. It's alive because it moves without electricity."

Story of the earth according to a Dakota: "Everything as it moves, now and then, here and there, makes stops. The bird as it flies stops in one place to make its nest, and in another to rest in its flight. A man when he goes forth stops when he wills. So the god has stopped. The sun, which is so bright and beautiful, is one place where he has stopped. The moon, the stars, the winds, he has been with. The trees, the animals, are all where he has stopped, and the Indian thinks of these places and sends his prayers there. . . ."

Stop and tell a story, trust in the stories behind names.

The Place of the Village Destroyer: Iroquois name for Washington, D.C., derived from their name for George Washington following the depredations of the Sullivan campaign. Some translate it "the Village Devourer." It became their name for all U.S. presidents thereafter. Cornplanter told Washington to his face, "When that name is heard, our women look behind them and turn pale."

Indian summer: our name—a tease, a false season, weather as Indian giver.

The other side of the creek: What the Iroquois say when they feel something is "none of our business." For example, says an Onondaga, the war in the Persian Gulf was very definitely "on the other side of the creek."

Horseheads: "In 1779 near this spot, General John Sullivan mercifully disposed of his pack horses worn out by faithful service in the campaign against the Six Nations of the Iroquois. The first white settlers entering the valley found the bleached skulls and named the place Horseheads. Some people say that the Indians found the skulls first and arranged them along the trail."

These are the authentic voices of place, the ground of poetry. It's poetry I can begin to make now from my attachment to this place, poetry which is a stay against the world's vanishing act, a stay against forgetfulness, poetry which belongs to its place as well as its moment in time. "Place induces poetry," says Eudora Welty, "and when the poet is extremely attentive to what is there, a meaning may even attach to his poem out of the spot of the earth where it is spoken, and the poem signify the more because it does spring so wholly out of its place, and the sap has run up into it as into a tree."

Well grounded now, I can say "Seneca"—and see a satellite dish poised in a stubbled field, the coy behinds of cows, hear the grapeshot of a passing train, the dull percussive of an army helicopter making its rounds in a pewtered sky, one pink smudge painted over the depot, a stain in the air—too much wine last night, rotting apples on the ground, the dog come home wreathed in bloodied fur.

I see raw truths along with gentle graces. I see the tracks of the eastern coyote right beside where I've punched my ski poles in the snow-filled cornfield across the road, the field where we gather ears left behind by the huge mechanical picker, the field owned by a well-dressed farmer who shows up three times a year in a white Mercedes and parks on the shoulder to watch as tractors and combines plow, plant, harvest. The rest of the time his field is owned by deer, coyotes, red-winged blackbirds, and me, musing.

Try instead the Seneca's true name, Nundawaono: a mist of chicory hovering over hay, alfalfa aswim with butterflies, leaves upturned in conversation, fifty thousand geese wintering on the lake (a city honking at the moon, black gauze skimming air and water), the mating dance of a pair of cardinals, two handfuls of flame flung at the sky.

Poetry: "a manifestation of landscape and climate," asserts John Elder, "just as . . . flora and fauna are."

———

A critic once accused Lawrence Durrell of writing as if the landscapes in his books were more important than the characters. Durrell pleaded guilty to seeing characters "almost as functions of a landscape." A place, he believed, "will express itself through the human being just as it does through its wild flowers."

People dwelling close to their land express that poetry through myths and place-names. In Keith Basso's long attention to Western Apache conversation, he's observed that not only do stories incorporating places serve to "stalk" people, but that place-names themselves stand in for stories, providing terse messages to tribal listeners. A place-name detaches a story from its physical anchor in the world and lets it function emblematically.

"Speaking with names," the Apache call their minimalist conversations—little more than an exchange of place-names—a way to talk to a person obliquely, and therefore politely. Instead of criticizing someone's behavior outright, say, one can respond with an appropriately didactic story evoked simply by the name of the place where that story happened: "It happened at whiteness spreads out descending to water, at this very place." The listener is thus given "pictures to work on in her mind." Silence follows, allowing her time to travel to the place, imaginatively stand in the exact vantage from which the name of the place derives, stand in the tracks of the ancestor who named it, and listen for the tale, understand why the story of the place is relevant to her situation. For someone to say more, more directly, would be seen as presumptuous, and it blocks a person's own thinking, "holding down the mind." This way, too, the ancestors themselves seem to make the point or judgment rather than the contemporary speaker.

The name and vision of the place are mnemonic, the trigger by which the story is roused. A story cannot "happen nowhere," Basso explains, and it can't be reinvoked without a reminder of its location. Stories like the one of the girl who disobeys her grandmother's warning about snakes, takes a shortcut at "white rock extends upward and out," falls, and is bitten, are just as compelling as our fairy tales, but they are also grounded in the communal territory of their telling in this valuable way. Children know that spot; they are going to listen!

The place-names used by the Apache for these stories, or "land names" literally, are precise guides to their locations— "Trail extends across a long red ridge with alder trees," "Cluster of big walnut trees stands bushing out." In contrast, says the Apache, "The Whiteman's names are no good. They don't give pictures to your mind." "Apaches don't need Polaroids. We've got good names!"

To stand imaginatively in a spot invoked by a place-name is to rejoin momentarily one's communal history. It is sometimes described as "daydreaming." The mention of the place-name sparks a response, though—not the complacency we ascribe to daydreams. A single name, says Basso, can "accomplish the communicative work of an entire saga." It is like literary allusion, the door that opens by mere mention. It has the density of poetry, the art of understatement, but uses the physical landscape as its vocabulary.

In the same vein, Chatwin proposes that the Australian songlines can be visualized as "a spaghetti of Iliads and Odysseys."

Gathering to sing a stretch of the ancestors' footprints, each owner in position along the songline . . . "To sing a verse out of order . . . was a crime. Usually meant the death penalty." "I can see that. . . . It'd be the musical equivalent of an earthquake." "Worse. . . . It would be to un-create the Creation."

Chatwin giving a lift to an aboriginal friend, the man flinging his head back and forth, window to window, frantically chanting the place-names along his songline in the twenty-five-miles-per-hour car, till the driver understands and slows down to the walker's pace of four miles per hour so the man can sing them properly.

Speaking right, knowing your land.

How much land have you got? "The grass of ten cows," says the rural Irish farmer. And it means much more than thirty-five acres. It tells the land's worth—another farm nearby would take sixty acres to feed those cattle.

An Onondaga looks at two acres of wild meadow. What does he see? "Two acres of medicine."

We see incoherence, a blur. Zoe, playing Auto Bingo on a long car trip, needs to locate for her game a cow, a gate, a railroad crossing, a house number on a post. Flings it aside in frustration—"All I see is empty land."

It used to be you could find your way by reading the land instead of route numbers—"Up to the great tumulus beneath the wild garlic wood, then . . . up along the stone way to the tall crucifix at Hawk Thorn, . . . to the third thorn tree at bogmyrtle hangar . . . up to the Hill of Trouble, then west. . . ."

The shift to a quantitative view of land—simple acres and miles, longitude and latitude—all but eliminated the old poetic relation to territory. It was no longer necessary to envision and name. It was no longer practical to define a piece of land by its flora, by its fertility, by what had happened on it. There was no longer any point in remembering the old landmarks and their stories. A map defined the single truth of the place.

When America's early settlers were cast into the New World, mapless, they had once again to rely on more immediate ways of knowing the land—the Indians' ways. Those lessons were one of the few fruits of the meeting between the two cultures, evidenced in remaining Indian place-names. But those names are now whimsical artifacts, unexamined. Few people are curious as to their meaning, what they might tell us. Given our own brand of place-names, we've lost the habit of thinking about names at all.

You can tell a lot about a people from their place-names—by how evocative and detailed the names are, whether they reflect local topography and incidents, by how many of them are possessives, asserting a strong sense of personal property, and by how many are deemed necessary to identify an area of land. A variegated landscape will tend to invite more names than a flat stretch of desert—it will appear to have more distinct places in it that can be separately identified. But, as is clear in the case of the Australian aborigines, it is more tellingly the relation of the culture to its land that influences the density of its named places than the visible variety of the topography. Researchers who've attempted to measure such density put the island of Fetlar in the Shetlands at the top of their list with 500 place-names per square mile—2,000 names on a mere four square miles, a density my Irish island probably approaches. Japan comes in high on the list with 140 names per square mile, the Ukraine with a hundred. And the United States? The estimate, averaging the entire country, is *one* name per square mile, a remarkably low figure. We overran the landscape quickly; our holdings were large; we didn't take the time, or feel the need, to name our fields, our small streams and hills.

Children, in contrast, greatly differentiate their land-scapes—by how they use them, by incidents that occur on them, by their features, and by how they lend themselves to fantasy—so that what for us is simply the backyard might be for them a world full of distinct places marked by bushes, flower beds, sprinklers, burrows. By the time we're adults, we think big, think little of the power of names.

American place-names were rushed into at the same speed the land was claimed. Most often, names were simply imported from the old country. Moving west, names were reproduced from the East. Many were given casually, humorously. (One town in the Adirondacks seems to have commemorated its founding father frankly by naming itself Speculator.) Names could be pulled from the book someone happened to be reading. We're distinctive, in fact, in that many of our namers were literate, in contrast to most of the world, where places were named before there were books to consult.

Sometimes naming was viewed as a ponderous chore, especially when a lot of names were needed at once. And so a committee of four was convened in New York State when the military tract townships had to be named. The four relied, like many with their task, on a thematic system—in their case classical heroes. The Spanish often used the calendar of saints, naming a place based on the date of its discovery. Others were less imaginative—the counties of Oklahoma were originally labeled simply with the letters of the alphabet, and there still remains a Kay County. Think how many towns and cities use bare numbers to name their streets. Some communities let addresses run to five digits on streets numbered in the hundreds, so loath are they to have to think up names. Or maybe they're just proud of their size. And, too, numbers are exact as names cannot be—their order is a given. They jibe well with our mechanistic view of nature—everything quantifiable, easy to identify.

Gridded, numbered streets were first used prominently in Philadelphia, where William Penn divided the new city into an orderly checkerboard and, eschewing the tradition of naming streets for the largest local householder, numbered the streets in one direction and then crossed them with neutral names, mostly of local trees. "Philadelphia became not only a city," claims George Stewart, "but the mother of many cities. The Americans, though far from an orderly people in everything, loved the orderly system of streets intersecting at right angles, and they carried it everywhere, even imposing it upon hilly sites to which it was not suited. Along with the plan went the naming, so that most American towns show numbered streets in one direction, and named streets in the other. Very often also the names are tree names, and even in the far-distant deserts, towns were laid out with streets called Chestnut, Spruce and Vine, though such plants never grew there." Though this classic American design has, as English critic Ian Nairn observes, the "superficial virtue of being able to tell you in a strange town exactly how to get from Main and Seventh to Walnut and Sixteenth," it has also ensured the visual monotony of American towns, where looking down a block almost inevitably yields an empty corridor rather than the inviting face of a building.

Topographically precise place-names are more frequently found in less developed places, especially where there's an agricultural peasantry, where small parcels of land have survived. Says Stewart: "In a mountain area such as Andorra a field of wheat may be no larger than a good-sized living-room in an American private home, and it can be an entity marked off by stone walls, and given a name." In the Shetlands, the numerous names evidently derive from the intimate knowledge of the land won by herding cattle and sheep—knowing every nook or mound an animal might hide behind or slip on. No doubt, as on my Irish island, and as with the Apache, those nooks and crannies have stories attached to them, past incidents retold for their humor and lessons. Native peoples use place-names and their stories both as vital information and as a key to their identity—they know where they are by the stories they hear, know where they belong by the stories they tell. Tales are cultural, but they are also in this way geographical; they create boundaries and rights.

The Tuscarora proved their ancestral connection to the Iroquois and won their place in the League in the eighteenth century by the evidence of place-names. Accurate descriptions of a great number of locales had survived in their language, enabling them to trace their tribal migration from Montreal through New York to Mississippi and finally to North Carolina, from which they were driven in 1712. Morgan marveled at such powers of preservation—"The era of their separation from the parent stock, and of this migration, they have entirely lost; but they consider the names of places on this extended route, now incorporated in their language, a not less certain indication of a common origin than the similarity of their languages [to the New York Iroquois]."

Stories and place-names were sometimes the only way Indians defined their territories. Morgan noted that even from exile on the reservations in the mid-nineteenth century, their places renamed by Europeans, the Iroquois' own names and mental geography had been "preserved among them with remarkable accuracy." But elsewhere, because many of the stories and names haven't been recorded, and have now, in many tribes around the country, been forgotten by the young, the "right" to territory has eroded. Native American activist Vine Deloria explains that "To name the land was for many Indians a way of claiming it, a way that proved more than adequate until Europeans arrived and started to claim the land for themselves with considerably harsher methods. Now, in litigation over the land, Indian claims can be disputed (and sometimes rejected) because many of the old names that marked tribal boundaries have been forgotten and lost." In the Cayuga land-claim case, hundreds of pages of documentation have been produced by lawyers and scholars to prove exactly where and when the tribe resided here.

Just as the Druids passed on their sacred and ritual knowledge to initiates by requiring them to memorize huge amounts of material (initiation could take twenty years), so Native American knowledge is a large undertaking. And like Druidic knowledge, now nearly lost to us because of the elimination of most of the population, so too Native American lore and ritual, often severed from its original landscape, is threatened with extinction. The symbiotic relation between the landscape and the oral tradition is crucial—without the land the stories will fade; without stories, land becomes less meaningful. Whenever the language of an indigenous people is lost, says Oren Lyons, the knowledge of a place is lost.

The transformation of a place's names under an occupying force can destroy a people's culture. Irish playwright Brian Friel depicts the phenomenon wrenchingly in his play *Translations*. The British army has come to rural Ireland in 1833 to survey it, map it, and translate the local place-names into English—the better to know their way around the country and control it. Owen, a local boy-done-well-in-the-city, comes home on the payroll of the army to aid in the linguistic work. He cavalierly sets out to remake the place-names of his childhood, dismissing the associations and tales they evoke.

It's the young English lieutenant Yolland who falls in love with the landscape and the musical, storied names Owen translates, and so begins to have qualms about "renaming a whole country overnight." He listens, too, as Owen's father, the drunken local schoolmaster, speechifies "that certain cultures expend on their vocabularies and syntax acquisitive energies and ostentations entirely lacking in their material lives." Plaintively watching his son and Yolland pore over the new place-names book, the schoolmaster laments that words "are not immortal. And it can happen . . . that a civilization can be imprisoned in a linguistic contour which no longer matches the landscape of . . . fact." Owen dismisses his father as pompous; Yolland thinks him astute.

YOLLAND: He knows what's happening.
OWEN: What is happening?
YOLLAND: I'm not sure. But I'm concerned about my part in it. It's an eviction of sorts.
OWEN: We're making a six-inch map of the country. Is there something sinister in that?

YOLLAND: Not in—

OWEN: And we're taking place-names that are riddled with confusion and—

YOLLAND: Who's confused? Are the people confused?

By the end of the play, Yolland having been abducted by rebels, likely murdered, and a violent revenge by the army imminent, it's the old schoolmaster who picks up the new place-names book and says, "We must learn where we live." A realist, he'll adapt, reconfigure his home landscape, unlearn the past, because, after all, "To remember everything is a form of madness."

It's a form of madness the contemporary Indian must embrace in order to survive culturally. The Iroquois still preserve their hardly recognizable landscape in their minds, in names and stories, even where the correspondence between name and place is no longer apt, even where the land has been bulldozed, built over, or flooded.

Like the British fumbling their way through Ireland, American settlers complained that Indian place-names were maddeningly imprecise. An early eighteenth-century land report in upstate New York bemoaned the vagueness of territorial boundaries among the Iroquois—names of brooks, hills, and falls were used to demarcate the land, and Europeans liked to assume that their names were "proper"; but they were revealed to signify only "a large brook, or broad brook, or small brook . . . so that the Indians show many such places by the same name." Of course the natives knew exactly what they meant, where they stood.

"White men need paper maps. We have maps in our minds," says an Apache. Until the age of treaties and surveyors, precise boundaries weren't really that important. Land was claimed by tradition, by continued use, with little conflict. There was, indeed, a general resistance to marking boundaries: "The country was made without lines of demarcation, and it is no man's business to divide it," said Nez Percé Chief Joseph. Home territory was a spacious concept including hunting grounds, gathering grounds, grazing land, living space, fishing places. Among the Navajo, it was only when the government ordered stock reduction and restricted people to defined grazing districts that possessiveness over land began. Before, "No one ever said 'This is my land' ... we just lived among each other. ..."

But the European geographical vision overwhelmed native tradition and gained legal weight. An 1832 ruling in the Alabama Supreme Court articulated the prevailing bias—the Indians did not have "what was essential to national character, they had no geographical boundaries." To have what in European property terms was "no permanent abiding place," to have movable villages and broad, seemingly undefined hunting grounds, communally held, made the Indians the equal of "the beast of the same forest that he habits." It was thus ruled that the Indians could have no legal possession of their inhabited land. Vine Deloria asserts that Indians were finally deemed people, rather than animals, only so they could have "the right to sell their lands."

While there was occasional intertribal tension over boundaries earlier, contact with Europeans and the development of, for instance, the fur trade created a much-increased consciousness of territory and a competitiveness over a dwindling resource that intensified the need to create firm boundaries. In order for land to be sold, it also had to have boundaries, and so the Indians had to make a huge shift in their concept of land occupation and ownership in order to negotiate with Europeans.

When they did have to define the borders of their territory, finally, they were able to do so quite clearly and definitively, usually using topographical landmarks, especially as expressed through use—"Where that river we fish from bends." A place-name in many Indian languages, explains Kim Stafford, is not typically "something that is, but something that happens," as with the old Kwakiutl names of the Northwest—Where Salmon Gather, Having Wind, Place of Homesickness. Children preserve this method of precise, experiential naming too, as when they call a neighborhood house "the house with the dog that bites." The Iroquois were exceptional among Native Americans, in fact, that in addition to local topographical landmarks they conceived of linear boundaries of great length between the tribal territories of the longhouse, upstate New York being neatly divided into five tribal strips, divisions that remained valid for centuries and are still cited in contemporary land-claim negotiations.

And despite the vagueness assumed by Europeans, Iroquois place-names do reveal a great sense of specificity about their topography. Outsiders would throw up their hands when the same lake was called by several different names; but Morgan explains that the Seneca word *te-car-ne-o-di* "means something more than 'lake.' It includes the idea of nearness, literally 'the lake at.' Hence, if a Seneca were asked the name of Lake Ontario, he would answer, *Ne-ah-ga* Te-car-ne-o-di; 'the lake at *Ne-ah-ga.'* This was a Seneca village at the mouth of the Niagara River. If an Onondaga were asked the same question, he would prefix *Swa-geh* to the word lake, literally 'the lake at Oswego.'"

So, *lake:* understood from a particular vantage point. From here on East Lake Road, in a cornfield of the military tracts, the city of Geneva a cheap necklace flung around the northern end of it, lead-bellied clouds trudging single file across. A place on the lake.

Elsewhere, seen from the highway, the lake's a silky glaze five men have been ice fishing the edges of, colorless figures through snow-limned branches, walking on water for all I know. I turn up the car heat. There are many kinds of lake.

Many tribes incorporate a compelling sense of relativity in their place-names. A Clatsop Indian explained how rivers were named in a letter published in 1900:

I wish to state this proposition, which cannot be overthrown, that the Indians in the Northwest country, extending as far back as the Rocky Mountains, never name a river *as* a river; they name localities. That locality may be of a greater or less extent, and they may say this water leads to such a place, or it will carry you to such and such a place, but never name a stream.

I know of some very good people who are hunting for the Indian names of the Columbia and its tributaries, and some who have even told me that they had found the name of the Columbia; but it is a mistake. . . .

The river as a whole, beyond the local, was unimportant. Intimate identification of its rapids, snags, and best fishing spots *within* the territory was, on the other hand, crucial. So those are what got named.

Lake: *lake at* . . . at that spot, from that point, with its particular set of associations and stories included in the name. As, *lake at Kashong:* ten miles south of Geneva on the western shore of the lake; where the weather splits according to locals, and if the first storm of winter keeps north of the creek, the whole winter will be milder south of it; where the Seneca sent their old people to live because it's a few degrees warmer there; Kashong, destroyed by a special detachment of Sullivan's army while the main group was busy burning corn at Ganundasaga; where Genevans of means have long had summer cottages, served early in the century by a steamer running four times a day to town so men could park their families down there and commute to work; Kashong, a place dwelt in for so long they're still finding graves when they plow, bones that predate the Iroquois found buried sitting upright, artifacts in their laps, bones that are mere gray outlines on the soil, quickly fading into the earth when touched by sunlight and air. Kashong, Creek of Two Branches, or Where the Limb Has Fallen, where healing herbs extinct elsewhere in the area still flourish along the banks and floor of the stream (so they say, if you can recognize them); where children can climb a small waterfall in summer and come home with tadpoles; where in April the smelt run thick as carpets to spawn upstream and men in waders go out at midnight with lanterns (seen from the road as swaying dots of light) to scoop them out with nets, fry them whole for breakfast; where in the nineteenth century some people thought enough of the place to want to make it a preserve, but the plan lost by one vote in the Geneva town council—all that and more: Seneca Lake at Kashong. More than you can fit on a map. More than you can get from a single book. A lived-in accumulation. Local knowledge. That is what ebbs away with forgotten tales, how the experience of place is impoverished.

"In coastal sailing guides," says Kim Stafford, "directions for crossing shoals to safe water often carry the refrain, 'local knowledge is advised.' Local knowledge is that story and place called 'Insufficient canoe.' The alternative to local knowledge is shipwreck."

For years now I have been studying the local poetry of lake, rising to each day's lesson of light. Month by month, season by season, I chart it, honing my language. Lake: flyway of geese, inhaler of sky, sulky gray inlet of a distant sea; or hung in lilac haze, the sky above dipped in apricot cream, glazed. Or, like today, blanked by fog, an abyss edged by mist-drowsed trees, silenced.

"Along this lake the eye is never tired," said an early visitor. And it is true.

I look, I write, I rip up pages. With as much as I've learned, I mistrust my metaphors, am alert to how every choice in words excludes some dimension of experience, emphasizes another. I go out with the lamp of myself shining brightly, illuminating a clearing, but I remain, implacably, its center. My fear is that I violate topography as I describe it, that I inject my own dream into what is, simply, there. (I am, admittedly, someone who once compared a particularly bright autumn treescape to a box of Trix!) Metaphor negates even as it carries us into new understanding. Because every act of depiction is inevitably interpretation, to turn the land into an emblem feels suspiciously like appropriating it.

Our metaphors reveal a lot about us. For centuries we've used theatrical metaphors for the landscape, thinking of places as scenes in our lives. Behind that inclination, suggests J. B. Jackson, lies an assumption that "the relationship between men and their surroundings could be so expertly controlled and designed as to make the comparison" to theatrical scenery apt. It requires such an assumption to undertake projects like enclosure and the building of dams. Even with our increasing self-examination, our relation to the land is still interestingly echoed in the theater—in modernist plays whose stage directions suggest they can happen "anywhere," and in plays whose bare stages represent an abstract *paysage interieur* or a nowhere. Jackson asserts that "if we are again to learn how to respond emotionally and esthetically and morally to the landscape," we will need to find a new metaphor for nature—or better yet, several.

Palimpsest, poultice, fugue . . . some days the desire to express this landscape in words seems futile; it feels as though I need another kind of language to do it in—perhaps one like the Hopi, in which you can't say "my house," but simply "here."

Younger, in Ireland, I felt the confidence to declare myself part of the landscape unabashedly. The Twelve Pin Mountains on the Connemara coastline were my daily muse. They hovered over my poems just as certainly as they defined my eastern horizon. They were the shape of my longing, the color of my experience. We're lucky to find places that become the unalterable on the daily borders of our lives, places we can entrust with the loyalty of our gaze, imaginative territory into which the mind may safely stray and return to tell its tale. Barring cataclysm or commercial development, the landscape is what remains reliably fixed. Only one loved place in my life has entirely disappeared—Spirit Lake beneath Mount St. Helens, where, before the volcano blew, I once rowed, listened, and wrote, so that it feels as if a piece of my life has been amputated there. But landscapes are, in general, one of the few predictables we have.

Trusting them, our perceptions have the freedom to blow their tops. Richard Hugo points out that when a writer uses a phrase like "noonday hillside," it suggests "that the world does not have rigid topography but optional configurations. At 4 p.m. it might not be a hillside at all." Such is the stance of the artist, the eye of the beholder claiming the prerogative to reconfigure the landscape, let it become a realm of private revelation—as Wallace Stevens famously did:

There it was, word for word,
The poem that took the place of a mountain.

He breathed its oxygen,
Even when the book lay turned in the dust of his table.

It reminded him how he had needed
A place to go to in his own direction,

How he had recomposed the pines,
Shifted the rocks and picked his way among clouds,

For the outlook that would be right,
Where he would be complete in an unexplained
    completion:

The exact rock where his inexactnesses
Would discover, at last, the view toward which they had
    edged,

Where he could lie and, gazing down at the sea,
Recognize his unique and solitary home.

Devoting ourselves to a place, we gain the boldness to name, project, reconstitute, see it in our own light. But my formal education has made me wary of that transformative impulse. I've been well warned, for example, to avoid the pathetic fallacy, that poetic error proclaimed by Ruskin in 1856 as the imposition of human feelings on the natural world, the betrayal of the "true appearance of things" under "the influence of emotion." Of course we now doubt such a singular thing as *the* true appearance of anything and know we're inevitably in the grip of our emotions, yet in our postromantic literary caution, perhaps we turn our backs on the vital connection between nature and the human, fail to express it, fail to rejuvenate it. To see oneself in blood relation to nature, the Iroquois notion of kinship, requires empathy and humility, a generous sense of community and family. On my best days, I feel as if this place *is* family now, almost as much so as my daughters, who've been born here. Yet it's easy to back off from such feelings out of fear of sentimentality. We probably, as Paul Shepard suggests, make distaste for the romantic an "excuse for our own lack of conviction."

Edmund Wilson, citing Alfred Whitehead, argues the wisdom of the romantic vision:

Those who make fun of the Romantics are mistaken in supposing that there is no intimate connection between the landscape and the poet's emotions. There is no real dualism, says Whitehead, between external lakes and hills, on the one hand, and personal feelings, on the other: human feelings and inanimate objects are interdependent and developing together in some fashion of which our traditional notions of laws of cause and effect, and dualities of mind and matter or of body and soul, can give us no true idea. The Romantic poet, then, with . . . his sympathies and passions which cause him to seem to merge with his surroundings, is the prophet of a new insight into nature: he is describing things as they really are; and a revolution in the imagery of poetry is in reality a revolution in metaphysics.

It's a return, really, to a way of regarding the physical world that predates the dissections of category and scientific analysis, an indigenous way that predates a vision of the world as full of natural resources. After all, no one thought of such a notion as the pathetic fallacy until the nineteenth century.

————

Contemporary poet Gary Snyder argues that to write full-heartedly from the vantage point of a well-known and loved territory is a vitally redemptive act. He urges commitment to a small bioregion, thoroughly learning it, responsibly caring for it, becoming its human voice.

It's that ideal I've moved toward, though imperfectly.

Staying in the Finger Lakes began as a practical choice—a job for each of us. To stay on now, to cancel job interviews elsewhere, has been a temperamental and ethical choice. The world needs our dedication—not just in the abstract global sense, but in local loyalties. It needs us to establish what Ted Relph calls "fields of care," the focused sites of our experiences, affections, and responsibilities.

But despite the strength of my attachment to this region, Geneva itself has never won my full affection. The town is floundering, its latest lakefront-development plans collapsing, its poverty worsening, and, as often in the past, Geneva has collaborated with its own decline. At its inception, it took a beautiful lakeshore and turned it into an industrial hub, and then into a dump to fill in defunct canals and to extend itself out onto water. Now, washed up, it wants the consolation of tourism, but soil tests for the hoped-for hotel revealed what shaky ground the whole enterprise rests on.

Ignoring its past, not keeping its feet on the ground, has this time cost Geneva millions (needlessly moving the highway and tearing down the Agway Tower). The history I've discovered here is virtually unknown to its inhabitants and politicians. Despite the great expressiveness of this landscape, the many lessons to be learned, Geneva remains adrift.

Our commitment to stay in the area has moved us finally to buy a house, to tie ourselves for the long term. But the contrary pull—our desire for a more lively, responsive human community, and our children's need for a more stimulating education— has led us forty miles southeast, to Ithaca, a small, warmhearted city, woven into its landscape in the way I'd always hoped Geneva would be. The decision wasn't easy. Despite how relatively nearby the move, it was still a move, and a severance. Like many, we made a decision based largely on our children's needs rather than our own. We've given up rural pleasures and purities in order to be in a neighborhood with other young children nearby. We've moved to have well-funded, progressive schools, music and dance lessons, plays, films, museums—all the activity of a university town—and a more heterogeneous, open-minded community.

We have shifted over one hearth in the League, to Cayuga territory at the southern end of Cayuga Lake. Ithaca is set in essentially the same landscape we lived in for eight years, only more dramatically cut with gorges and waterfalls, the city perched on three big hills. From where we live, it's a five-minute walk to a city-center pedestrian mall; five minutes in the other direction and we're in a wildflower preserve beside a deep gorge and rushing creek, seemingly miles from human effort, for all you can hear or see. The beauty of the land around the city is prized, protected in dozens of parks and preserves. Ithaca seems, miraculously, to be one of those rare places left in the country that is not, in Durrell's phrase, living at right angles to the land. Its unusual social and environmental conscience, and strong sense of self, make it a truly distinctive place.

Semiurban, it is a world closer to David's heart, and a world we feel right in providing our children. Perhaps, as a family, we've found our balance, found our place—I hope for more than a while. I do miss the constant presence of the lake; so does Zoe. My need for rootedness was shaken once again. But having stayed with one job and circle of friends in a known region this long, I feel closer to rootedness now than I have since Ireland. I am a full-fledged citizen, if not of a town, at least of a bioregion. Geneva has given me that, perhaps by throwing me back on the land instead of distracting me with urban amenities. It has been as vital to my making myself at home here as Ithaca now seems to be.

I still spend most of the working week and many evenings and holidays in Geneva. I am part of a web of people who, like David and me, have come here from elsewhere and stayed. Through our shared experiences, we continually bind ourselves to this place. We've been here long enough to watch children grow, move on, return, find their footing; we've buried friends together and return to their graves to keep them present among us. Working together, demonstrating at the depot or the Women's Rights Park, hiking the lakeshore, or visiting the schools to bring Seneca traditions into the classroom, we are part of the ongoing story of the place. The world holds still in our hands a moment, stops vanishing.

Commuting two hours a day now, I drive through a landscape resonant with all I've learned about it after so many years of driving around. I go through Kendaia, follow along Sullivan's route. I pass Rose Hill, get on the longhouse trail near Border City Road. When I crest a hill to find Seneca Lake laid out before me, my heart pings with a sense of hitting center. The lake is where I first fell in love with this place, and it is still what opens a keenness in me, what makes lines of poetry leap into my head. It is where I know my most generous impulses, my greatest optimism. Driving, I am grounded too by new patterns that mark the land for me: the hawk on the wire I pass each day south of Ovid, always facing east to Cayuga Lake in the morning, west to Seneca at sunset. I am warmed by the dark countryside revealing its houses in Christmas lights each December, by the mud-clogged fields brightening each May. I speed past the monolithic miles of the depot's barbed-wire fence, watch a jet roar into the crotch of Orion.

The act of staking a place here has been fraught with everything I know stands cocked against it. I've taken the fragile notion of home territory and stretched it, possessed it by will-power. Doing so, I've found my way to a vibrant, responsible life inside a piece of America I knew nothing about, a place more my own than Ireland would finally have been.

I've lived in the Finger Lakes region for ten years now, longer than anywhere else in my life. Though in the past I loved best places where the human touch is least evident—untamed mountain and sea, the detail-diminished vista—I have learned to love as well the dock- and cottage-dotted lakeshores, the shapings of gardens, home ground. This place has taught me anew how to look and how to live, just as Ireland did. With everything it has revealed to me, when I walk out into the land now, I know, more deeply than I thought possible, where I stand.

Notes

I

p. 5   On the geology of the Finger Lakes—O. D. von Engeln, *The Finger Lakes Region: Its Origin and Nature* (Ithaca, N.Y.: Cornell University Press, 1961), p. 2.

9   "But you get so tired . . ."—*The New Yorker*, quoted by David Lowenthal, "Is Wilderness 'Paradise Enow'?: Images of Nature in America," *Columbia University Forum* 7, no. 2 (1964), p. 34.

"The idea that the world contains scenery . . ."—Paul Shepard, *Man in the Landscape: A Historical View of the Esthetics of Nature* (New York: Knopf, 1967), p. 117.

10   "Strictly speaking . . ."—D. W. Meinig, *The Interpretation of Ordinary Landscapes* (Oxford: Oxford University Press, 1979), p. 2.

On the term landscape—Leslie Marmon Silko, "Landscape, History, and the Pueblo Imagination," *Antaeus* 57 (Autumn 1986), p. 84.

15   "If we think of space . . ."—Yi-Fu Tuan, *Space and Place: The Perspective of Experience* (Minneapolis: University of Minnesota Press, 1977), p. 6.

17   On stories and the land—Silko, pp. 88–9.

18   On the Western Apache—Keith H. Basso, *Western Apache Language and Culture: Essays in Linguistic Anthropology* (Tucson: University of Arizona Press, 1990), pp. 99–137.

19   "anyone who leaves . . ."—Amos Rapoport, *House Form and Culture* (Englewood Cliffs, N.J.: Prentice-Hall, 1969), p. 76.

On the Ronga ritual—Lucien Levy-Bruhl, *Primitive Mentality*, trans. Lilian A. Clare (New York: The Macmillan Co., 1923; reprint, Boston: Beacon Press, 1966), p. 214.

21 "My brothers . . ."—Khethaahi, quoted by T. C. McLuhan, *Touch the Earth: A Self-Portrait of Indian Existence* (New York: Outerbridge and Dienstfrey, 1971), p. 156.

"The practice of giving . . ."—Arthur Minton, "Names of Real-Estate Developments: III," *Names* 9, no. 1 (March 1961), p. 9.

22 "linguistic landscaping"—David Lowenthal, "Not Every Prospect Pleases," *Landscape* 12, no. 2 (Winter 1962–63), p. 22.

23 "Many Europeans have spoken . . ."—Amos Rapoport, quoted by E. Relph, *Place and Placelessness* (London: Pion, 1976), p. 15.

On the songlines—Bruce Chatwin, *Songlines* (New York: Viking, 1987), pp. 2 and 13.

24 Attitudes toward mountains—Relph, p. 124.

"History, as yet . . ."—Henry James, *Hawthorne* (New York: Harper & Brothers, 1880; reprint, Ithaca, N.Y.: Cornell University Press, 1956), p. 10.

"The ancient landscape . . ."—Yi-Fu Tuan, "Geopiety: A Theme in Man's Attachment to Nature and to Place," in David Lowenthal and Martyn J. Bowden, eds., *Geographies of the Mind: Essays in Historical Geosophy* (New York: Oxford University Press, 1976), p. 18.

27 "the business of this campaign . . ."—Barbara Graymont, quoted by Thomas S. Abler and Elisabeth Tooker, "Seneca," in Bruce G. Trigger, ed., *Northeast*, vol. 15 of *Handbook of North American Indians* (Washington, D.C.: Smithsonian Institution, 1978), p. 508.

On the Three Sisters—Lewis Henry Morgan, *League of the Iroquois*, ed. and ann. Herbert M. Lloyd (New York: Dodd, Mead and Co., 1904), pp. 152–3.

29 "Is not the door . . ."—quoted in Morgan, *League of the Iroquois*, Appendix B, pp. 301–2.

On the Navajo visit to Iroquois territory—Irving Powless, Jr., "The Sovereignty and Land Rights of the Houdenosaunee," in Christopher Vecsey and William A. Starna, eds., *Iroquois Land Claims* (Syracuse, N.Y.: Syracuse University Press, 1988), p. 159.

On the foundation of the Iroquois League—Christopher Vecsey, "The Story and Structure of the Iroquois Confederacy," *Journal of the American Academy of Religion* 54, no. 1 (Spring 1986), p. 97.

30   Quotations from the condolence ceremony—Frank G. Speck, *Midwinter Rites of the Cayuga Long House* (Philadelphia: University of Pennsylvania Press, 1949), pp. 160–1.

32   "Have we, the first holders . . ."—Cayuga chief Peter Wilson, quoted in McLuhan, p. 100.

"We stand a small island . . ."—Red Jacket, quoted by John Delafield, "History of Seneca County," in *State Agricultural Report* (1850), p. 386.

33   On the grid system's "remorseless rectangularity"—Wilbur Zelinsky, *The Cultural Geography of the United States* (Englewood Cliffs, N.J.: Prentice-Hall, 1973), p. 47.

On the symbolism of the grid system—John B. Jackson, *American Space: The Centennial Years 1865–1876* (New York: Norton, 1972), p. 25; and Ervin H. Zube, ed., *Landscapes: Selected Writings of J. B. Jackson* (Amherst, Mass.: University of Massachusetts Press, 1970), pp. 4–5.

34   On centralized authority—Alexis de Tocqueville, *Democracy in America*, vol. 2 (New York: Vintage Books, 1945), p. 312.

On the problems of the grid system—Peirce F. Lewis, "The Northeast and the Making of American Geographical Habits," and Hildegard Binder Johnson, "Towards a National Landscape," in Michael P. Conzen, ed., *The Making of the American Landscape* (Boston: Unwin Hyman, 1990), pp. 96–7 and 127–9.

On the clearing of the land in New York State—Ulysses Prentiss Hedrick, *A History of Agriculture in the State of New York* (Albany: New York State Agricultural Society, 1933), p. 99.

35   "As I stand . . ."—quoted by Eric Sloane, *Our Vanishing Landscape* (New York: Funk and Wagnalls, 1955), p. 10.

35 "No army in the history . . ."—Hedrick, p. 18.
36 "The aim of the farmers . . ."—George Washington, quoted by Hedrick, p. 75.

"*Resolved,* that none of us . . ."—quoted by Paul Shepard, *Nature and Madness* (San Francisco: Sierra Club Books, 1982), p. 2.

"There is as yet . . ."—quoted by Christopher Vecsey, "American Indian Environmental Religions," in Christopher Vecsey and Robert W. Venables, eds., *American Indian Environments: Ecological Issues in Native American History* (Syracuse, N.Y.: Syracuse University Press, 1980), p. 34.

On the destruction of animals—W. H. McIntosh, *History of Ontario County, N.Y.* (Philadelphia: Everts, Ensign and Everts, 1876), p. 47.

38 "A handsome sheet . . ."—from the archives of the Geneva Historical Society.

39 On the state restocking program—Bureau of Fisheries, *A Strategic Fisheries Management Plan for Seneca Lake* (Albany: New York State Department of Environmental Conservation, October 1980).

40 "The theory advanced . . ."—undated, unidentified newspaper clipping from the archives of the Geneva Historical Society.

41 "Seneca water . . ."—Arch Merrill, *The Lakes Country* (reprinted from *The Democrat and Chronicle*, Rochester, 1944), p. 78.

43 On the building of the Seneca Army Depot—Hilda R. Watrous, *The County Between the Lakes: A Public History of Seneca County, New York, 1876–1982* (Seneca County Board of Supervisors, 1983).

46 On the remains of the Manhattan Project—*Finger Lakes Times*, August 4, 1987.

47 "In part, at least . . ."—Richard Wilbur, in introduction to Alan Gussow, *A Sense of Place: The Artist and the American Land* (New York: Friends of the Earth, Seabury Press, 1971), p. 25.

II

51   "Geneva is a pretty place . . ."—*Penn Yan Democrat* article of
1835, quoted by G. David Brumberg, *The Making of an
Upstate Community, Geneva, New York* (Geneva Bicentennial
Commission, 1976), p. 92.

54   "Everyone in Geneva . . ."—Arthur Dove in a letter to
Alfred Stieglitz, in Ann Lee Morgan, ed., *Dear Stieglitz,
Dear Dove* (Newark: University of Delaware Press, 1988),
p. 395.

55   "Variety is disappearing . . ."—Tocqueville, vol. 2, p. 240.

       "If we eat . . ."—Den Fujita, quoted by *Mother Jones* (July
1976), p. 6.

59   "which left me . . ."—Stephen Potter, quoted by David
Lowenthal, "Geography, Experience, and Imagination,"
Annals of the Association of American Geographers 51, no. 3
(September 1961), p. 252.

       "In Princeton . . ."—Edward Witten, quoted by K. C. Cole,
"A Theory of Everything," *New York Times Magazine* (October 18, 1987), p. 25.

60   "They are spending . . ."—Morgan, *Dear Stieglitz, Dear Dove,*
p. 393.

61   "the most radical American painter . . ."—Sasha M. New-
man, *Arthur Dove and Duncan Phillips: Artist and Patron* (New
York: Braziller, 1981), p. 24.

       Georgia O'Keeffe on Arthur Dove—quoted by Barbara
Haskell, *Arthur Dove* (San Francisco Museum of Art,
1974), p. 77.

       "It is swell . . ." and "Think I'd better . . ."—Morgan, *Dear
Stieglitz, Dear Dove,* p. 382.

62   Descriptions of early Geneva—letters of Elkanah Watson,
quoted by E. Thayles Emmons, *The Story of Geneva* (Geneva, N.Y.: The Geneva Daily Times, 1931), p. 341.

63   Description of Geneva in 1804—Robert Munro (a pseudo-
nym for Charles Williamson), "A Description of the
Genesee Country" (Geneva, N.Y., 1804).

       "Not only an elegant . . ."—Elkanah Watson, in Emmons,
p. 343.

63   Charles Williamson on Genesee Country—Anonymous (but known to have been written by Williamson), "Description of the Settlement of the Genesee Country, in the State of New York, in a series of letters from a Gentleman to His Friend" (Geneva, N.Y., 1799).

64   On criticism of Williamson—William Wyckoff, *The Developer's Frontier: The Making of the Western New York Landscape* (New Haven: Yale University Press, 1988), p. 69.

    "The very slightest . . ."—Charles Dickens, quoted by Sloane, p. 57.

65   "When the colonial charters . . ."—Brumberg, p. 17.

66   Diary entries—quoted by A. G. Hilbert, "The Pre-Emption Line—Fraud, Error, or Hard Liquor" (unpublished manuscript, Geneva Historical Society archives, 1969).

67   "I have always maintained . . ."—quoted by A. G. Hilbert.

    "Father . . ."—quoted by McLuhan, pp. 131–3.

69   "that moment of unspecified love . . ."—Peter Handke, *Slow Homecoming* (New York: Farrar, Straus and Giroux, 1985), p. 179.

70   On Endymion—Lucile M. Harford, *The Country Cousin* (Geneva, N.Y.: Bicentennial Commission of the Town of Geneva, 1976), p. 140.

72   On the legend of the mound—Morgan, *League of the Iroquois*, Book 3, p. 90.

73   "It matters very little . . ."— Ely Parker to Governor Hill, quoted by George S. Conover, *Reasons Why the State Should Acquire the Famous Burial Mound of the Seneca Indians Adjacent to the State Agricultural Experiment Station* (pamphlet, Geneva, New York, 1888), manuscript file of Hobart and William Smith Colleges Library.

74   "That land of Ganono-o . . ."—Peter Wilson, quoted in McLuhan, p. 100.

    Description of Ganondagan in 1687—publicity poster for Ganondagan State Historic Site.

78   On Mary Jemison, and quotations from her—James E. Seaver, ed., *Dehhewamis: Life of Mary Jemison* (New York: Miller, Orton and Mulligan, 1856).

84   On the autobiography of Mary Jemison—Annette Ko-
       lodny, *The Land Before Her: Fantasy and Experience of the
       American Frontiers, 1630–1860* (Chapel Hill: University of
       North Carolina Press, 1984), pp. 80–1.

85   "right angles to the land"—Lawrence Durrell, *Spirit of
       Place*, ed. Alan G. Thomas (New York: Dutton, 1969),
       p. 161.

III

89   On the word "dwell"—John B. Jackson, *Discovering the Ver-
       nacular Landscape* (New Haven: Yale University Press,
       1984), p. 91.
       On centennial homes—Zelinsky, p. 91n.
       On American mobility—Zelinsky, p. 56.

90   "Many people prefer moving . . ."—quoted by Vance Pack-
       ard, *A Nation of Strangers* (New York: David McKay Co.,
       1972), p. 1.
       "I have repeatedly seen . . ."—Harold F. Searles, *The Nonhu-
       man Environment in Normal Development and in Schizophrenia*
       (New York: International Universities Press, 1960),
       pp. 82–3.

91   On Pratolini's novel—David Lowenthal, "Geography, Ex-
       perience, and Imagination," p. 259.
       "The Germans had . . ."—Harvey Cox, "The Restoration
       of a Sense of Place: A Theological Reflection on the
       Visual Environment," *Ekistics* 25 (1987), pp. 422–3 (first
       published in *Religious Education*, January 11, 1966).

92   On *Landschaft*—John R. Stilgoe, *Common Landscape of America,
       1580–1845* (New Haven: Yale University Press, 1982),
       pp. 12–13.
       "This obligatory submission . . ."—John Barrell, *The Idea of
       Landscape and the Sense of Place 1730–1840: An Approach to the
       Poetry of John Clare* (Cambridge: Cambridge University
       Press, 1972), pp. 95–6.

93   On John Clare—John Barrell; and John Lucas, "Places and
       Dwellings: Wordsworth, Clare and the Anti-Pictur-
       esque," in Denis Cosgrove and Stephen Daniels, eds., *The*

Iconography of Landscape (Cambridge: Cambridge University Press, 1988), pp. 83–97.

94   "Nature was scarcely seen . . ."—Samuel H. Monk, quoted by David Lowenthal and Hugh C. Prince, "English Landscape Tastes," *The Geographical Review* 55, no. 2 (1965), p. 195.

"a self-conscious observer . . ."—Raymond Williams, *The Country and the City* (New York: Oxford University Press, 1973), p. 124.

On the landscape of mobility and hierarchy of land-owners—J. B. Jackson, *Discovering the Vernacular Landscape*, pp. 152–6.

95   "Homelessness . . ."—Martin Heidegger, quoted by James M. Houston, "The Concepts of 'Place' and 'Land' in the Judaeo-Christian Tradition," in David Ley and Marwyn S. Samuels, eds., *Humanistic Geography: Prospects and Problems* (Chicago: Maaroufa Press, 1978), p. 225.

"perpetual exile"—as envisioned by Edward Said, Tzvetan Todorov, and Julia Kristeva, is described by Lee Quinby, *Freedom, Foucault, and the Subject of America* (Boston: Northeastern University Press, 1991), pp. 147–8.

"To be rooted . . ."—Simone Weil, *The Need for Roots: Prelude to a Declaration of Duties Toward Mankind*, trans. Arthur Wills (New York: G. P. Putnam's Sons, 1952; reprint, New York: Harper Colophon Books, 1971), p. 43.

96   Congressmen on grid system—quoted by Stilgoe, p. 104.

On social impact of life on the grids—Zelinsky, pp. 47–9.

"Mobility is always . . ."—Harvey Cox, *The Secular City* (New York: Macmillan, 1966), p. 45.

97   "To be tied to place . . ."—Yi-Fu Tuan, "American Space, Chinese Place," *Harper's Magazine* (July 1974), p. 8.

"Roots are ruts . . ."—quoted by Packard, p. 183.

"To be rooted . . ."—David E. Sopher, "The Landscape of Home: Myth, Experience, Social Meaning," in D. W. Meinig, p. 137.

"As for relatives . . ."—Morgan, *Dear Stieglitz, Dear Dove*, p. 291.

"encounters and obligations . . ."—Houston, p. 226.

98 "We shall not cease . . ."—T. S. Eliot, "Little Gidding," *The Complete Poems and Plays, 1909–1950* (New York: Harcourt, Brace and World, 1950), p. 145.

"Before any choice . . ."—Eric Dardel, quoted by Relph, p. 41.

"If you are in Chicago . . ."—Richard Hugo, *The Triggering Town: Lectures and Essays on Poetry and Writing* (New York: Norton, 1979), p. 7.

99 "Why should we take . . ."—Alastair Reid, *Notes on Being a Foreigner* (San Francisco: North Point Press, 1988), p. 15.

101 "Theories have proliferated . . ."—Elizabeth Pepper and John Wilcock, *Magical and Mystical Sites: Europe and the British Isles* (New York: Harper and Row, 1977), pp. 183–4.

102 "the skeleton of a dead place"—Relph, p. 32.

103 On practices in the region of Carnac—Mircea Eliade, *Patterns in Comparative Religion*, trans. Rosemary Sheed (New York: New American Library, 1958), p. 223.

106 "Their spatial existence . . ."—Stephen Kern, *The Culture of Time and Space 1880–1918* (Cambridge: Harvard University Press, 1983), p. 51.

On the Yiddish language—Maurice Samuel, quoted by Houston, p. 228.

"arose in the social context . . ."—Cox, *The Secular City*, p. 47.

"The places that we have known . . ."—Marcel Proust, quoted by Relph, p. 144.

107 "If there is a single illusion . . ."—Kern, p. 50.

"Most individuals feel almost naked . . ."—Zelinsky, p. 55.

"Freud moved theory . . ."—E. V. Walter, *Placeways: A Theory of the Human Environment* (Chapel Hill: University of North Carolina Press, 1988), p. 97.

109 "Today, archeological relics . . ."—Suzanne C. Bernfeld, "Freud and Archeology," *American Imago* 8 (1951), p. 110.

On Freud and hysteria and cities—Joseph Rykwert, summarized and quoted by Walter, p. 108.

"as though the human race . . ."—Searles, p. 3.

110   "The lost identity . . ."—Wendell Berry, *The Unsettling of America: Culture and Agriculture* (New York: Avon Books, 1977), p. 111.

111   On Sati—Diana L. Eck, "Shiva and Shakti in the Land of India," Larwill lectures in religion, Kenyon College, 1982, p. 37.

112   "official, government-promoted . . ."—Eleanor Munro, *On Glory Roads: A Pilgrim's Book About Pilgrimage* (New York: Thames and Hudson, 1987), p. 20.

         "the countless dedicated pilgrims . . ."—Surinder Mohan Bhardwaj, *Hindu Places of Pilgrimage in India: (A Study in Cultural Geography)* (Berkeley: University of California Press, 1973).

         On mythical geography—Diana Eck, "Living Myth: Landscape of Hindu Pilgrimage," Hobart and William Smith Colleges lecture, May 9, 1989.

         On Indian sense of place—David E. Sopher, "Place and Landscape in Indian Tradition," *Landscape* 29, no. 2 (1986), p. 2; and Sopher, "The Landscape of Home," in Meinig, p. 135.

114   "one of the finest examples . . ."—National Park Service, quoted in *Finger Lakes Times*, April 29, 1987.

         "At night when the streets . . ."—Chief Seattle, Surrender Statement, 1855.

116   "Other lives . . ."—Adrienne Rich, "From an Old House in America," *Poems: Selected and New, 1950–1974* (New York: W. W. Norton and Co., 1975), p. 235.

117   "It is well . . ."—Pablo Neruda, "Towards an Impure Poetry," quoted in Seamus Heaney, "Place, Pastness, Poems: A Triptych," *Salmagundi* 68–69 (Fall 1985/Winter 1986), p. 31.

         On Pablo Neruda—Seamus Heaney, p. 31.

118   "the dead have no rights . . ."—Thomas Jefferson, quoted by Lowenthal, "The Place of the Past in the American Landscape," in Lowenthal and Bowden, p. 91.

         On the centennial celebration—Jackson, *American Space*, p. 235.

119   "Americans *love* their country . . ."—Francis J. Grund, in *The Americans* (1837), quoted by Lowenthal, "The Place of the Past in the American Landscape," in Lowenthal and Bowden, p. 96.

"All our implements . . ."—Berry, p. 57.

On the building of Washington, D.C.—Tocqueville, vol. 2, p. 56.

120   On the sesquicentennial celebration of the Sullivan campaign—Harford, pp. 85–6.

On nostalgia—Jean Starobinski, "The Idea of Nostalgia," *Diogenes* 54 (1966), pp. 97–8; David Lowenthal, *The Past Is a Foreign Country* (Cambridge: Cambridge University Press, 1985), p. 11; Willis H. McCann, "Nostalgia: A Review of the Literature," *Psychological Bulletin* 38, no. 3 (March 1941), p. 166; and David Lowenthal, "Past Time, Present Place: Landscape and Memory," *The Geographical Review* 65, no. 1 (January 1975), p. 2.

121   "The decline of the theory . . ."—Starobinski, p. 102.

"Where are the snows . . ."—François Villon, quoted in Robert B. Heilman, "We're Here: Heresay and Other Versions of the Place Sense," *Gettysburg Review* 1, no. 1 (1987), p. 95.

"Asian villagers . . ."—François Villon, quoted and commented on by Russell Baker, "Past Shock," *New York Times Magazine* (May 4, 1975), p. 6.

122   "I am looking . . ."—Mayor Richard Daley, Sr., quoted by Fred Davis, *Yearning for Yesterday: A Sociology of Nostalgia* (New York: The Free Press, 1979), p. 12.

"fenced off . . ."—David Lowenthal, "The American Way of History," *Columbia University Forum* 9, no. 3 (1966), p. 27.

On *Architecture Worth Saving*—Peirce F. Lewis, "The Future of the Past: Our Clouded Vision of Historic Preservation," *Pioneer America* 7 (1975), p. 1.

124   "The most ancient . . ."—David Lowenthal, in David Lowenthal and Marcus Binney, eds., *Our Past Before Us: Why Do We Save It?* (London: Temple Smith, 1981), p. 214.

IV

129 "If you do not feel like working . . ."—quoted in Carl
Carmer, *Listen for a Lonesome Drum* (New York: Farrar and
Reinhart, 1936), p. 366.

130 "The slightest excuse . . ."—John B. Jackson, "Ghosts at the
Door," in Paul Shepard and Daniel McKinley, eds., *The
Subversive Science: Essays Toward an Ecology of Man* (Boston:
Houghton Mifflin, 1969), pp. 160–4.

"Once in each . . ."—Early laws in the archives of the
Geneva Historical Society. (Geneva was part of the
"Town of Seneca" from 1789 until it was incorporated
in 1812.)

"that is at once . . ."—Michael Pollan, *Second Nature* (New
York: The Atlantic Monthly Press, 1991), p. 53.

"In the night . . ." and "A singular proof . . ."—*The Complete
Poetical Works of Henry Wadsworth Longfellow*, Cambridge
Edition (Boston: Houghton Mifflin, 1906), pp. 143 and
666.

132 On traditional Iroquois agriculture—Christopher Vecsey,
"American Indian Environmental Religions," in Vecsey
and Venables, eds., p. 22.

On contemporary Iroquois agriculture—Jorge Quintana,
"Agricultural Survey of New York State Iroquois Reservations, 1990," *Northeast Indian Quarterly* 8, no. 1 (Spring
1991), p. 35.

"is certainly to make the crop thrive . . ."—Eliade, *Patterns
in Comparative Religion*, pp. 332–3.

"Another method . . ."—Pliny, quoted by Hedrick,
pp. 36–7.

On the need for symbolic centers—Yi-Fu Tuan, *Topophilia:
A Study of Environmental Perception, Attitudes, and Values* (Englewood Cliffs, N.J.: Prentice-Hall, 1974), p. 27.

"About an hour . . ."—Frederick Church in a letter to
Erastus Dow Palmer, July 7, 1869, quoted by David C.
Huntington, *The Landscapes of Frederick Edwin Church: Vision
of an American Era* (New York: George Braziller, 1966),
p. 114.

133   "That is why . . ."—Rykwert, *The Idea of a Town* (Princeton, N.J.: Princeton University Press, 1976), p. 90.

134   On the perambulation and sanctity of boundaries—Nigel Pennick, *The Ancient Science of Geomancy: Man in Harmony with the Earth* (London: Thames and Hudson, 1979), p. 59; and Eliade, *Patterns in Comparative Religion*, p. 371.

     On the legend of Jack-o'-Lantern—John R. Stilgoe, "Jack-o'-Lanterns to Surveyors: The Secularization of Landscape Boundaries," *Environmental Review* 1 (1976), p. 14.

135   On privileged place—Mircea Eliade, *The Sacred and the Profane* (New York: Harper Brothers, 1959), p. 24.

     On San Francisco gangs—*San Francisco Examiner*, June 10, 1989, quoted in *Landscape* 30, no. 3 (1990), p. 12.

     On the ancient spirit of place—Vincent Scully, *The Earth, the Temple and the Gods* (New Haven: Yale University Press, 1962); and Walter, p. 70.

136   On *nemos* and *moira*—Erich Isaac, "God's Acre," in Shepard and McKinley, p. 152.

     On Greek gods and their landscapes:—Paula Philippson, in Erich Isaac, "Religion, Landscape and Space," *Landscape* 9, no. 2 (Winter 1959–60), p. 14.

137   "Among the braves . . ."—George Conover, in the archives of the Geneva Historical Society.

139   On power points—William Irwin Thompson, *Passages About Earth: An Exploration of the New Planetary Culture* (New York: Harper and Row, 1974).

140   On the traditional Chinese view of the earth—Michael Loewe, "Geomancy," in Brian Hook, ed., *Cambridge Encyclopedia of China* (Cambridge: Cambridge University Press, 1982), p. 306.

141   "You have to infer . . ."—Maxine Hong Kingston, *The Woman Warrior* (New York: Vintage, 1977), pp. 34–5.

     "Even the slightest shift . . ."—quoted by J. L. Watson, "Cosmology," in Hook, p. 304.

     On *feng-shui*—John Michell, *The View Over Atlantis* (London: Sago Press, 1969), pp. 46–9.

142   On geomancy and environmental consciousness—Paul

Devereux, John Steele, and David Kubrin, *Earthmind: A Modern Adventure in Ancient Wisdom* (New York: Harper and Row, 1989), pp. 112–3 and 168.

142 On the Gaia hypothesis—James Lovelock, *Gaia: A New Look at Life on Earth* (Oxford: Oxford University Press, 1979), p. 11.

"I find that country people . . ."—James Lovelock, quoted by Clare Cooper Marcus, "Alternative Landscapes: Ley-Lines, Feng-Shui and the Gaia Hypothesis," *Landscape* 29, no. 3 (1987), p. 10.

143 On the Nazca lines—Pennick, pp. 73–4 and 86; and George Kubler, *The Art and Architecture of Ancient America* (New York: Penguin Books, 1984), p. 299.

On the root *reg*—Devereux, *Earthmind*, pp. 100–1.

144 On Celtic fairy tracks—Michell, p. 26.

"a worldwide blank . . ."—Paul Devereux and Ian Thomson, *The Ley Hunter's Companion* (London: Thames and Hudson, 1979), p. 60.

145 On fault lines—Devereux, *Earthmind*, pp. 101–2.

On spirit walls—Pennick, p. 66.

"The lines of the dragon current . . ."—Michell, p. 51.

"strayed across a connection . . ."—Eleanor Munro, p. 4.

On unusual magnetic conditions—Devereux, *Earthmind*, pp. 111–2.

146 On earth lights and UFOs—Devereux, *Earthmind*, pp. 102–3 and 192–7.

On Michael Persinger's experiments—Devereux, *Earthmind*, p. 197.

147 On the redesigning process of megalithic monuments—Francis Hitching, *Earth Magic* (New York: William Morrow & Co., 1977), pp. 286–7.

148 *"disruption* of the earth's crust . . ."—Robert Smithson, quoted by Mark Rosenthal, "Some Attitudes of Earth Art: From Competition to Adoration," in Alan Sonfist, ed., *Art in the Land* (New York: Dutton, 1983), p. 64.

"built into . . ."—Gutzon Borglum, quoted by Rex Alan

Smith, *The Carving of Mount Rushmore* (New York: Abbeville Press, 1985), p. 21.

149 *When to plant . . .*—Quintana, p. 35.

151 "Land doesn't belong . . ."—Oren Lyons, quoted by Lisa Aug, "Humans and the Earth," *Turtle Quarterly* 3, no. 2 (Spring–Summer 1989), p. 13.

"Father! . . ."—Cornplanter, quoted in McLuhan, p. 131.

"a special hell . . ."—Handsome Lake, quoted by George S. Snyderman, "Concepts of Land Ownership Among the Iroquois and their Neighbors," in William N. Fenton, ed., *Symposium on Local Diversity in Iroquois Culture*, Smithsonian Institution, Bureau of American Ethnology Bulletin no. 149 (Washington, D.C., 1951), p. 28.

"The unequaled monument . . ."—Aug, p. 5.

"The virgin land rhetoric . . ."—Vecsey, "American Indian Environmental Religions," p. 8.

152 "more than bullets . . ."—Aug, p. 7.

On early American treatment of the land—William T. Hagan, "Justifying Dispossession of the Indian," in Vecsey and Venables, eds., p. 67; and Peter Nabokov, ed., *Native American Testimony* (New York: Thomas Y. Crowell, 1978), p. 40.

On Indian conservation—Vecsey, "American Indian Environmental Religions," p. 9.

"The real historical Indian . . ."—John Mohawk, quoted by Aug, p. 6.

153 On the Tewa—Vecsey, "American Indian Environmental Religions," p. 9.

"Indians have another reality . . ."—Oren Lyons, quoted by Aug, p. 8.

"I am very sorry . . ."—quoted by Aug, p. 8.

154 On *orenda*—Rosalie and Murray Wax, "The Magical World View," *Journal for the Scientific Study of Religion* 1, no. 2 (Spring 1962), p. 182.

155 "In the minds of European . . ."—Peter A. Thomas, "Contrastive Subsistence Strategies and Land Use as Factors

for Understanding Indian-White Relations in New England," *Ethnohistory* 23, no. 1 (Winter 1976), pp. 4–5.

155   On the "land utilization" argument—Hagan, p. 67.

"These people must die out . . ."—Horace Greeley, quoted by Hagan, p. 71.

On the linking of the Indians with nature—Vecsey, "American Indian Environmental Religions," pp. 36–7.

156   On the association of the earth with woman—Carolyn Merchant, *The Death of Nature: Women, Ecology, and the Scientific Revolution* (New York: Harper and Row, 1980), pp. 3–4.

On the term "natural resources"—Vecsey, "American Indian Environmental Religions," p. 33.

"Not only did Europeans . . ."—Lisa Aug, "A Cry for Understanding," *Turtle Quarterly* 3, no. 2 (Spring–Summer 1989), p. 23.

157   "We know the sap . . ."—attributed to Chief Seattle, claimed to be a letter to President Millard Filmore, quoted by Aug, "A Cry for Understanding," p. 23.

V

162   On Jemima Wilkinson—Herbert A. Wisbey, Jr., *Pioneer Prophetess: Jemima Wilkinson, The Publick Universal Friend* (Ithaca, N.Y.: Cornell University Press, 1964); and Whitney R. Cross, *The Burned-Over District: The Social and Intellectual History of Enthusiastic Religion in Western New York, 1800–1850* (Ithaca, N.Y.: Cornell University Press, 1950).

165   On Walter Taylor—his own promotional material, newspaper clippings, and a documentary, *Baron of Bully Hill*, produced and directed by Christopher Zimmerman for WXXI-TV.

167   "Something about the land . . ."—Paul Horgan, quoted by Carmer, p. 359.

168   On the Hill Cumorah Pageant—promotional material and *Finger Lakes Times*, July 21, 1988.

On the burned-over era—Whitney Cross.

170   On Matilda Gage—Sally Roesch Wagner, in introduction

to Matilda Gage, *Woman, Church & State,* Reprint Edition (Watertown, Mass.: Persephone Press, 1980).

On patent records—Darrell Norris, "The *New,* New England," Geneva Historical Society lecture, September 8, 1988.

171 "When the cultural geography . . ."—Wilbur Zelinsky, "Classical Town Names in the United States: The Historical Geography of an American Idea," *Geographical Review* 57, no. 4 (1967), pp. 469 and 486.

On the character of nineteenth-century New Yorkers—Michael Barkun, "Religious Fervor in Central New York: The Burned-Over District," Geneva Historical Society lecture, October 20, 1988.

On Joseph Smith—Thomas F. O'Dea, *The Mormons* (Chicago: University of Chicago Press, 1957), pp. 1–21; and Cross, pp. 142–3.

172 Emerson and Thoreau on the Fox sisters—quoted by John B. Wilson, "Emerson and the Rochester Rappings," *New England Quarterly* 41 (1968), pp. 248–9.

175 On the super collider proposal—*Finger Lakes Times,* June 30, 1987.

176 Canandaiguans about Bare Hill—*Finger Lakes Times,* various issues.

On Lewis Henry Morgan—Elisabeth Tooker, "Lewis H. Morgan: The Myth and the Man," *University of Rochester Library Bulletin* 37 (1984), p. 32.

178 "the most catalytic book . . ."—Elman Service, quoted by John R. Lee, "The Life and Times of Lewis Henry Morgan," in Russell Judkins, ed., *Iroquois Studies: A Guide to Documentary and Ethnographic Resources from Western New York and the Genesee Valley* (Geneseo, N.Y.: Department of Anthropology, State University of New York, and The Geneseo Foundation, 1987), p. 49.

Engels on Morgan—Frederick Engels, *The Origin of the Family, Private Property and the State in the Light of the Researches of Lewis H. Morgan* (New York: International Publishers, 1972), pp. 6 and 16.

178 Engels on the Iroquois—Engels, p. 85.

179 On David Cusick—Russell A. Judkins, "David Cusick's Ancient History of the Six Nations: A Neglected Classic," in Judkins, ed., p. 26.

180 "vain enough to hope . . ."—Arthur Parker, quoted by William N. Fenton, ed., *Parker on the Iroquois* (Syracuse, N.Y.: Syracuse University Press, 1968), p. 25.

"set a standard . . ."—Fenton, ed., pp. 46–7.

184 "the truth of the matter . . ."—George Heron, quoted by George H.J. Abrams, *The Seneca People* (Phoenix, Ariz.: Indian Tribal Series, 1976), p. 98.

"not possible to halt . . ."—President Kennedy, quoted by Abrams, p. 98.

185 "Even today . . ."—Laurence M. Hauptman, *The Iroquois Struggle for Survival: World War II to Red Power* (Syracuse, N.Y.: Syracuse University Press, 1986), pp. 89–90.

186 "Relocation is a word . . ."—Pauline Whitesinger, quoted by Anita Parlow, *Cry, Sacred Ground: Big Mountain, U.S.A.* (Washington, D.C.: Christic Institute, 1988), p. 9.

"is about the worst . . ."—Thayer Scudder, quoted by Hattie Clark, "Lands Lost: Navajo Exile in the Arizona Desert," *Christian Science Monitor*, October 22, 1987, pp. 16–17.

187 "I'd rather have a nuclear . . ."—quoted by Michael Winerip, "Perennial Hope of the Scattered Cayuga Nation—Land," *New York Times*, August 10, 1984.

188 On pollution at Akwesasne—Mary Francis Hoover, "Mohawk Land Under Attack," *Turtle Quarterly* 1, no. 4 (Fall 1989), pp. 20–3; and Mary Esch, "Mohawks' Food Sources Threatened," *Democrat and Chronicle*, Rochester, N.Y., December 26, 1987, p. 7B.

190 "Woe! Hearken! . . ."—from Iroquois condolence ceremony, H. Hale, *The Iroquois Book of Rites* (Philadelphia: D. G. Brinton, 1883), p. 153.

VI

193   On community welcome signs—Wilbur Zelinsky, "Where Every Town Is Above Average: Welcoming Signs Along America's Highways," *Landscape* 30, no. 1 (1988), pp. 1–10.

194   On here versus there—Robert Heilman, p. 96.

"remove its exogenous . . ."—Yi-Fu Tuan, "Geopiety: A Theme in Man's Attachment to Nature and to Place," p. 34.

"In the beginning . . ."—tale paraphrased from Harriet Maxwell Converse, *Myths and Legends of The New York State Iroquois*, ed. Arthur C. Parker (Albany, N.Y.: State of New York, Education Department, December 15, 1908, bulletin no. 437); and Hazel W. Hertzberg, *The Great Tree and the Longhouse: The Culture of the Iroquois* (New York: Macmillan, 1966).

195   On prohibitions against storytelling—Arthur C. Parker, in introduction to Converse.

197   "This is a beautiful . . ."—Morgan, *Dear Stieglitz, Dear Dove*, p. 363.

"They are a wonderful people . . ."—Charles Alexander Eastman, quoting his uncle on the subject of whites, in *Indian Boyhood*, quoted by Nabokov, ed., pp. 25–6.

198   "Everything as it moves . . ."—a Dakota, quoted by McLuhan, p. 37.

"In 1779 near this spot . . ."—Horseheads tourist pamphlet.

199   "Place induces poetry . . ."—Eudora Welty, "Place in Fiction," *South Atlantic Quarterly* 55 (January 1956), p. 63.

200   "a manifestation of landscape . . ."—John Elder, *Imagining the Earth: Poetry and the Vision of Nature* (Urbana, Ill.: University of Illinois Press, 1985), p. 39.

A place "will express itself . . ."—Lawrence Durrell, "Landscape with Literary Figures," *New York Times Book Review*, June 12, 1960, p. 1.

On Apache use of place-names—Basso, pp. 138–73.

201   On the songlines—Chatwin, p. 58.

202   "The grass of ten cows . . ."—*Tipperary Star*, January 2, 1960, reprinted in *Landscape* 9, no. 3 (Spring 1960), p. 20.

202   "Two acres of medicine . . ."—Onondaga chief Irving
          Powless, in conversation.
          "Up to the great tumulus . . ."—944 A.D. English land
          charter, quoted by Lowenthal, *The Past Is a Foreign Country*,
          p. 257.

203   On place-names—George R. Stewart, *Names on the Globe*
          (New York: Oxford University Press, 1975), pp. 18–19.

204   "Philadelphia became not only . . ."—George R. Stewart,
          Names on the Land (New York: Random House, 1945;
          reprint, Boston: Houghton Mifflin, 1958), pp. 105–6.

205   "superficial virtue . . ."—Ian Nairn, *The American Landscape:
          A Critical View* (New York: Random House, 1965),
          pp. 11–12.
          "In a mountain area . . ."—Stewart, *Names on the Globe*, p. 19.

206   "The era of their separation . . ."—Morgan, *League of the
          Iroquois*, Book 3, p. 77.
          "To name the land . . ."—Vine Deloria, quoted by Basso,
          p. 179.

207   On losing indigenous languages—Onondaga chief Oren
          Lyons, interviewed on PBS by Bill Moyers, July 3, 1991.
          From Brian Friel, *Translations*, in *Selected Plays* (London: Faber
          and Faber), 1984, pp. 419–20.

208   "a large brook . . ."—Cadwallader Colden, 1732, quoted by
          William M. Beauchamp, *Aboriginal Place Names of New York*,
          New York State Museum Bulletin no. 108 (Albany,
          N.Y.: 1907), p. 8.
          "White men need . . ."—Apache, quoted by Basso, p. 105.
          "The country was made . . ."—Chief Joseph, quoted by
          McLuhan, p. 54.

209   "No one ever said . . ."—Navajo, in Rock Point Commu-
          nity School, *Sun Tracks* (Chinle, Ariz.: Rock Point Com-
          munity School, 1982), p. 187.
          On Alabama Supreme Court ruling—Caldwell v. State,
          quoted by Donald W. Large, "This Land is Whose
          Land? Changing Concepts of Land as Property," *Wiscon-
          sin Law Review* 1973:1039, no. 4, p. 1042.

"the right to sell . . ."—Vine Deloria, *Custer Died for Your Sins* (New York: Avon, 1970), p. 7.

On Indian place-names—Kim R. Stafford, *Having Everything Right* (New York: Penguin Books, 1987), p. 3.

210 On children's place-naming—Roger Hart, *Children's Experience of Place* (New York: Irvington Publishers, 1979), p. 150.

On the Seneca word for "lake"—Morgan, *League of the Iroquois*, Book 3, p. 79.

211 "I wish to state . . ."—Silas B. Smith, quoted in Morgan, *League of the Iroquois*, Appendix B, p. 242.

212 "In coastal sailing guides . . ."—Stafford, p. 4.

213 On metaphors for the landscape—J. B. Jackson, "Landscape as Theatre," *Landscape* 23, no. 1 (1979), pp. 3–7.

214 "The world does not have . . ."—Hugo, p. 8.

"There it was . . ."—Wallace Stevens, "The Poem that Took the Place of a Mountain," *The Collected Poems* (New York: Vintage, 1982), p. 512.

215 On romanticism—Paul Shepard, "Place in American Culture," *North American Review* 262, no. 3 (Fall 1977), p. 22.

"Those who make fun . . ."—Edmund Wilson, *Axel's Castle,* (New York: Charles Scribner's Sons, 1931), p. 12.

216 "Fields of care . . ."—Relph, p. 38.

A Note About the Author

Deborah Tall has lived in upstate New York since 1982, teaching writing and literature at Hobart and William Smith Colleges, and editing the poetry journal, *Seneca Review*. She is the author of three books of poems and a memoir, *The Island of the White Cow*, about the five years she lived in rural Ireland in the 1970s. Educated at the University of Michigan, where she won the Hopwood Award, and at Goddard College, she is married to the poet David Weiss. They live in Ithaca, New York, with their two daughters, Zoe and Clea.

A Note on the Type

The text of this book was set in a digitized version of Centaur. Originally designed by Bruce Rogers in 1914 as a private type, it was named for the book in which it was first used (*The Centaur* by Maurice de Guérin). Monotype made it generally available in 1929.

Rogers based his design on the 1470 font of Nicolas Jenson, the Venetian printer, introducing refinements lacking in the original. Typographers consider Centaur to be one of the finest roman types currently available, a superb revival of the Jenson letter, which has served as an inspiration for all designers of roman type.

Composed by ComCom, a division of
Haddon Craftsmen, Allentown, Pennsylvania

Printed and bound by Arcata Graphics/Fairfield,
Fairfield, Pennsylvania

Designed by Robert C. Olsson